CASS LIBRARY OF AFRICAN STUDIES

AFRICAN PREHISTORY
No. 2

General Editor: Professor BRIAN FAGAN

Department of Anthropology, University of California, Santa Barbara

THE STONE AGE CULTURES
OF KENYA COLONY

AFRICAN PREHISTORY

No. 1. Gertrude Caton Thompson
The Zimbabwe Culture. Ruins and reactions (1931).
With a new introduction by the author.
Second Edition

No. 2. L. S. B. Leakey
The Stone Age Cultures of Kenya Colony (1931).
With a new introductory note by the author.
New Impression

No. 3. David Randall-MacIver
Mediaeval Rhodesia (1906).
With an introductory note by Brian Fagan.
New Impression

No. 4. James Theodore Bent
The Ruined Cities of Mashonaland: being a record of excavation
and exploration in 1891 (1892; 3rd ed. 1895).
New Impression

No. 5. Richard Nicklin Hall
Great Zimbabwe, Mashonaland, Rhodesia: an account of two
years examination work in 1902–4 on behalf of the Government
of Rhodesia (1905).
New Impression

No. 6. Edward Humphrey Lane Poole
The Native Tribes of the Eastern Province of Northern
Rhodesia. Notes on their migrations and history (2nd ed. 1938).
New Impression

No. 7. Miles Crawford Burkitt
South Africa's Past in Stone and Paint (1928). With a new
preface by the author.
New Impression

**No. 8. Astley John Hilary Goodwin and Clarence Van
Riet Lowe**
The Stone Age Cultures of South Africa (1929).
New Impression

No. 9. Louis Péringuey
The Stone Ages of South Africa as represented in the collection
of the South African Museum (1911).
New Impression

No. 10. Anthony John Arkell
Shaheinab. An account of the excavation of a Neolithic
occupation site carried out for the Sudan Antiquities Service
in 1949–50 (1953).
New Impression

THE

STONE AGE CULTURES
OF KENYA COLONY

BY

L. S. B. LEAKEY

with Appendices by

J. D. SOLOMON   C. E. P. BROOKS   A. T. HOPWOOD

H. C. BECK   and   M. CONNOLLY

With a new Introductory Note
by the Author

FRANK CASS & CO. LTD.

1971

Published by

FRANK CASS AND COMPANY LIMITED

67 Great Russell Street, London WC1B 3BT

by arrangement with Cambridge University Press

All rights reserved

First edition   1931
Reprinted with a new
Introductory Note   1971

ISBN 0 7146 2465 9

Printed in Great Britain by Clarke, Doble & Brendon Ltd.
Plymouth and London

NEW INTRODUCTORY NOTE

This book was published in 1931 as a result of five years' preliminary work on the Prehistory of Kenya. Since then, a very great deal has happened and much additional knowledge has been accumulated and published. The value of the book, therefore, lies not so much in the information it contains, but because it represents the first serious attempt to review the Prehistory of Kenya, at a time when it was almost unknown.

The basic facts set out in the book remain, of course, true; but most of the deductions drawn from those facts are no longer valid. The prehistoric site at Kariandusi, for example, was excavated in much greater detail during 1945/46, and it became clear that the cultural material at the site represents an advanced stage of the Acheulean. There is no "Chellean" material there at all. Even the abraded specimens (some are heavily rolled, and some are lightly rolled) do not represent a different cultural stage from the unrolled material. The interpretation, rather, is that this ancient shore-line was occupied, periodically, for several hundreds of years, at times when the water level had dropped sufficiently for the beach to be exposed. At other times, the lake waters were standing right at the site, and all specimens on the beach were thus subjected to battering and rolling in the sandy gravels. The beautiful unrolled specimens which rest on the top of the beach, and which were later sealed in by fine sands, represent the last occupation of this site, before it was finally covered up. It is thus doubtful whether there is a difference of more than a few hundred years between the age of the most rolled specimens and that of the unrolled ones.

A limited amount of faunal remains was found in the new excavations and these, taken in conjunction with the cultural material indicate a geological age at the end of the Middle Pleistocene, comparable to the higher levels of Bed IV at Olduvai. The site is now open to the public as a "Museum on the Spot".

The cultural material which is described in this book as Nanyukian, is now referred to as a Kenya variant of the Fauresmith. It represents one of the end stages of the Hand-axe culture when the climate began to get drier, at the end of the Middle Pleistocene. Many sites of this culture are now known in Kenya and it is only found at high altitudes near forested mountains. Elsewhere in Kenya, at the same time, a different, but corresponding, end-product of the Hand-axe culture occurs around Lake Victoria, and is referred to as the Kenya Sangoan.

The material described in this book as Levalloisian is nowadays regarded as a local variant of what is commonly called "The Middle Stone Age Complex" of East and South Africa. The same is true of the Kenya Stillbay. At the time of writing this preface considerable revision of this whole complex is being undertaken.

The Kenya Aurignacian is no longer referred to by that name, but is called the Kenya Capsian. It must be clearly understood that the use of the term "Capsian" in no way implies that the early part of this culture, in Kenya, is as young as the Capsian in North Africa. A very detailed report on the Capsian from Gamble's Cave II, was sent to press in Paris, just before the outbreak of World War II, but the whole report and all the illustrations and diagrams were mislaid or destroyed during the German Occupation. A number of additional excavations of Upper Paleolithic have been carried out in Kenya.

Very little new work has been done on the Elmenteitan and Kenya Wilton Mesolithic Cultures, and there is urgent need for additional study of this part of Kenya's Prehistory.

By way of contrast, much study of the Kenya Neolithic has been carried out, and there are now several special reports as well as many smaller papers dealing with the subjects. Of particular importance are the reports on the excavations at Hyrax Hill and the Njoro River Rock Shelter by Mrs. M. D. Leakey.

The appendices dealing with Geology and Palaeontology which appear in this volume are now out of date, and are of historical interest only.

Nairobi   L.S.B.L.
August, 1970

CONTENTS

v

CONTENTS

LIST OF ILLUSTRATIONS

LIST OF ILLUSTRATIONS

TEXT-FIGURES

LIST OF ILLUSTRATIONS

Fig.

ix

LIST OF ILLUSTRATIONS

PREFACE

THE East African Archaeological Expedition has carried out two seasons' excavations and as a result we now know something of the sequence of Stone Age cultures in Kenya, and of their relation to each other. We have also been able to work out a number of clear subdivisions in Pleistocene and recent times, based upon climatic changes, and to establish in most cases the relation of the cultures found to these time divisions.

This book is intended not only for the archaeologist, but also for the more general reader in East Africa and in England who wishes to know the results of the Expedition's work in Kenya up to date; and for this reason no attempt is made to discuss the details of the excavations of any of the sites, and I have confined myself to giving an account of the culture sequence as we know it, and to describing a characteristic type series of tools for each culture. A more detailed study of the individual sites and of the many surface finds is now in progress, and it is intended to publish these shortly, probably in book form, or possibly as a number of papers in scientific journals.

Nor have I attempted to discuss the skeletal remains that were found associated with some of the cultures. These, too, are now being studied under the guidance of Sir Arthur Keith, F.R.S., and will be published in a special volume.

I wish to record my very sincere thanks to all the members of my two expeditions; without their co-operation only a tithe of the work could have been done. Mr B. H. Newsam was my colleague throughout the first season, 1926–7, while Mr T. W. Powys Cobb, Mrs Creasy (Mrs Shaw), Miss Kitson, Mr D. G. B. Leakey, Mrs L. S. B. Leakey, Mr D. G. MacInnes, and Mr J. D. Solomon were with me for periods varying upwards from four months during the 1928–9 season. Mr Solomon in particular contributed very largely to the value of the second season's work by his study and interpretation of the Pleistocene geology, and by establishing the relationship of various implementiferous horizons to each other. An important appendix has been prepared by him for this volume, and the results of his work will also be published in greater detail elsewhere.

PREFACE

I cannot sufficiently express my gratitude to Dr A. C. Haddon, F.R.S., or to Sir Arthur Keith, F.R.S., who have from the beginning helped me in every possible way, and without whose constant advice, help, and encouragement the Expedition could never have been carried out.

In work of this nature the problem of finance is never far out of sight. Financial assistance to *both* Expeditions was generously given by the Percy Sladen Memorial Trustees, the Royal Society, the Government of Kenya, and Sir John Ramsden; and to the second season's Expedition by the Rhodes Trust, the Royal Geographical Society, and by Dr Tapp also; and I hereby express my sincere gratitude to them all. I also have to thank the Council of St John's College, Cambridge, the Goldsmiths' Company, and the Commissioners for the Royal Commission of the 1851 Exhibition for awarding me research studentships tenable in the field, which not only covered my personal expenses, but contributed considerably to the general research expenses of the Expeditions.

In England many friends have helped me in every sort of way, but I would especially thank Mr Benians, Senior Tutor of St John's College, Mr M. C. Burkitt, Mr A. T. Hopwood, Miss Tyldesley and Mr L. C. G. Clarke, who have on many occasions given most excellent help and advice. Mrs Burkitt has most kindly done a number of drawings for this book; Mr Ross Munroe has generously allowed me to use his farm at Elmenteita as the headquarters camp of the Expedition since January 1927; to these I would record thanks, as well as to many others whose names I cannot list here, but to whom I am none the less grateful.

Many friends in East Africa have also helped, and again I offer my heartiest thanks, and would like to make special mention of His Excellency Sir Edward Grigg, Mr C. Juxon Barton, Mr E. J. Wayland, Dr Erik Nilsson, Dr C. J. Wilson, Mr Dunlop, Mr Abbott, Mr Sikes, Dr van Someren, Archdeacon Maynard, and Mr Rickman. I also thank Major and Mrs A. J. Macdonald, Mr and Mrs Gamble, Colonel and Mrs Deighton, Captain and Mrs Long, Mr and Mrs Keeling, and the Hon. Mrs Galbraith Cole for permission to work on their land. Finally I would thank the many people who have sent me tools or other prehistoric remains from their farms, or who have given me information concerning possible sites. This material will be published as soon as it is worked out.

The Union Castle Steamship Company has on each occasion generously

PREFACE

allowed the crates of specimens to be shipped at special rates, while their staff have given every possible assistance to insure that delicate specimens should not suffer from careless handling. Besides contributing to the expenses of the Expeditions, the Kenya Government has, through the officers and the staffs of the various Departments—especially the Customs, the Railways, the P.W.D., the Medical Department and the Game Department —given help in many ways.

In connection with the task of working out the material published in this book, I have profited greatly from discussions with my friends Professor Fleure, F.R.S., Miss Caton Thompson, Dr Dorothy Garrod, Dr Hans Reck, M. l'Abbé Breuil, M. Péyrony, Mr C. van Reit Lowe, Mr Leslie Armstrong, Dr C. E. P. Brooks, Mr Horace Beck and Major Connolly, and many others. The last three, and also Mr Solomon, have contributed Appendices to this book, for which I thank them.

Finally I offer my warmest thanks to my parents who have frequently given hospitality to members of my Expedition, and who have allowed me to store boxes of specimens in their house; and last but not least do I thank my wife for having cheerfully undertaken much of the dullest work of the Expedition and of preparation.

The archaeological study of East Africa is as yet but in its infancy, and I look forward to many more years of work in Kenya and in other East African Territories. When I return in 1931 I hope to start an East African Archaeological Society, and I hope that many of those who have already shown interest in the work in Kenya will join it.

L. S. B. LEAKEY

January 1931

CHAPTER I

DISCOVERIES IN KENYA PRIOR TO 1926

U P to the time when the East African Archaeological Expedition started excavations in Kenya in August 1926 no detailed archaeological investigations had been carried out in that colony, although a considerable number of important surface finds had been made, as well as a few discoveries of stone tools *in situ*. There had been no attempt whatever to work out the culture sequence, although several people—notably Professor J. W. Gregory, F.R.S., and Mr C. W. Hobley—had recognised the existence of several distinct phases. On the other hand, some of the statements made in connection with the discovery of tools in Kenya are astonishing, and the true significance of many of the discoveries had not been realised at all.

As far as is known, Professor J. W. Gregory was the first European to recognise a Stone Age tool in Kenya, and this was as far back as 1893, when he found a worked obsidian flake in the Ulu Mountains.[1] He at first suspected it of being a gun flint. He later found a number of other tools and flakes in various parts of East Africa. In his book, *The Rift Valleys and Geology of East Africa*, he devotes a whole chapter to the subject of "Prehistoric Man in British East Africa", and this is quoted verbatim in Appendix E, by kind permission of the publishers and author.

Professor Gregory's arguments in that chapter are often exceedingly puzzling. He seems to have been convinced that all the *obsidian* tools which he found were of Neolithic age. True, the late Sir John Evans had described a series submitted to him as being of that date, but his other evidence is less convincing. He says,[2] "*Conclusive evidence* [the italics are mine] of the Neolithic character of the *obsidian* implements is given by the discovery of two ground stone axes. The first, which has a weather-roughened surface, was found by Major C. Ross in 1913 at a depth of three feet at the Eldoma Ravine. It has been described by Mr Hobley, who regards it as the same age as the obsidian implements found at Njoro, *only twenty-five miles distant*". [The italics are again mine.] But although he apparently regarded all the obsidian tools which he found as of Neolithic age, Professor Gregory and Mr Hobley did find one site with tools which they considered to be of

I

Palaeolithic workmanship. This was at Ol Kejo Nyiro near Mt Olgasalic. Once again the statements are remarkable.

Although Professor Gregory regarded the implements which he found as indications of "the occupation of the Rift Valley north of Magadi by Palaeolithic Man", he says, "The specimens collected were lying on a bank of white diatomaceous earth which seemed to have been dug by such implements. The earth was probably used as a paint, and these thin stone axes would make effective hand hoes in digging it. One specimen was in two pieces lying four feet apart, showing that it had been broken at the place. These flakes are certainly suggestive of Palaeolithic workmanship".

I have not seen these tools, but three of them are figured by Professor Gregory3 and they have been described to me as coups-de-poing; but it is hard to see how the marks of the diggings of Palaeolithic man in a soft exposed bank of diatomaceous earth—how else is one to interpret the words, "which seemed to have been dug by such implements"?—should not have been eroded beyond recognition.

But Professor Gregory was not the only man who had described stone tools in East Africa, prior to 1926.

Mr C. W. Hobley in various notes and articles in the *Journal of the East Africa and Uganda Natural History Society* drew attention to discoveries made by himself and by others, and he also published a note in *Man*.4 Among the more important of the discoveries thus described by him were the finds made by a settler named Harrison in 1913.5 Harrison apparently found a site rich in rolled examples of coups-de-poing, and took a series of these down to the Nairobi Museum. He seems to have been told that they were worth a good price, and so he refused to say where he had obtained them, though he left them temporarily at the Museum. Later on he was killed in the war, and no one knows of the site. A big collection of tools had been made by Mr W. Tunstall at Njoro, and Mr Hobley published some notes on tools from this and other sites in 1912.6 Since then Mr Tunstall has given me a large series of tools from this same site, and these will be described at a later date.

Another keen East African collector is Captain Montague of Kyambu, and he too gave a series of tools to Mr Hobley to be described.

In 1925 Sir John Ramsden presented the Cambridge Museum of Archaeology and Ethnology with a very fine example of a polished Stone

Age axe from Kipipiri, very similar indeed to that which Mr Hobley recorded from Eldama Ravine,[7] where it was found by Major Ross.

In *Man*, 1909,[8] Mr Seton Kerr published a note on some stone tools found by him in a railway cutting east of Nairobi. Another important find was that made by Mr Dowson at the Morendat River, Naivasha. (The tools were actually found in gravels exposed by the Malewa River near the old Government Farm at Naivasha.) These same gravels had yielded the lower jaw of a fossil equine described as *Equus hollisi*.[9]

Besides these published finds of stone implements, several people had discovered stone tools in various parts of East Africa but had not published them, and a few of the English museums possessed small collections of obsidian tools. There had also been found several stone bowls. These were roughly classed as Neolithic, but apparently no associated finds were made, with the exception of one or two stone rings resembling the so-called "digging-stones" so common in South Africa. Several notes on these were published by Mr Hobley[10] and by Mr Dobbs.[11]

In 1923 there appeared in the *East African Standard* of April 14 a letter from Major Macdonald of Nakuru, describing a find which he had made on his farm.[12] He had made a partial excavation of the site and had found a number of stone bowls, pestles and mortars, animal bones, etc., and he asked for information on the subject of his discovery. The editor of the *East African Standard* put a footnote to Major Macdonald's letter, suggesting that the site should be left as far as possible *in statu quo*, and about a month later, as soon as I saw the letter in Cambridge, I both wrote and cabled to Major Macdonald begging him to keep the site intact for detailed examination. This he very kindly did. It seemed fairly certain to me that this site would throw much light concerning the makers of those stone bowls previously found in Kenya; nor were we disappointed. (See Chapter IX.)

The published prehistoric discoveries in Kenya prior to 1926 may be summed up as follows.

The existence of a Palaeolithic phase was recognised by Professor Gregory and others, but none of the obsidian tools found in Kenya were considered to belong to that phase. All the obsidian tools, together with the polished stone axes and stone bowls which had been found, were classed together vaguely as Neolithic. No human remains had been found associated with any of these finds, and no attempt had been made to work out any sequence, or to sub-divide either the Palaeolithic or the Neolithic phases.

The position was better than this in Uganda and Tanganyika Territory. In both of these areas a certain amount of actual excavation work had been carried out by geologists. In Tanganyika Territory Professor Dr Hans Reck had discovered a fossil skeleton of a prehistoric man in the Pleistocene deposits at Oldoway,[13] but had found no stone tools with it. A note on this discovery was published in the *Illustrated London News*[14] and various comments on it appeared from time to time in publications on prehistory. Dr Reck and Dr Arning also published notes on one or two other interesting sites, notably some burial mounds in Ngorongoro crater which yielded stone bowls, beads and human skeletons.[15]

In 1924 I discovered a number of stone tools in the neighbourhood of Lindi and Tendaguru in south-east Tanganyika Territory, and a note on some of these was published in 1926.[16]

In Uganda, Mr E. J. Wayland, the Director of the Geological Survey, took a deep interest in the archaeology of his territory from the time of his appointment, and he has made an extensive collection of tools of various periods and cultures. He has published a number of notes on these from time to time, and has shown that Uganda is a rich field for archaeological investigation. Unfortunately, as Director of the Geological Survey, he has to do his archaeological work mainly in his spare time, so that he has not been able to carry out any very detailed excavations of cave sites. Prior to 1926 his published accounts indicated that he had evidence of three main culture groups which he called Kafuan, Sangoan and Magosian,[17] and he was already suggesting the idea of a glacial-pluvial correlation as a basis for dating the East African cultures.

REFERENCES

1. *The Rift Valleys and Geology of East Africa*, by J. W. Gregory, p. 219.
2. *Ibid.* p. 220.
3. *Ibid.* facing p. 39.
4. *Man*, June 1925, no. 51.
5. *Journal of the East Africa and Uganda Natural History Society*, vol. VI, no. 11, p. 189.
6. *Ibid.* vol. III, no. 5, pp. 20 *et seq.*
7. *Ibid.* vol. III, no. 6, p. 60.
8. *Man*, 1909, p. 152.

9. *The Rift Valleys and Geology of East Africa*, by J. W. Gregory, p. 221. Also *Proceedings of Zoological Society*, 1909, p. 586, a paper by Ridgeway.

10. *The Akamba*, by C. W. Hobley, p. 130.

11. *Journal of the East Africa and Uganda Natural History Society*, vol. IV, no. 8, pp. 145 *et seq.*

12. *East African Standard*, April 14, 1923.

13. "Erste Vorläufige Mitteilung über den Fund eines fossilen Menschenskelets aus Zentralafrika", by Hans Reck, in *Sitzungsberichte der Gesellschaft naturforschender Freunde*, Berlin, 1914.

14. *Illustrated London News*, April 1914.

15. "Prähistorische Grab- und Menschenfunde und ihre Beziehungen zur Pluvialzeit in Ostafrika", by Hans Reck, in *Mitteilungen aus den deutschen Schutzgebieten*, Band XXXIV, Heft 1, Berlin, 1926.

16. *British Museum, Stone Age Antiquities Guide*, 1926, p. 185.

17. *Proceedings of the Prehistoric Society of East Anglia*, vol. IV, part 1, paper by E. J. Wayland; and *Man*, November 1924, no. 124, note by E. J. Wayland.

CHAPTER II

CLIMATIC CHANGES

IN Kenya the story of prehistoric man is as intimately bound up with climatic changes as it is in European prehistory.

In Europe the Pleistocene was marked by a series of glacial and inter-glacial periods, and these climatic changes had a very marked influence upon the movements and distribution of the fauna and upon the types of vegetation; and since Stone Age man was at first essentially a hunter, dependent upon wild animals and plants for food, he too came under the direct influence of the climate, despite the fact that he could adapt himself to the cold of the glacial periods, thanks to the discovery of fire, and of the use of skins as clothing.

The sequence of glacial and inter-glacial changes was worked out in detail in the Alps by Penck and Brückner, and the results of their investigations have been applied (with certain modifications) to most of the other regions of Europe which were affected by the advances and retreats of the ice. The various advances of the ice sheet resulted in boulder clays and moraines, while the warm inter-glacial phases were marked by river gravels and by alluvial deposits. Fossils representing the fauna of the different periods are frequently found in the boulder clays, gravels and sands, as are also the stone weapons and implements of the Stone Age hunters of the various periods. Consequently it has been possible to work out the cultural sequence with considerable accuracy and to determine whether the makers of a given culture lived during a glacial or an inter-glacial phase, or whether they arrived during one climatic phase and continued on into the next, adapting themselves and their mode of life to the changing climatic conditions.

Unfortunately, there is still no absolute agreement between various archaeologists, or between archaeologists and geologists, as to the exact relation of the deposits in different parts of Europe to each other, and this is partly because each succeeding advance of the ice sheet tends to obliterate and mix up earlier deposits and so complicate the evidence. However, there now seems to be some measure of agreement that the biggest inter-glacial phase was that known as the Mindel-Riss inter-glacial, and there are many who tend to regard the Günz and Mindel glaciations of the Penckian scheme as the two maxima of a single major glaciation, separated from each other by a warm inter-glacial which did not necessarily involve a complete retreat of the ice from the northern parts of Europe. The Riss and Würm glaciations of the Penckian scheme are likewise regarded by many as the maxima of a single major event, but the warm period between these two was probably longer and more marked than that between the Günz and Mindel glacial phases. At the end of the Würm glaciation was a period of warmer climate known usually as the Achen retreat, but this was interrupted for a time by a renewed advance of the ice sheet which was responsible for what is known as the Bühl Stadium. The subsequent climatic fluctuations which led up to present-day conditions have also been worked out but need not concern us here.

It is often stated that the fauna of Europe during the glacial periods was essentially arctic in character, but that during the warm inter-glacial phases a tropical fauna with marked affinities with the African fauna of the present day (as well as of the African Pleistocene) came north into Europe, only to be driven back or exterminated with each return of the arctic conditions. In the broad sense this is essentially true, but it must be borne in mind that the southern parts of Europe did not have an ice cap even if they were subject to very cold winters, and certain species may well have successfully adapted themselves to the changed climatic conditions, and so persisted in the south of Europe, whence they would eventually spread northwards again when the ice cap and its influence were once more in retreat.

During the warm inter-glacials we find that the fauna of Europe included species of lion, hippopotamus, rhinoceros, elephant and hyena, etc., some of them closely related to the living African forms; while the fauna of the glacial periods included mammoth, woolly rhinoceros, reindeer, musk ox, cave bear, etc.; but even during a glacial period it is not impossible that some of the former persisted in the southern parts of Europe.

Very many reasons have been adduced to account for the glacial and inter-glacial changes, and they cannot be examined here, but whatever the cause or causes may have been, meteorologists are agreed that the climatic changes of the Northern Hemisphere must have been accompanied by changes of climate in the other parts of the world.

This fact is of the greatest importance to the study of African archaeology, for Africa is yielding considerable evidence of great climatic fluctuations during the Pleistocene, and the deposits which correspond to the different climatic periods are frequently found to be rich in fossil bones and teeth of animals and in the stone tools of prehistoric man. Theoretically therefore, it should sooner or later be possible to correlate the climatic changes of Europe and Africa, and so to learn much concerning the comparative dating of the various Stone Ages in these two continents.

In 1893 Professor J. W. Gregory, the pioneer of East African geology, discovered much evidence of former pluvial periods in that area and he also recognised that these were connected with the greater extension of the ice sheets on Mount Kenya, and he suggested in his book *The Great Rift Valley*, in 1896, that there must be some correlation between these pluvial periods which had resulted in great extensions of the lakes and the successive glaciations of Mount Kenya. He wrote as follows:[1]

The second series of faults which made the main Rift Valley probably happened at the same time and increased its size and depth while others enlarged that of the Albert Nyanza. The climate of Africa must have been less arid than at present. The snow fields of Kenya were certainly larger and great glaciers flowed from these for several thousand feet down the flanks of the Mountain. The heavier rainfall helped the growth of the lakes which extended over places which are now sandy deserts.

But in his table on p. 235 he shows that he considered at that time (1896) that this extension of the glaciers and the rise of the lakes, and the second series of faults, were Pliocene events, so I conclude that he did not then connect them with the European Ice Age. At a later date, however, he did come to this conclusion. In May 1919 he wrote in the *Journal of the East Africa and Uganda Natural History Society* as follows:[2]

The conclusion that Mount Kenya was dead and desiccated before the beginning of the Pleistocene is based on the natural assumption that the former great size of the Kenyan glaciers was during the great Ice Age in Europe.

He also had realised that there had been considerable fluctuations in climate during that period, for in the same article he wrote:

The climatic variations of Kenya and the variations of the lakes were probably not due to a progressive desiccation, but to alternations of drier and wetter periods. Thus on the floor of the Endariki Valley is a deep young gorge now being cut out by floods after storms; but this gorge is being made by the re-excavation of an old gorge which has been filled by löess, a wind carried deposit, during some recent period drier than the present or during the formation of the original gorge.

CLIMATIC CHANGES

In 1926 Dr C. E. P. Brooks, the meteorologist, in his book *Climate through the Ages*, laid stress on the fact that, during the glacial advances in the northern parts of Europe, the climate of the land to the south must have been wetter. He says,[3] "Outside the limits of the ice sheets on the peripheral zone of ice winds, the weather was probably much as we know it to-day but more stormy", and he continues:

This applies especially to the Mediterranean region which must have had a heavy rainfall distributed more or less evenly throughout the year instead of a moderate or scanty rainfall limited to the winter months as at present. . . . Wandering storms penetrated into the Sahara which was then one of the most genial regions on the globe, and this region, now a desert, appears to have been one of the main centres in which the human race rose to a dominant position in the world. The Equatorial regions in general had a greater rainfall than at present though with local exceptions. . . . There is abundant evidence that the lakes in Equatorial regions were probably much more extensive than at present, especially in Equatorial Africa, and it seems probable that this pluvial period coincided with the glacial period. At the same time the glaciers descended to a lower level than to-day.

But although in 1919 Professor Gregory had appreciated that the change of climate from the maximum extension of the lakes to the present-day conditions was not a continuous, gradual desiccation, but was rather a sequence of alternating wet and dry periods, and although Brooks was able to write in 1926 that there was abundant evidence that the lakes in Central Africa were once more extensive than to-day, and to suggest that this was during the period of the Ice Age, no really detailed study of the Pleistocene climatic changes of Kenya had been made. In Uganda however Mr E. J. Wayland had already done some detailed work which had led him to certain tentative conclusions which he summarised in a paper to the Prehistoric Society of East Anglia published in 1923[4] and in a note in *Man* in 1924.[5] He recorded stone tools in various high-level pluvial deposits and suggested the possibility of correlating the European glacial phases with pluvial periods in Uganda. When the East African Archaeological Expedition started work in Kenya in 1926 we concentrated our investigations mainly upon the lake basins of Nakuru, Elmenteita and Naivasha.

Here we found evidence which seemed to me to prove conclusively that during the Pleistocene there had been at least three pluvial periods, separated from each other by arid periods. In working out the geological evidence during the first season's work, I was very much helped, first by the Swedish geologist Dr Erik Nilsson, who had come out on an expedition to study the geology of the Rift Valley, and then also by Mr Wayland, the Director of the Geological Survey of Uganda, who kindly came down from Uganda to give us his advice, and he examined some of our sites and wrote me a short report, which was not however published. Although we obtained a considerable amount of evidence for alternating dry and wet periods, the details were not sufficiently clear to justify publication, and so when I returned for my second season's work in 1928–9 I arranged to have on the expedition a geologist, and a surveyor. Mr J. D. Solomon came out as the geologist of the Expedition in December 1928 and he did a great deal of very valuable work on the pluvial sequence, while my brother, Mr D. G. B. Leakey, undertook all the levelling which was necessary to ascertain the height of the various high-level lake terraces.

The geological evidence is now in course of preparation for publication by Solomon, and a summary of it is published as an Appendix to this book, so that I need not discuss the geological evidence here in any detail, but refer my readers to that Appendix. For convenience, however, I will here give an outline of the results of the geological investigation.

In 1926 we discovered water-laid deposits which were earlier than those three pluvial periods which we had then distinguished, but I did not take them into account, as I believed that they were part of a series of deposits laid down in what Professor Gregory named the Kamasian Lake or Kamasian Sea, and which he regarded as being part of his Nyasan series, which he had described as of Miocene date.[6] Solomon's work, however, has demonstrated that although these deposits do belong to the Kamasia series of lake deposits, which extend from the region of Lake Baringo to the Njorowa Gorge at Naivasha and probably farther, they are of Pleistocene date, and in fact it seems that part at any rate of Professor Gregory's Kamasia series should be brought into the first half of the Pleistocene and should not be regarded as the equivalent of the Karungu bone beds which are Miocene. Solomon further showed that the two pluvial periods, which in 1926 I had called "first" and "second", are really simply maxima of a single major pluvial period which had a small period of drier conditions in the middle. He has also shown that my old "third pluvial period" was not of sufficient size and duration to justify the term "pluvial period", and so we now designate it a post-pluvial wet phase, somewhat comparable to the re-advance of the ice in Europe during what is known as the Bühl Stadium. A second small post-pluvial wet phase was also traced, separated from the former by a dry period. The interval between the first major pluvial period and the second was marked by earth movements and volcanic activity on a large scale, and must have been of very long duration, for many of the stratified deposits laid down in the lake (or lakes) of the first pluvial were not only heavily faulted, but were eroded into foot hills and valleys before the waters of the lakes of the second major pluvial cut terraces into them. Many volcanoes too came into being at that time and poured lava sheets over the deposits of the first major pluvial period, as may be seen in the section exposed at the Njorowa Gorge, or near Baringo. We have not yet made a sufficiently detailed study of the first major pluvial period to enable us to establish any sub-divisions, but it seems probable that they do exist. The break between the two maxima of the second pluvial was not long enough to result in complete desiccation, but it caused a very considerable lowering in the level of the waters of the then existing lake in the Nakuru-Elmenteita basin. The level dropped from about seven hundred feet above the present lake to a point below the three hundred foot level, and then during the second maximum rose again to the height of about five hundred and ten feet.

At the end of the second major pluvial period there was a period of complete desiccation in the Rift Valley during which the lakes seem to have dried up completely and all exposed land surfaces were reddened. Deposits of aeolian sand were formed at this time, some of which have been preserved in sheltered places, but which were mainly washed away by the succeeding wet phase. This in turn was terminated by a new period of desiccation, after which came a further wet period when the waters in the Nakuru-Elmenteita basin rose to one hundred and forty-five feet above their present level, since which time they have gradually dwindled. This gradual change to present-day conditions must certainly have been accompanied by a number of minor fluctuations, but no attempt has been made to work these out.

We published a short note on this sequence in *Nature* in 1929,[7] giving provisional names to the various pluvial periods and to the post-pluvial wet phases. We have now decided that some of these names should be altered; for example, whereas we called the deposits of the first major pluvial Eburrian, they should obviously be called Kamasian, since they have been shown to be the same as Gregory's Kamasia deposits and his name must take precedence. Similarly the two maxima of the second pluvial should not be distinguished by separate names, but should rather be termed Lower Gamblian and Upper Gamblian. The sequence may be shown in a table, thus:

The climatic changes of the Pleistocene in Kenya

Height of water in Lake Nakuru basin above present level	Old name	New name	Period
145 ± feet	Nakuran	Nakuran	Second post-pluvial wet phase
Period of aridity and deposition of aeolian sand			
375 ± feet	Makalian	Makalian	First post-pluvial wet phase
Period of intense aridity marked by deposition of aeolian sand, reddening of all exposed land surfaces, formation of kunkar			
510 ± feet	Gamblian	Upper Gamblian	The two Gamblian periods
300 ± feet	Period of decreased rainfall.	Fall of lake levels	together form the second
700 ± feet	Enderian	Lower Gamblian	major pluvial
Long period of earth movements, faulting, volcanic eruptions and also of erosion. Dry			
	Eburrian	Kamasian. Sub-divisions not worked out, but a very long period, probably much longer than the Gamblian	First major pluvial

Unfortunately plans for enabling Solomon to work on the old moraines of Mount Kenya were frustrated, but we have the work which was done by Dr Nilsson[8] in 1927 to help us. He has not yet published full details, but a small paper by Lonnberg[9] published in 1929 gives some of the more important findings. Dr Nilsson apparently found clear evidence of four glaciations on Mount Kenya. The first of these is represented by a very low terminal moraine previously noted by Professor Gregory, and by others; the other three were of less size and did not extend as far as the first. Dr Nilsson found similar evidence on Mount Kilimanjaro, but here one small moraine was not noted. Mount Elgon gave similar evidence, but the smaller glaciations were less clearly marked because of the relatively low altitude of that mountain. Nilsson suggests that the glaciations should be correlated with the pluvials. He is not aware of our new terminology, and the correlation which he suggests is not absolutely clear. I suggest that it is likely that the greatest glaciation should correspond to the Kamasian, the next to the Gamblian, and the two smaller ones to the Makalian and Nakuran post-pluvial wet phases, both of which must have involved sufficiently increased precipitation to affect the glaciers to some extent.

These pluvial periods, with their great extensions of the ice sheets on all the higher mountains, must have had a marked effect on the temperature of the Highlands in Kenya. Even with conditions as they are to-day, slight frosts are by no means unknown in those areas which stand over 7000 feet above sea level, and even at the 6000 feet level black frosts have been recorded in the cold season. It is therefore almost certain that when the glaciers on the mountains like Kenya and Kilimanjaro were down to the 10,000 feet level, and when mountains like Elgon were glaciated, the Highlands areas over 6000 feet had snow and frost, at any rate during the cold season, besides having had a very much greater rainfall.

This probability has to be borne in mind when we consider the habits of prehistoric man who lived in the country during the pluvial periods. Similarly we may conclude that during the dry inter-pluvial periods, when the lakes in the Rift Valley dried up, the areas round the base of big mountains, like Mount Kenya, would still have a small rainfall, besides having streams fed from the smaller snowfields on the mountain itself. Thus in theory at any rate one would expect that the prehistoric tribes moved to the high land round the base of the big mountains during the inter-pluvials but that they evacuated that country and moved down to the Rift Valley areas during the pluvials, since they were less cold, besides being well watered.

It has been suggested on more than one occasion that the climatic changes of which we have such clear evidence in Kenya were really only *local* events. Were this the case, it would of course not be permissible to attempt any correlation with the northern climatic changes. But whereas a very great deal more detailed work is still needed in areas where evidence of pluvial and inter-pluvial periods has been noted, already there is a sufficient weight of facts to show that the pluvial and inter-pluvial periods were events which left their mark on the whole of Central East Africa. In Uganda Mr E. J. Wayland has worked out a tentative pluvial sequence which fits in with our evidence in all essential details.[10] His most recent views on this subject were published in *Man*, July 1929, no. 88. In the Albertine basin he has a big series of lake deposits which he calls the Kaiso series, and which culminate in an arid period, during which the Kaiso bone beds were formed. The Kaiso series overlies unconformably the Kisegi series, which is

13

considered to be probably of Miocene age, and contemporary with the Karungu lake beds which have yielded an extensive Miocene fauna. Subsequent to the Kaiso series and the arid period, there was a fresh rise of the lake which laid down beds of sand and gravel over the Kaiso series. These are probably the equivalent of the Gamblian beds. Deposits corresponding to the Makalian and Nakuran post-pluvial wet phases do not occur in the Albert basin, but this is probably because the Albert basin had at that time an outlet somewhere about the same level as at present, and therefore, unlike the Nakuru and Naivasha basins, would not record the increased rainfall of the smaller wet periods. But I understand that there is evidence of them in other parts of Uganda.

In Tanganyika Territory, Solomon and I found evidence of three terraces for Lake Manyara, and Lake Tanganyika, but no detailed work was done owing to lack of time.

At Oldoway in Tanganyika Territory Professor Hans Reck found a series of beds which yielded an extensive extinct fauna, and also a fossil human skeleton. Unfortunately no Stone Age tools were noted in any of the deposits. Reck has already published a series of preliminary reports on the geology of the Oldoway beds.[11]

The sequence of his six main beds is given below:

Top. (6) Calcareous deposit of "Steppe lime".

(5) Tufa and sand, with only dry fauna, antelopes, land deposit.

(4) Clay of grey colour, with fish and wet fauna very similar to (2).

(3) Stratified sands and gravels, heavily reddened and containing concretions, fauna now includes dry climate forms as antelope.

(2) Grey-brown loam with fragments of lava, fossiliferous, wet fauna. Appears to have been laid down under water.

(1) Tufa lower part and land deposit and upper part water laid. slightly fossiliferous.

Bottom. Lava.

He holds that this whole series of beds represents a single continuous period, but I am not prepared to agree with him, and I may perhaps be permitted to suggest my interpretation of his strata. I agree of course that the sequence

14

is continuous, but I see in his deposits evidence of several alternating wet and dry periods.

Reck regards layer (1) as mainly a land surface deposit, but its upper levels may have been laid down in water. I am prepared to agree thus far and look on (2) and (3) as essentially a single deposit, although varying in colour and texture. I regard the lower beds as laid down during the height of a pluvial (their fauna suggests this), but I suggest that layer (3) represents the closing stages, as it includes more antelopes, showing that the forests were giving way to open plains. So far we are in agreement, I think. But Reck, as I understand him, holds that there was no break between the formation of beds (3) and (4). I think that the intense reddening of bed (3), and the presence of lime concretions (kunkar?), must be taken as indications that the deposition of bed (3) was followed by a period of intense desiccation and some erosion. This was in turn followed by renewed wet conditions which resulted in the deposition of bed (4), which is a water-deposited grey clay and must have been laid down after the reddening. It should, if I am right, lie unconformably upon some of the lower beds, and might well contain derived fossils. (It is worth noting here that Reck especially remarks that it resembles bed (2) very closely in appearance.) Bed (5) marks a further period of dry conditions, as is shown by its fauna, which consists almost entirely of antelopes, some of them extinct, and the deposit is an aeolian one.

Now, Reck claims that the human skeleton which he found lay in bed (2), but he shows by his description that at the point where it occurred the deposits of the supposed bed (2) were *at the same level* and *alongside of* the reddened beds of (3), and *not beneath* them. This he attributes to erosion and tectonic influence, in which I cannot follow him. Instead, I am more inclined to consider that the deposit in which the human skeleton occurred was in fact a pocket of bed (4)* (which he himself says closely resembles bed (2)), lying unconformably against bed (3), owing to erosion having taken place before bed (4) was deposited. I also incline to the idea that if this is the true interpretation, the bones of *Hipparion* found in the same pocket of deposits as the human skeleton (in bed (4) as I believe) were derived fossils which belong to bed (2) or (3) (where I understand they also occur).

I entirely agree with Reck that the idea of the skeleton having been a

* Reck is certain that the skeleton does belong to bed (2), in which case it would seem to be of Kamasian age.

15

later burial into the deposits in which it was found is untenable, but on the other hand I regard it as of later date than the fossils of beds (1), (2) and (3), and as an integral part of the deposit (4), for the reasons given above.

As to the correlation of these beds with those of Kenya and of Uganda, I think that my interpretation renders such a correlation more possible. On the evidence of the fossils from beds (2) and (3), especially the elephants, hippopotami and *Hipparion*, these would seem to be contemporary with the Kaiso beds, the aridity which marks the end of the Kaiso period corresponding to that which resulted in the intense reddening of bed (3) at Oldoway. I think we may also correlate, *tentatively*, these three lowest Oldoway beds with our Kamasia series. Bed (4) then becomes the equivalent of the post-Kaiso beds in Uganda, and the Gamblian beds of Kenya, while the dry period which is marked by bed (5) would correspond with the dry period which marked the end of the Gamblian. The cutting of the Oldoway gorge which is many kilometres long and very deep was probably started in the Makalian post-pluvial wet phase, and the stratified deposits were then exposed. It seems that the Balbal depression to the east of Oldoway was formed about this time, so that during the Makalian wet phase a gorge was cut through the old lake deposits by a river draining into the Balbal depression, instead of the Makalian wet phase resulting in a new series of lake deposits at Oldoway. Even to-day a marsh forms in the Balbal depression during the wet season, and I am inclined to think that during the Makalian and Nakuran wet phases it was in the newly formed Balbal depression that a lake formed, and that a study of this depression would reveal deposits and beaches corresponding to these two wet phases.

Even the dry period which marks the break between the Makalian and the Nakuran left its mark at Oldoway, for Reck describes an aeolian deposit sometimes attaining a depth of from six to eight metres which fills in some of the depressions formed after the gorge was cut. This aeolian deposit is overlain by the hard layer of "steppe lime" which also overlay and sealed in the deposit containing the human skeleton (after it had been subjected to a considerable erosion, as evidenced by the fact that bed (4)—according to Reck, bed (2)—had been laid bare of any trace of bed (5)). The "steppe lime" is overlain by humus. If my interpretation of Reck's sequence is accepted, it means that the Oldoway skeleton (which is certainly *Homo sapiens*, and which has some marked resemblances to the skulls which

I obtained from Gamble's Cave II) is of Gamblian date. Otherwise if it really belongs to bed (2) and not bed (4) it must be considered as being probably of Kamasian date and contemporary with the Acheulean.*

But if the theory of climatologists is correct and the periods of glacial advance in the Northern and Southern Hemispheres were due to increased precipitation over more or less the whole globe, the evidence of pluvial and inter-pluvial periods in Africa ought to extend much farther than Kenya, Uganda and Tanganyika, and it is therefore interesting to find that there is similar evidence from Nyasaland, Rhodesia and South Africa on the one hand, and from Egypt and the Sudan and the Jordan Valley[11] on the other. Evidence of climatic fluctuations is now being put forward from all these countries, and we may hope that in a few years' time a very considerable degree of correlation will be possible in Africa as a whole, especially as considerable attention is now being paid to Stone Age cultures which belong to each deposit.

NOTE. Blanckenhorne's evidence for the Jordan Valley[12] is particularly interesting as it compares very closely indeed with ours for East Africa. He says that in the Jordan Valley the sequence is (from oldest to youngest) Older Diluvium followed by a period of rift faulting and desiccation and then Younger Diluvium which has two maxima separated by a short dry period. He equates the Older Diluvium with Günz and Mindel, and the Younger Diluvium with Riss and Würm.

REFERENCES

1. *The Great Rift Valley*, by Prof. J. W. Gregory, p. 232.
2. *Journal of the East Africa and Uganda Natural History Society*, vol. VI, no. 15, p. 438.
3. *Climate through the Ages*, by C. E. P. Brooks, p. 315.
4. *Proceedings of the Prehistoric Society of East Anglia*, vol. IV, part 1.
5. *Man*, 1924, no. 124.
6. *The Rift Valleys and Geology of East Africa*, by Prof. J. W. Gregory, pp. 114, 203 *et seq*.
7. *Nature*, July 6, 1929.

* Since writing this discussion of the Oldoway beds I have been over to Berlin to discuss the whole question with Reck once again.

He insists that beds (2), (3) and (4) form a single unit and since they include his Oldoway Skeleton, an advanced *Homo sapiens*, it is difficult to believe that they are of Kamasian date. It may be that these beds equal our Lower Gamblian—which has an early Aurignacian culture—and that his bed No. (5) is the equivalent of our Mid-Gamblian break in the fluvial conditions. This would make it easier to understand the difference between the fauna from our Upper Gamblian and Reck's Oldoway series.

I have invited Professor Reck to accompany me to Oldoway in 1931 and examine all the evidence with me again on the spot.

8. *Preliminary Report on the Quaternary Geology of Mt Elgon and some parts of the Rift Valley*, by E. Nilsson.

9. "The development and distribution of the African fauna in connection with and depending on the climatic changes", by Lonnberg, Stockholm, 1929.

10. *Man*, July 1929, no. 88.

11. (*a*) "Erste Vorläufige Mitteilung über den Fund eines fossilen Menschenskelets aus Zentralafrika", by Prof. Hans Reck, in *Sitzungsberichte der Gesellschaft naturforschender Freunde*, Berlin, 1914.

(*b*) "Prähistorische Grab- und Menschenfunde und ihre Beziehungen zur Pluvialzeit in Ostafrika", by Prof. Hans Reck, in *Mitteilungen aus den deutschen Schutzgebieten*, Band xxxiv, Heft 1, Berlin, 1926.

(*c*) "Untersuchungen über den Oldowayfund", by Gieseler and Mollison, in *Verhandlungen der Gesellschaft für physische Anthropologie*, Band iii.

12. Krenkel, *Geol. Afr.* vol. 1, pp. 73–74.

CHAPTER III

PLEISTOCENE FAUNA

ALREADY there have been a number of discoveries of animal remains in East Africa in close association with traces of prehistoric man. Sometimes these traces are his stone tools, and sometimes, as at Oldoway in Tanganyika Territory, no tools were found, but the finding of actual human bones indicates the presence of man at the period during which the deposits were laid down.

In view of these facts it is necessary that we should determine how far we may safely use fossil animal remains in our efforts both to date the East African implementiferous deposits, and to correlate them with implementiferous deposits in Europe. First we must examine the position of fossil fauna for dating in Europe, and consider the limitations of the evidence, and also the type of information that it may yield.

In Europe the Pleistocene period underwent alternating glacial and inter-glacial phases. During the height of a glacial, most of Europe had an arctic or sub-arctic climate, and during the height of an inter-glacial the climate was more or less tropical. But these changes were not sudden, and between these two extremes, during the gradual oncoming of a glaciation or the gradual oncoming of an inter-glacial period, every degree of climatic variation must have been experienced.

It would seem that during the height of a glaciation the greater part of Europe had an arctic fauna, while during the maximum of an inter-glacial a tropical fauna flourished. But this does not mean that arctic and tropical forms were not present long after the climatic conditions best suited to them had ceased to exist, for very many animals are capable of a considerable degree of adaptation, *provided that the climatic changes are not too sudden.* Yet even keeping this capacity for adaptation well in mind, the study of any big series of fossils from any single Pleistocene deposit in Europe usually enables the Palaeontologists to fix with a fair degree of certainty the climatic conditions of the period during which that deposit was formed.

What is still more important is that a detailed study of numerous sites during many years has suggested that certain animals can be considered to be characteristic of certain periods, and equally it has been found that certain associations of faunal types are characteristic of certain phases. Apart from this, however, the most that fauna does is to indicate the climate and temperature, and it is frequently left to other evidence such as stratigraphy and associated palaeolithic cultures to determine the exact period of a deposit. Certain species of animals associated with Palaeolithic man in Europe are extinct to-day, but many others still survive either in Europe or in distant parts of the world, represented by closely allied if not by identical forms. For example, the list of fauna found associated with the young Neanderthal child of the Devil's Tower, Gibraltar,[1] consists almost entirely of forms either identical or very similar to animals living in the world to-day; and practically not one of the fossils found there, if taken out of the assemblage, could be used as evidence for dating purposes.

Even when fauna can be used for the dating of a deposit, we must remember that the geography of the area is very largely responsible for making this possible. At various times, from late Pliocene onwards, there have been land bridges connecting Europe and North Africa which made possible movements of animals and of early man from Africa to Europe, and *vice versa*. But these land bridges were not always in existence when they were most needed, and there is every indication that the warm fauna of the mid-Pleistocene inter-glacial did not return to North Africa with the first advance of the ice, but either stayed in the southern parts of Europe and adapted itself to the colder conditions, or else died out.

As far as I am aware no one has yet made a complete study of the relations of the North African and European Pleistocene fauna to each other, with special reference to the problem of the land bridges, although much light might thereby be thrown on the question. The notes published by Romer[2] in his study of the North African animals are very suggestive of the possibilities of such an investigation.

Unfortunately there is very considerable divergence of opinion among writers as to the number of times during the Pleistocene that land connections between North Africa and Europe have existed, nor is it agreed whether they occurred during the glacial or the inter-glacial phases. Romer tends to support the theory that land bridges came into being during the inter-glacial periods, while the arguments in favour of glacial land bridges are considered by Peake and Fleure[3] to be more conclusive.

As far as I can see two facts stand out clearly. There is ample evidence of a land connection during the warm period at the end of the Pliocene before the onset of the Ice Age, for the fauna of North Africa was then almost identical to that of Europe. There also seems to be some evidence that in very early Mousterian times there was a land bridge, for at this period many animals that have previously only been recorded from Europe, such as *Rhinoceros merkii*, *Elephas iolensis*, bear, deer, fox and wild cat, make their first appearance in North Africa.* Simultaneously a number of new forms arrive in North Africa from farther south, and among these are included wart-hog, water-buck, reed-buck, serval cat, and jackal. The combination of these two facts seems on the whole to favour the opinion that the Mousterian land bridge existed during a cold period, probably the beginning of the Würm glaciation, for warmth-loving animals such as the zebra and *Elephas atlanticus* (which had been in North Africa for some time), and also the newly arrived forms from farther south, do not seem to have crossed over into Europe at this period as they surely would have done if this so-called Mousterian land bridge had existed during an inter-glacial.

From the archaeological point of view the important question is to decide whether this land bridge continued to exist during the closing stages of the Würm, when the Aurignacian culture seems first to have entered southern Europe from North Africa. Many writers postulate the existence of such a bridge at this time, and of another one during the Bühl Stadium, on the ground of the arrival in Europe first of the Aurignacian culture and later of the Azilian.

The difficulty of accepting this hypothesis is that there is certainly no evidence that any of the African animals crossed over at the same time, for there seems to be no record of animals such as the wart-hog, jackal or zebra ever occurring in south-western Europe. This may possibly be explained by the fact that the land bridges may only have existed during the cold periods, in this case, the closing stages of the Würm and the period of the Bühl advance of the ice—so that it was only man with his knowledge of fire and of skin clothing who would move northwards in search of fresh hunting fields, while the contemporary African fauna did not cross over. There is another possible explanation which ought to be borne in mind, namely that

---

* This can however be explained by infiltration of these animals via Palestine, so that a land bridge in early Mousterian times is not an essential explanation. This is the view of Vaufray and others in France.

subsequent to the maximum of the Würm glaciation no land bridge existed, but that as the population increased in North Africa a few of the Aurignacian families, seeing land across the fairly narrow strip of water,* made rafts and contrived to cross in search of new hunting fields.

But whereas in Europe the presence and absence of land bridges, the movements of the ice sheets, and the accompanying great changes of temperature all contributed to the distribution and extermination or alteration of fauna during the various phases of the Pleistocene, the story on the African continent was somewhat different. Africa is not only of vast size, it also extends over a wide latitudinal range, and has large areas of highland plateaux where altitude counteracts the effects of latitude on climate and temperature, to a marked degree. Even to-day, within this range of altitudes and latitudes, almost every type of climatic variation can be encountered, from the permanent snows and glaciers of such mountains as Kilimanjaro, Kenya, and Ruenzori, to the desert sands of the Sahara or the Kalahari. Moreover, whereas the world-wide periods of increased precipitation in the Pleistocene resulted in glaciations in Europe because of her latitudinal position, in Africa they mainly resulted in pluvial periods, although in the regions of higher altitudes, that is of land over 12,000 feet, this increased precipitation involved the formation of snow and ice caps on mountains which to-day have no ice, and in great advances of existing glaciers.[3] But in all the other vast lower lying areas the actual temperature change was not excessive, although the mean temperature was probably lowered owing to the greater amount of cloud. Again, it would seem that the world-wide periods of precipitation resulted in a proportionately increased rainfall all over the world, so that in Africa, areas such as the Sahara, which are deserts to-day, were probably open grass lands on which herds of antelopes and zebra could flourish, even though there was not enough rainfall for the growth of forests.

According to Dr Simpson's theory[4] there was only one world-wide period of decreased precipitation which corresponded to the Mindel-Riss inter-glacial, while the smaller inter-pluvials of which we have record in Africa (such as that which sub-divides our Gamblian pluvial) would be more or less local, and due to *secondary* meteorological causes, and not to *primary*

* The archaeological evidence suggests that the early African Aurignacians crossed into Europe via Malta and Sicily rather than via Gibraltar and Spain. Even if there was no actual land bridge the straits of sea must have been narrower at this time.

world changes of climate. If this view is correct, it follows that theoretically the most likely time for the extinction of animal species during the African Pleistocene should be the Middle Pleistocene inter-pluvial period corresponding to the Mindel-Riss inter-glacial, while those species which survived that period should most of them have survived up to the present day in some part of the continent, even if the smaller and more localised inter-pluvial periods resulted in a different distribution of the fauna from that which it had during a previous pluvial phase. In fact we may say that on theoretical grounds the presence of many extinct forms in a fossil fauna in Africa in Pleistocene times probably indicates a date prior to the big Middle Pleistocene inter-pluvial, while at any point subsequent to that major inter-pluvial comparatively few extinct forms are likely to be found in Africa, although the study of the present distribution of the forms in any such deposit should be very useful as indications of the climatic conditions.

Before we turn to the actual discoveries of fauna in Pleistocene deposits in East Africa, we may profit by a brief examination of certain facts from North Africa.[1] Up to the Chellean period, a certain number of forms existed which are extinct to-day. Among these special note must be made of *Hipparion* (which in Europe died out much earlier), *Hippopotamus hipponensis* and *Equus stenonis*. After the Middle Pleistocene, although many of the forms found in geological deposits do not occur in North Africa to-day, the majority of them represent species still living in some other part of Africa, while the truly extinct forms are few, and consist chiefly of animals like *Rhinoceros merkii*, *Ursus spelaeus*, and *Elephas iolensis*, which migrated into North Africa from Europe at the beginning of the Würm and died out there. In fact in North Africa the vast majority of the animals found in deposits later than the Middle Pleistocene are living to-day, and the deposits in which they occur as fossils can only be dated with certainty as Pleistocene if by chance one of the few extinct forms is found associated with them, or if the deposit can be dated on stratigraphical or cultural grounds, or else if the forms found though living elsewhere in Africa are known not to continue in North Africa after a given period.

In the preceding chapter we have seen that the Middle Pleistocene in East Africa was marked by a period of intense aridity, and that both in Mr Wayland's collection[5] from Kaiso in Uganda, and in Dr Reck's collection from Oldoway in Tanganyika Territory, the fauna which antedates this period of aridity includes a fairly high percentage of extinct forms, including in each case *Hipparion*. This mid-Pleistocene period of aridity seems to correspond to the end of the Kamasian pluvial. In Kenya, with the exception of the Homa bone bed, we have as yet no fossiliferous beds of Kamasian date, and the fauna so far found in deposits of the next—that is the Gamblian—pluvial, although fairly extensive, has not as yet been fully worked out. From Mr A. T. Hopwood's preliminary study (see Appendix C) of the collections from deposits of Gamblian pluvial date which we brought home last season we can say that there are very few extinct forms present, although the modern distribution of some of the species found is interesting. This finding is entirely in keeping with what was to be expected on theoretical grounds. Before I began to investigate the question of the Pleistocene fauna in North Africa, and before going into the question of pluvial-glacial correlation with Dr Simpson and with Dr Brooks, I believed and hoped that we should find a large number of extinct species in the Gamblian pluvial fauna.* This I now see was a hope based on a misunderstanding of the whole question of Pleistocene fauna, due to a study of the late Pleistocene fauna of Europe without a full appreciation of the local effects of latitude, climate, and land bridges problems. If a *high* percentage of extinct species of animals were to be found in supposed Gamblian deposits in East Africa, the date of the deposits would have to be carefully considered (unless the fossils could be shown to be derived from earlier beds).

In Kenya Colony the fossil beds that can be placed in the Pleistocene sequence with any degree of certainty are few. The Homa bone bed near Kisumu is regarded by Hopwood as probably of the same age as the Kaiso beds, and is therefore probably of Kamasian date. The Gamblian beds exposed in the Malewa River Valley, Naivasha (also called the Morendat River), have yielded a number of fossil bones. The first fossil recorded from here was a fragment of lower jaw of an equine, which was named by Professor Ridgeway *Equus hollisi*.[6] Here, too, Dr Nilsson found a complete skeleton of an extinct buffalo, *Bos bubalus antiquus* sp.[7] We collected a large number of bones from this area, including remains of rhinoceros and of hippopotamus, etc. (See Appendix C.)

The bones from the Aurignacian levels of Gamble's Cave II, Elmenteita, and of Lion Hill Cave are of Upper Gamblian date and a large number of

* This may be seen by a study of my monthly field reports.

mammals are represented, and also a number of molluscs and birds and fish. A provisional list of mammals and mollusca from Upper Gamblian deposits is given below, but specific identification of the mammals is not yet possible as the material has not been fully worked out. The birds and fish have not yet been examined.

With a very few exceptions all the Upper Gamblian fauna is living to-day either in East Africa or in neighbouring Territories, and, but for its stratigraphical position, would be of no use for dating purposes. As corroborative evidence of the climatic conditions it is very instructive however, nearly all the forms being those which like a wet climate with forest or thick bush, few if any of the typical plains animals being found.

Provisional list of mammals of the Upper Gamblian pluvial period in Kenya

Several large carnivores	Porcupine
Jackal	Cane rat
Otter (two species at least)	Many antelope forms
Hippopotamus	Buffalo
Rhinoceros	Many small rodents
Wart-hog	Several bats
Forest hog	Several insectivores
Bush pig	Several small carnivores
Hyrax	Aard vark
Hare	Several monkeys

Also:

Bos bubalus antiquus sp.   *Equus hollisi*

Provisional list of mollusca of the Upper Gamblian pluvial period

FRESH-WATER SPECIES:

1. *Melanoides tuberculata* (Müll.).
2. *Corbicula africana* (Krs.) (= *radiata* Phil.).
3. *Lymnaea elmeteitensis*? Smith.
4. *Bulinus*, species. Fragments.
5. *Bulinus syngenes*? (Prest.). One shell.
6. *Planorbis*, species.
7. *Segmentina planodiscus*? (M. and P.). One shell.

25

PLEISTOCENE FAUNA

LAND SPECIES:

1. *Marconia elgonensis* (Prest.).
2. *Gulella ugandensis* (Smith) (= *optata*, Prest.).
3. *Cerastus lagariensis*, Smith.
4. *Opeas aphantum*, Conn.
5. *Subuliniscus adjacens* ? Conn.
6. *Halolimnohelix bukobae* (Mts.).
7. *Homorus*, species.
8. *Subulina*, species.
9. *Opeas psephenum*, Conn.
10. *Limicolaria flammea*? (Müll.).
11. *Opeas tangaense* d'Ailly.

NOTE. For the above identifications of mollusca I am indebted to Major Connolly. (See Appendix D.)

Makalian fauna

A certain number of animal remains have been found in Makalian deposits, but it is not yet possible to say whether they include any extinct species or not, nor to give the complete list of species which have been found. Such details as are at present possible are given in Appendix C, but the following provisional list may be given here.

Mammals found in Makalian deposits

Hyrax	Many antelopes
Baboon	Many rodents
Wart-hog	*Bos* sp.
Hippopotamus	

REFERENCES

1. "Excavation of a Mousterian rock shelter at Devil's Tower, Gibraltar", by D. A. E. Garrod and others, in *Journal of Royal Anthropological Institute*, Jan. and June 1928.
2. "Pleistocene mammals of Algeria", by A. S. Romer, in "A contribution to the study of prehistoric man in Algeria, North Africa", in *Beloit College Bulletin*, vol. XXIV, no. 5, pp. 92 *et seq.*
3. *Hunters and Artists*, by Peake and Fleure, pp. 12 *et seq.*
4. "Past climates", by C. S. Simpson, paper to the British Science Guild, 1929.
5. "A review of the fossil mammals of Central Africa", by A. T. Hopwood, in *American Journal of Science*, vol. XVII, 1929.
6. *Proceedings of Zoological Society*, 1909, p. 586, a paper by Ridgeway.
7. "The development and distribution of the African fauna in connection with and depending on the climatic changes", by Lonnberg, Stockholm, 1929.

CHAPTER IV

OUTLINE OF THE KENYA CULTURE SEQUENCE

MANY archaeologists when describing the cultures and industries found in areas other than the classic ones of Central and Western Europe tend to use a new terminology of their own, instead of retaining the earlier names. They argue that the original terminology should not be used unless contemporaneity as well as similarity is demonstrable. In other words, names such as Mousterian or Chellean are held not only to denote a type of culture, but also a definite date. This argument seems to me to be essentially a false one, and I am not prepared to subscribe to it. Even in East and Central Europe it would be absurd to say that all Chellean implements were contemporary, for the period during which they were made must have spread over many thousands of years, and one certainly cannot logically argue that the earliest Chellean implements in South Spain were absolutely contemporary with the earliest Chellean implements in France or England. Neither can it be argued that the terminology necessarily implies a definite sequence, even if a particular sequence has always been found in Europe. I therefore prefer to regard the words Chellean, Acheulean, Mousterian, Aurignacian, etc., as each denoting a very definite culture phase, within which there may be variations of detail in different areas.

If we are to treat archaeological terminology scientifically, we must follow the precedent of the older sciences in our naming of cultures and industries, and only employ new names for them when they are so different from those which have been already named that they cannot be regarded simply as local variations.

There is of course always a slight danger that workers in other countries who are not well acquainted with the cultures and industries of the type stations, and who only have drawings and photographs available for comparative purposes, may be liable to regard a culture or industry which they have found as identical to one already described and use the earlier name when in point of fact theirs is quite different, but this difficulty is not insuperable nor is it foreign to other sciences. Those in favour of new terminologies for new areas lay stress on this argument, but surely the confusion caused by a totally new terminology is far worse than such possible mistakes, and with the ever-increasing diffusion of type series of tools to museums of other parts of the world this difficulty should soon be removed altogether.

Where a culture or industry in a new area is found to be very similar to one already described and named, I contend that it should be named after that culture or industry, but with an adjective denoting the country in which it is found prefixed to the name. In addition care should be taken that in all publications the statement is made that the culture name used does not imply any date, or even of necessity a culture contact. If a culture is not similar to one already named and described elsewhere, it must of course be given a new name. Moreover a kind consideration for archaeological students favours the restricted terminology, for the work of mastering even necessary local names must in any case entail great increase of labour.

In accordance with this principle I have named the cultures and industries in Kenya after their European equivalents whenever possible, only prefixing the word Kenya. In instances where there is no European equivalent, but where there is a similar culture previously named in South Africa, I adopt their name, again with the prefix Kenya. In a few instances it has been found necessary to use new names where a culture or industry is not really the equivalent of any known to me previously.

The culture sequence as at present known to us in Kenya is as follows, the oldest culture being at the bottom:

> Njoroan
> Gumban B (the Nakuru culture of my earlier reports)
> Gumban A
> Kenya Wilton
> Elmenteitan
> Kenya late Aurignacian ⎱ contemporary
> Kenya Stillbay ⎰
> Kenya Aurignacian ⎱ contemporary
> Kenya Mousterian ⎰
> Nanyukian
> Kenya Acheulean
> Kenya Chellean

OUTLINE OF THE KENYA CULTURE SEQUENCE

Before proceeding to the description of these various cultures it is necessary to state the evidence upon which the sequence is based, and to indicate the relation of the cultures to the various climatic periods.*

Kenya Chellean and Kenya Acheulean

So far the Kenya Chellean is very poorly represented by implements found *in situ* in deposits of a known horizon, in fact none of the *earlier* types of Kenya Chellean tools have so far been found in deposits whose relation to the pluvial sequence can be proved. At one site, however, tools of *late* Chellean type are found in a heavily rolled condition in the same beds as completely unrolled tools of Acheulean type, and we thus have clear evidence that the former are the earlier. That the early Chellean types are older than the late Chellean types can at present only be argued on the basis of typology, but there is little doubt that the typological evidence is correct.

The beds in which the rolled late Kenya Chellean and the unrolled Kenya Acheulean tools are found *in situ* consist of faulted lake deposits belonging to the closing stages of the Kamasian period. (See Appendix A.) It therefore follows that these cultures cannot be later than that time. The unrolled Kenya Acheulean tools are in such perfect condition that they cannot have been made very long before they became embedded in the deposit in which they were found, but the late Kenya Chellean tools are so heavily rolled that they may well belong to a considerably earlier date. We may thus say that the Kenya Acheulean belongs to the closing stages of the Kamasian pluvial, and that the Kenya Chellean can be assigned to an earlier part of the same pluvial period.

The Nanyukian

So far there is no positive evidence on which to date this industry, which really represents a very advanced development of the Kenya Acheulean with a marked tendency towards a very early Mousterian type. The regions in which it has been found, so far, are away from the Great Rift Valley, which, as we have seen, underwent a period of earth movements and volcanic activity at the close of the Kamasian period. The typology of the industry together with its locality suggest that it belongs to the period separating the

* In a publication called *Cahiers d'Art* published in Paris, 1930, M. L'Abbé Breuil has recently given an outline of the Stone Age cultures of the whole of Africa and has included many references to my work. Unfortunately these references are based on my preliminary field reports only and naturally therefore, as was inevitable, L'Abbé Breuil's account is not entirely accurate or complete.

Kamasian from the Gamblian pluvial, but its position in the sequence must be regarded as only provisional, pending further work next season.

The Kenya Mousterian and the Kenya Aurignacian

There is no doubt whatever as to the position of these two cultures in the pluvial sequence. There is no trace of tools of either of these two types in the deposits of the Kamasian period, but they both occur all through the deposits of the Gamblian period, throughout which there is a marked development of both cultures from the lower to the upper beds. Tools of the Mousterian type tend to be more common than those of the Aurignacian in the gravels and silts of the Gamblian period, but this is probably due not so much to a predominance of the makers of the former industry, as to a consideration of their mode of life. Cave excavations have shown that the Aurignacians were essentially a cave-dwelling people, and it is therefore only natural that their tools should not be common in the gravels and silts. It may well be that further excavations in other caves will show that the makers of the Kenya Mousterian tools also lived in caves, but evidence of this is at present wanting. Moreover since habitable caves must have been limited, and since the evidence shows that the makers of these two distinct cultures were occupying the country simultaneously, we may presume that the superior race would monopolise the caves (at anyrate the better ones) to the exclusion of the less advanced race. We must believe that the Kenya Aurignacians were the more advanced race, since we know from their skeletons that they were of the *Homo sapiens* type, and from the excavation of their caves that they had a wide range of specialised tools. Nevertheless it is not safe to imply that the makers of the Kenya Mousterian tools were of the Neanderthal race, but we must consider them as having been more primitive than the contemporary Kenya Aurignacians, since they seem to have had far fewer specialised tools. I am inclined to believe that when a skull is eventually found which does belong to this culture, it will prove to be a modified form of the Broken Hill skull type (*Homo rhodesiensis*).

That the two cultures were contemporaneous is shown by the fact that whenever silts and gravels of Gamblian date are found to be implementiferous, tools of one or other or of both types occur, and it cannot be held that the one is earlier than the other, or that one type of tool is merely derived from earlier beds, because both cultures show a very marked evolution from the lower to the upper beds of deposits of Gamblian date. That the two cultures were not intermixed is proved by the cave excavations. At Gamble's Cave II, in deposits of Upper Gamblian date (see Ch. VII), we found some 59,000 tools of upper Kenya Aurignacian type exactly similar to those found in the silts and gravels of Upper Gamblian date, but there was no trace whatever of the tools of upper Kenya Mousterian type with them, such as occur side by side with the upper Kenya Aurignacian tools in gravels and silts of this period.

Kenya Stillbay and Kenya late Aurignacian

The Kenya Stillbay is a direct development from the upper Kenya Mousterian, and the Kenya late Aurignacian is derived from the ordinary upper Kenya Aurignacian. Both these industries are found stratigraphically later than the upper Kenya Mousterian and upper Kenya Aurignacian, and they belong to the period of the decline of the Gamblian pluvial, some time after the maximum of the Upper Gamblian.

Elmenteitan

This culture is found in the lake deposits which lie unconformably upon the deposits of the Gamblian period, and which belong to the Makalian wet phase. It was also found in the sequence in Gamble's Cave II, separated from the deposits of the period of Upper Gamblian by a deposit of aeolian sand, indicative of arid conditions. It is therefore unquestionably later than the Gamblian, and belongs to the Makalian wet phase.

The Kenya Wilton

The earliest deposits in which the Kenya Wilton is known to occur are the silts and muds which belong to the very close of the Makalian wet phase. Branches of this culture probably persisted until much later times, and it seems likely that the Gumban cultures are the result of a development of a Kenya Wilton under outside influence.

The Gumban A

This is the provisional name which I have given to a culture which is distinguished by a remarkable type of pottery with very characteristic decoration. It has been found at one point buried in the muds of the 145 foot lake, and it apparently belongs to the early part of the Nakuran wet phase. Associated with this pottery one finds crude stone-bowls suggesting an affinity with the Gumban B culture (my old "Nakuru Culture").

31

The Gumban B ("Nakuru Culture" of my earlier reports)

So far the Gumban B has only been examined at one site, where its date can be fixed with some degree of certainty. The site rests upon an old beach of Makalian times, and is therefore of later date than that. During the excavation of the site beads were found which are not earlier than 3000 B.C., and so a backward limit may be fixed in that way. The site is far from any stream or spring to-day, but only about half a mile away from the old beach of Lake Nakuru of the time of the Nakuran wet phase, when the lake stood one hundred and forty-five feet higher than it does to-day; and it is more than probable that this was the water supply of the Gumban B folk. The site moreover contains fish bones, whereas to-day Lake Nakuru has no fish, nor are there known to be fish in any of the streams running into the lake. It seems certain, therefore, that the occupation of the Nakuru site coincided with the period of the one hundred and forty-five foot lake, or at any rate with a time before it had dwindled so far as to have a soda percentage too great to be drinkable or to contain fish.

We know that between the end of the Makalian and the rise of the Nakuran lakes there was a period of intense desiccation, and this would seem to coincide very well with what Brooks[1] describes as the Climatic Optimum. Brooks suggests that this period was probably dry in Equatorial regions, and he dates it about 4000 to 3000 B.C. This fits our evidence very well. The drying up during the Climatic Optimum was followed by gradually renewed wet conditions, and Lake Nakuru rose to one hundred and forty-five feet by about 1000 B.C., or even later, since when, with various fluctuations, it has gradually sunk to its present low level.

The Njoroan

I am tentatively suggesting this name for the polished axe culture, signs of which have been found in Kenya. We have not yet enough evidence to say whether it was earlier, contemporary with, or later than the Gumban cultures, which are also Neolithic, but it seems most probable that they were roughly contemporary.

We may summarise the relation of the cultures in Kenya to the climatic changes in the following table:

OUTLINE OF THE KENYA CULTURE SEQUENCE

Climatic phase	Culture phase
Nakuran post-pluvial wet phase	Njoroan ⎫ Gumban B ⎬ contemporary? Gumban A ⎭
Makalian post-pluvial wet phase	(2) Kenya Wilton (1) Elmenteitan
Decline of Upper Gamblian	Kenya late Aurignacian ⎫ contemporary Kenya Stillbay ⎭
Upper Gamblian ⎫ Second major pluvial Lower Gamblian ⎭	Upper Kenya Aurignacian ⎫ contemporary Upper Kenya Mousterian ⎭ Lower Kenya Aurignacian ⎫ contemporary Lower Kenya Mousterian ⎭
Period between Kamasian and Gamblian	Nanyukian
Kamasian (late) ⎫ Kamasian (middle) ⎬ First major pluvial Kamasian (early) ⎭	(2) Kenya Acheulean (1) Upper Kenya Chellean Lower Kenya Chellean ?

REFERENCE

1. *Climate Through the Ages*, by C. E. P. Brooks, p. 415.

CHAPTER V

THE KENYA CHELLEAN, THE KENYA ACHEULEAN AND THE NANYUKIAN

WE have already seen in Chapter IV that tools of early Chellean type have not so far been found in Kenya in deposits which can be fitted into any place in the climatic sequence, but since we have tools of late Chellean type which can be fitted into that sequence we may take it as a safe working hypothesis that the early Chellean types are of earlier date than the more advanced types which are found in a rolled condition in the upper deposits of the Kamasian series.

The only tool I know which is of definite early Kenya Chellean type found *in situ* in Kenya is a very large coup-de-poing found by Mr Wayland in a gravel-bed at Koru.* This specimen he sent to the Cambridge Museum of Archaeology and Ethnology, and he also sent me a note about it, which the Curator of the Cambridge Museum has kindly allowed me to publish.

It is the large tool shown in Plate I and it is formed of a big pebble of lava,† which has been trimmed at one end so that it has a flattened point, at the butt end the pebble surface is left intact. This tool weighs 4 lb. 9 oz. and must have required a giant to handle it. Tools of a somewhat similar type have been found in several parts of Kenya on the surface, and there can be no doubt that they will one day be found *in situ* in beds which show their true relation to the upper Kamasian series. But whereas the lower Kenya Chellean is thus poorly represented, the upper Kenya Chellean tools are more abundant, and their position in the sequence is known. The type station for these upper Kenya Chellean tools is the same as that for the Kenya Acheulean, namely the exposure of the Kamasian deposits near the point where the Kariandusi River runs into Lake Elmenteita. The late Kenya Chellean and the Kenya Acheulean tools occur side by side, but the former are all rolled whilst the latter are quite unrolled. A few of the rolled tools have been less abraded than the others and are probably intermediate in date between the two series. There are, however, not enough of these less rolled tools to establish an intermediate series on purely typological grounds.

* Since this was written many others have been found in Kenya.
† The tool is too weathered for it to be possible to determine the exact nature of the lava without slicing, but it is possibly a dolerite.

As the deposits in which all these tools occur belong to the closing stages of the Kamasian period,[1] we may say that the Kenya Acheulean represented by the unrolled tools was roughly contemporary with that time, whereas the upper Chellean was somewhat earlier, and presumably the lower Chellean earlier still.

Before describing those types from this site which belong to the late Kenya Chellean series, we must examine the material of which they are made. The material is lava, chiefly quartz-trachyte, and even the unworked pieces from the site can mostly be termed flakes rather than cores. Some of these are natural flakes, but more often they are the result of an intentional detaching blow. The significance of this lies in the fact that the simplest way to obtain suitable pieces of lava to work into coups-de-poing was to batter the outcrop, and to detach large pieces, which came off in the form of flakes. Hence nearly all the implements of lava are made on flakes, but this fact has little effect on the type of tool.

There was a time when it was considered a *sine qua non* of Chellean and Acheulean industries that the tools were core tools, but this theory has long since been exploded. It originated in the fact that Chellean and Acheulean tools were first found in flint areas, and since flint is by nature often nodular, if early man wanted to make large tools of coup-de-poing type his simplest way was to make them by chipping off flakes and using the central core as his tool. But in areas where flint was not available early man had to use other material, such as quartzite and lava, and although he sometimes made his tools of pebbles of these materials, he more frequently made them from big flakes of either natural origin, or from flakes intentionally struck off an outcrop. Even in the flint areas, if Chellean man found large enough pieces, he sometimes made his coups-de-poing on flakes. This digression has been necessary because in spite of clear statements by authorities such as Burkitt[2] and others, many people still hold to the old-fashioned view that all Chellean and Acheulean tools must be core tools.

The upper Kenya Chellean series at the Kariandusi River includes the following three main types of coup-de-poing:

(1) Coups-de-poing trimmed over both surfaces leaving little or no trace of original flake surface.

(2) Coups-de-poing with most of the lower flake surface untrimmed.

(3) Coups-de-poing trimmed at the points only and with thick blunt butts.

35

There are also a certain number of cleavers and a few very crude side-scrapers. All the tools are of rather crude workmanship, with more or less irregular cutting edges. Among the coups-de-poing there are no two which are sufficiently similar to be described as made to a pattern, and there is every shade of workmanship ranging from a tool worked all over both surfaces and with a sharp edge all round, to tools with a sharp edge only at one end.

Some of the coups-de-poing have the bulbs of percussion trimmed away, sometimes these bulbs are left. In almost all cases where the position of the bulb of percussion can be located it is at the side of the flake, a little to one end, and this is very characteristic of the Kenya Chellean of this site. Whether this is simply due to material or was intentional it is impossible to say. The cleavers consist of very roughly made rectangles, one end of which has a sharp edge formed by the intersection of two cleavage faces. The sides of the rectangle are roughly trimmed by oblique blows where necessary so as to give more or less of a parallelogram section across the middle of the tool.

Plates I, II and III, and Figs. 1 and 2, illustrate the Kenya Chellean types.

The Kenya Acheulean

As I have already stated, the type station for the Kenya Acheulean is the same as that for the late Kenya Chellean. One of the chief features of the Kenya Acheulean at the Kariandusi site was the use of obsidian for making the finest coups-de-poing. Lava such as quartz-trachyte was also used, but by far the greatest number of the good tools are made of obsidian, though there are a considerable number of less well-made tools of other lavas. The first impression was that the obsidian was so much easier to work that tools made of it were always more highly finished than the specimens made of other lavas, which material could not be worked into such perfect tools. But this cannot be the true explanation, for there are two specimens in a lava other than obsidian (it is probably quartz-trachyte) which are far superior in workmanship to any of the obsidian tools found. The real explanation is probably that obsidian, which is more brittle than the other lavas, was used chiefly for fine tools which were intended for delicate work, whilst the coarse lavas were used for tools required for rougher work, and which were not therefore made with such care. Occasionally, however, a good piece of ordinary lava would be worked into a really fine tool.

36

The unrolled Kenya Acheulean series includes many poorly made specimens which if found alone would be classed as late Kenya Chellean, owing to the irregular working edge and general crude workmanship. But the unrolled series must be considered as a whole, and the number of well-made tools with straight working edges and of generally good workmanship is high, in fact more than half of the total number of unrolled coups-de-poing from the site.

The tools may be sub-divided as follows:

(1) Coups-de-poing worked over the whole of both surfaces and with a sharp edge all round.

(2) Coups-de-poing with a plain untrimmed flake surface on one side, and a worked surface on the other.

(3) Coups-de-poing trimmed all over one surface and partially trimmed on the lower flake surface in order to remove the bulb of percussion.

(4) Coups-de-poing with a thick blunt butt, and worked to a point by trimming on one or both faces at one end.

(5) Cleavers.

(6) Crude side scrapers.

There are also a number of tools which are intermediate between some of these types and which do not easily fall into any special category.

The most peculiar type is the second group, which can be best understood by a study of the photographs on Plate VII, nos. 1 to 4. Although not a common type, it does occur in Acheulean deposits in Europe and I have seen flint coups-de-poing which match the Kariandusi examples exactly.

The cleavers, too, are worthy of special note. In Europe this type has received little attention until recently, but it undoubtedly occurs in Europe in late Chellean and Acheulean sites; it is, however, common in the later Stellenbosch sites (South African Acheulean) in South Africa, and in the Acheulean of North Africa. In fact it is one of the type tools of this culture.

The crude side scrapers are rare and are not a very well-defined category, but they are worthy of mention because in the next phase they are a very distinct type, and I am therefore inclined to regard these as the prototypes of those found in the Nanyukian industry.

THE NANYUKIAN

The Nanyukian

As pointed out in Chapter IV, there is as yet no direct stratigraphical evidence upon which to decide the exact point in the climatic sequence to which this industry should be assigned. Typologically, however, there can be no doubt of its position, as it is certainly derived, in part at least, from the Kenya Acheulean culture. Its geographical distribution too would seem to indicate that it belongs to some time during the break between the end of the Kamasian pluvial and the beginning of the Lower Gamblian, for it has so far only been found in areas which were little affected by the earth movements and volcanic upheavals which mark the close of the Kamasian. The type station for this industry is a site up in the forest above Nanyuki to the north of Mount Kenya near the forester's hut. The implements are washing out from a hill-wash, and the unweathered tools of the Nanyukian are accompanied by some weathered tools which may either represent an earlier phase of the Nanyukian, or may be a very late phase of the Acheulean. The geology of the site is described by Solomon in Appendix A. The industry consists of the following tool types:

(*a*) Flat triangular coups-de-poing worked on both surfaces.
(*b*) Ovates.
(*c*) Discs.
(*d*) Cleavers.
(*e*) Scrapers.
(*f*) Points.
(*g*) Rough balls of stone.

The flat triangular coups-de-poing are very remarkable. At this site they are made of various materials, some of which are most unpromising, and yet quite good tools are achieved, showing that considerable skill had been acquired by the workman. The materials are all lavas, but they are too weathered for determination without slicing. There is a considerable range of size in the flat coups-de-poing, some being as long as eight inches, whilst others are quite small. Some of the ovates are very well made, as are the cleavers which show a very marked improvement on those of the Kenya Acheulean period. They tend to be smaller, and are usually trimmed all round the butt end and sides so that they are U-shaped, but this is not invariable. The side scrapers are Mousterian in form with very typical

38

"step-flaking" and if found alone would certainly be classed as such. It has been suggested to me that the Nanyukian industry was perhaps the result of contact between an early Kenya Mousterian and a late Kenya Acheulean. While not denying the possibility of this explanation I prefer to regard it as a transitional phase between the Kenya Acheulean and Kenya Mousterian. This point will be discussed further in Chapter x, and so need not be developed here.

The points are triangular with little or no secondary working, and with an unprepared striking platform at a very wide angle, rather similar to that associated with the Clacton industry in England. This, too, may be taken as an indication of development in the direction of the Mousterian type of culture. The rough balls of stone are curious because, although they suggest hammer stones, none of them show any trace of having been used as such. I am myself inclined to regard them as having been used as weights for "bolas" for hunting game. Unless this is their use the whole industry includes no effective weapons of offence, and yet the makers must surely have been hunters, and I suggest that their means of catching game was by "bolas" and by game pits dug with the coups-de-poing; they doubtless also used the coups-de-poing to make wooden clubs and pointed wooden spears.

Plates IV, V, VI, VII, VIII, and IX, and Figs. 3, 4, 5, 6, 7, 8, 9, and 10, illustrate the Kenya Acheulean and the Nanyukian.

REFERENCES

1. The geological evidence is given in Appendix A.
2. *Prehistory*, by M. C. Burkitt, p. 68.

39

PLATE I

Large rolled coup-de-poing from a gravel-bed at Koru, Kenya. This tool was found by Mr E. J. Wayland who gave it to the Museum of Archaeology and Ethnology at Cambridge.

Although the deposit in which it was found cannot be fitted with certainty into the Pluvial sequence, on typological grounds this tool is assuredly earlier than the upper Kenya Chellean series which belongs to the closing stages of the Kamasian pluvial.

The dimensions of the tool are: Length, 177 mm.; Width, 114·5 mm.; Thickness, 111 mm. Its weight is 4 lbs. 9 ozs.

Material. Dolerite?

PLATE I

PLATE II

Rolled coups-de-poing from the Kariandusi River site, Elmenteita. They are of upper Kenya Chellean type and belong to the last part of the Kamasian pluvial.

Note. Each tool was photographed separately and, as they are therefore not all to the same scale, the measurements of each specimen are given separately in millimetres.

No.	Field number	Material	Length	Width	Thickness
1, 2	M.209. 1929.	Quartz-trachyte	167	66	32
3, 4	M.282. 1929.	,,	179·5	96	37
5, 6	M.278. 1929.	,,	171	89	43
7, 8	M.208. 1929.	,,	197	101	44·5

PLATE II

1   2   3   4

5   6   7   8

PLATE III

Rolled coups-de-poing from the Kariandusi River site, Elmenteita. They are of
upper Kenya Chellean type and belong to the last part of the Kamasian pluvial.

Note. Each tool was photographed separately and, as they are not, therefore, all to the
same scale, the measurements of each specimen are given separately in millimetres.

No.	Field number	Material	Length	Width	Thickness
1, 2	M.264. 1929.	Quartz-trachyte	142	82	43
3, 4	M.295. 1929.	,,	168	101·5	36
5, 6	M.296. 1929.	,,	163·5	98	34
7, 8	M.277. 1929.	,,	178	92	33

PLATE III

1   2   3   4

5   6   7   8

PLATE IV

Coups-de-poing (unrolled) from the Kariandusi River site, Elmenteita. They are of Kenya Acheulean type and belong to the closing stages of the Kamasian pluvial.

Note. Each tool was photographed separately and, as they are not therefore all to the same scale, the measurements of each specimen are given separately in millimetres.

No.	Field number	Material	Length	Width	Thickness
1, 2	M.39. 1929.	?	178	88·5	37·5
3, 4	L.873. 1929.	?	173	93·5	43
5, 6	M.210. 1929.	Phonolitic lava	164	82·5	45
7, 8	M.31. 1929.	?	181	87	49

The tools marked ? are of lava, but the exact nature of the lava cannot be determined without slicing.

PLATE IV

1   2   3   4

5   6   7   8

PLATE V

Coups-de-poing (unrolled) from the Kariandusi River site, Elmenteita. They are of Kenya Acheulean type and belong to the closing stages of the Kamasian pluvial.

Note. Each tool was photographed separately and, as they are not therefore all to the same scale, the measurements of each specimen are given separately in millimetres.

No.	Field number	Material	Length	Width	Thickness
1, 2	M.33. 1929.	Quartz-trachyte	173·5	87	37
3, 4	M.212. 1929.	,,	177·5	81	42·5
5, 6	M.47. 1929.	?	156	87	37
7, 8	M.28. 1929.	Phonolite	177·5	108	39·5

PLATE V

1   2   3   4

5   6   8

PLATE VI

Coups-de-poing (unrolled) from the Kariandusi River site, Elmenteita. They are of Kenya Acheulean type and belong to the closing stages of the Kamasian pluvial.

Note. Each tool was photographed separately and, as they are not therefore all to the same scale, the measurements of each specimen are given separately in millimetres.

No.	Field number	Material	Length	Width	Thickness
1, 2	M.350. 1929.	Obsidian	194·5	109	38
3, 4	L.868. 1929.	,,	198·5	103·5	40
5, 6	M.347. 1929.	,,	110	51·5	28
7, 8	M.56. 1929.	,,	117	64	39·5

PLATE VI

PLATE VII

Coups-de-poing (unrolled) from the Kariandusi River site, Elmenteita. They are of Kenya Acheulean type and belong to the closing stages of the Kamasian pluvial.

Note. Each tool was photographed separately and, as they are not therefore to the same scale, the measurements of each specimen are given separately in millimetres.

No.	Field number	Material	Length	Width	Thickness
1, 2	M.40. 1929.	Obsidian	172	101	41
3, 4	M.42. 1929.	,,	154	83	36·5
5, 6	M.54. 1929.	,,	127	79·5	25
7, 8	M.336. 1929.	,,	154	81	41

PLATE VII

PLATE VIII

Tools from the Kariandusi River site, Elmenteita. Numbers 1 to 6 inclusive are cleavers, and numbers 7 and 8 are rough side-scrapers. Numbers 1, 2, 3, and 7 are rolled, and must therefore be associated with the rolled coups-de-poing of upper Kenya Chellean date from this site, but numbers 4, 5, 6, and 8 are unrolled and belong to the Kenya Acheulean series.

Note. Each tool was photographed separately and, as they are not therefore all to the same scale, the measurements of each specimen are given separately in millimetres.

	No.	Field number	Material	Length	Width	Thickness
Rolled cleavers	1	M.322. 1929.	Quartz-trachyte	148	106	43
,,	2	M.323. 1929.	,,	141	87	32
,,	3	M.320. 1929.	,,	183	115	48
Unrolled cleavers	4	M.319. 1929.	,,	141	100	32
,,	5	M.88. 1929.	Obsidian	175·5	99	38
,,	6	M.110. 1929.	,,	131	74·5	33·5
Side-scrapers	7	L.883. 1929.	Lava*	143	79	44·5
,,	8	M.149. 1929.	Obsidian	127	95	31

* Too weathered for exact determination, probably quartz-trachyte.

PLATE VIII

1

2

3

4

5

6

7

8

PLATE IX

Tools from Forest Station site, Nanyuki. The tools of this site seem to represent a late development of the Kenya Acheulean, and the industry has been provisionally termed Nanyukian. As yet there is no positive evidence by which to date the deposits in which these tools occur, but there are indications which suggest that it belongs to the period of earth movements which separated the Kamasian pluvial from the Gamblian.

Note. Each tool was photographed separately and, as they are therefore not all to the same scale, the measurements of each specimen are given separately in millimetres.

	No.	Field number	Material	Length	Width	Thickness
Coup-de-poing	1, 2	M.217. 1929.	Made of various	185·5	112	26·5
,,	3, 4	M.215. 1929.	lavas which are	119	97	39
,,	5, 6	M.214. 1929.	too weathered	123	100	35
Cleaver	7	M.216. 1929.	for accurate	151	93	20
Side-scraper	8	M.213. 1929.	determination	135	84	37

PLATE IX

FIGURE 1

Two views of a rolled coup-de-poing of upper Kenya Chellean type from the Kariandusi River site. This tool is reproduced approximately natural size, and is the same tool as Nos. 1 and 2 in the photograph on Plate II.

The field catalogue number is M.209, 1929.

Material: quartz-trachyte?

(Drawings by Mrs Burkitt)

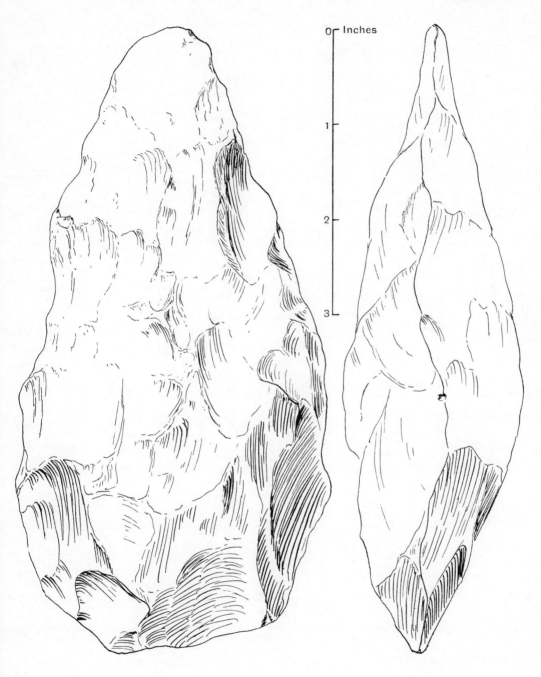

FIGURE 1

0 Inches
1
2
3

59

FIGURE 2

Two views of a rolled coup-de-poing of upper Kenya Chellean type from the Kariandusi River site.

This tool is typical of the larger examples of the coups-de-poing of this period. The drawing is reproduced approximately natural size, and the tool is the same as that in photographs Nos. 3 and 4 on Plate II.

Its field catalogue number is M.282, 1929.

Material: quartz-trachyte.

(Drawings by Mrs Burkitt)

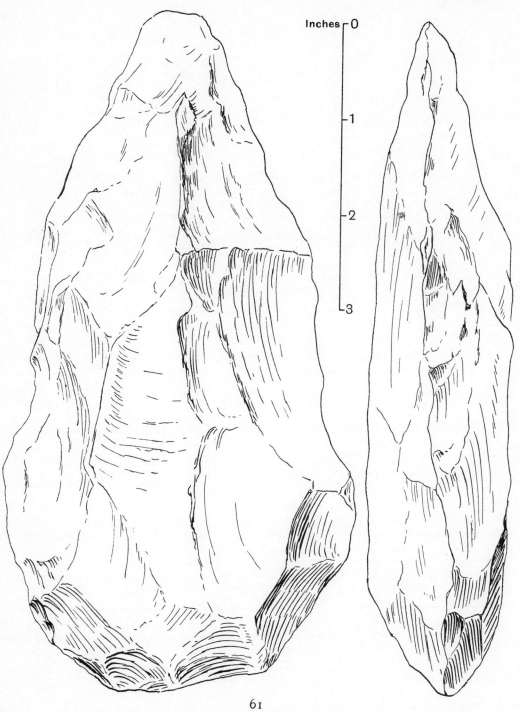

Inches 0

1

2

3

FIGURE 2

61

FIGURE 3

Two views of a coup-de-poing of Kenya Acheulean type from the Kariandusi River site. This tool is the same as that in photographs Nos. 1 and 2 on Plate IV. Its field catalogue number is M.39, 1929. The drawing is reproduced at approximately natural size.

Material: Lava (not determinable).

(Drawings by Mrs Burkitt)

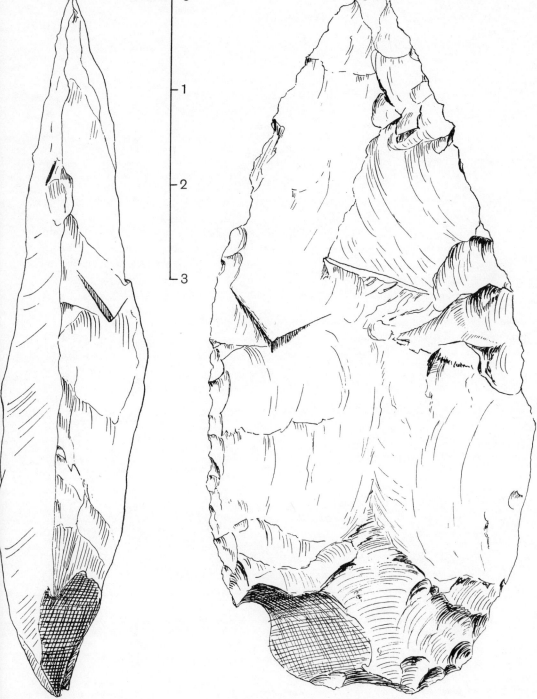

Inches

FIGURE 3

63

FIGURE 4

Two views of a coup-de-poing of the Kenya Acheulean type, from the Kariandusi River site. This tool is the same as that in the photographs Nos. 5 and 6 on Plate IV. The field catalogue number is M.210, 1929. The drawing is reproduced at approximately natural size.

Material: Phonolite (?).

(Drawings by Mrs Burkitt)

FIGURE 4

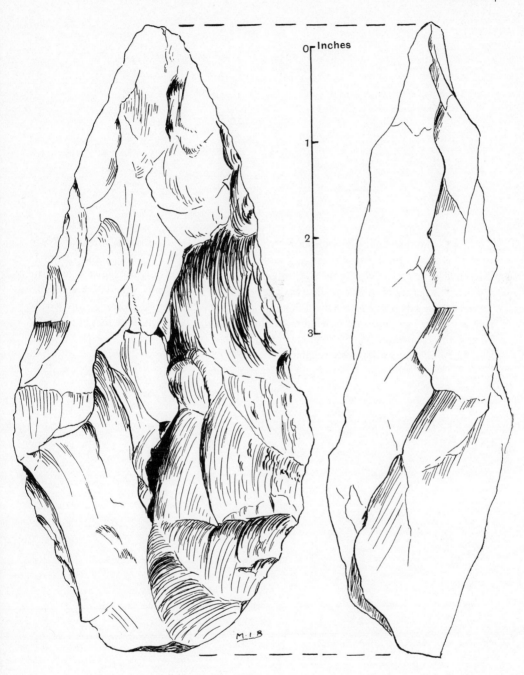

M.I.B

0 — Inches
1
2
3

FIGURE 5

Two views of a coup-de-poing of Kenya Acheulean type from the Kariandusi River site. This tool, unlike those in Figs. 3 and 4, is essentially a flake and not a core tool. The frequent occurrence of large coups-de-poing made on flakes in the Kenya Acheulean is due to the nature of the material, lava of various kinds, from which the tools were made. In this case a part of the lower main flake surface has been trimmed away. Compare this tool with the obsidian one in Figure 7. This drawing is of the tool in photographs Nos. 5 and 6 on Plate V. Its field catalogue number is M.47, 1929.

Material: Lava (not determinable).

(Drawings by Mrs Burkitt)

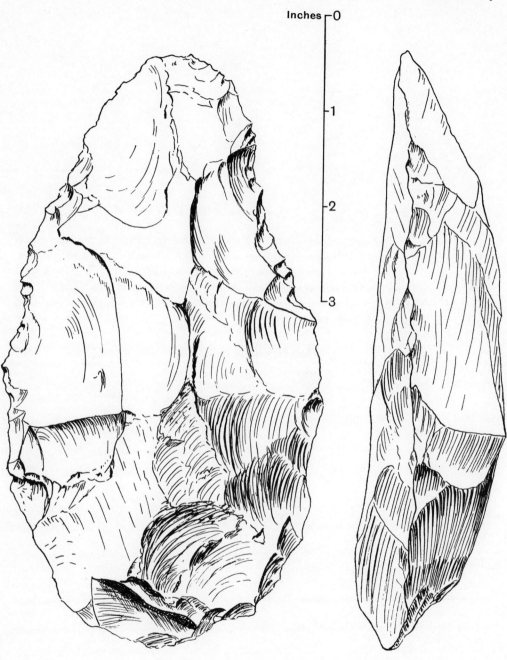

Inches

0

1

2

3

FIGURE 5

67

FIGURE 6

Two views of a large coup-de-poing of Kenya Acheulean type from the Kariandusi River site, Elmenteita. Although made from a large flake of obsidian, this tool has been trimmed all over the lower flake surface so that it has every appearance of being a core tool. This specimen is the same as that in the photographs Nos. 3 and 4 on Plate VI, but the side view in the drawing is the opposite one from that in the photograph. The field catalogue number is L.868, 1929.

Material: obsidian.

(Drawings by Mrs Burkitt)

0 Inches

1

2

3

FIGURE 6

M.18

69

FIGURE 7

Two views of a very fine obsidian coup-de-poing of the Kenya Acheulean type from the Kariandusi River site. This tool is made on a flake, but the greater part of the lower main flake surface has been left intact, although there has been some trimming at the lower end.

This tool is the same as that in photographs Nos. 7 and 8 on Plate VII, and is reproduced approximately natural size. Field catalogue number, M.336, 1929.

Material: obsidian.

(Drawings by Mrs Burkitt)

FIGURE 7

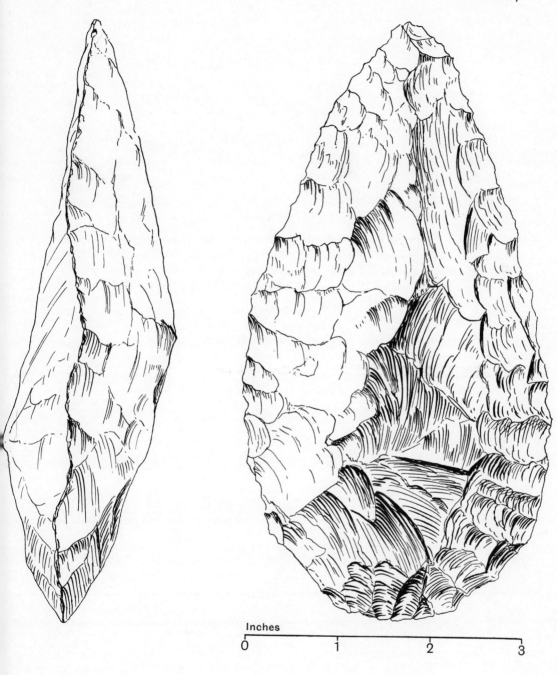

Inches
0   1   2   3

71

FIGURE 8

A cleaver from the Kenya Acheulean at the Kariandusi River site. The cutting edge is the natural sharp edge of a large flake, and both sides of the tool have been trimmed by the removal of a number of flakes in such a way that the section is a parallelogram.

The tool is the same as that in the photograph No. 4 on Plate VIII. The field catalogue number is M.319, 1929.

Material: quartz-trachyte.

(Drawing by Mrs Burkitt)

FIGURE 8

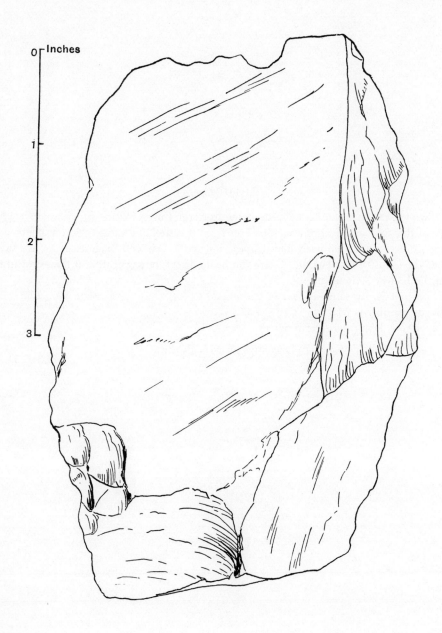

0 ⌐ Inches

1

2

3 ⌐

FIGURE 9

Two views of a large, flat coup-de-poing from the Forest Station site, Nanyuki. The shape of this tool is typical of a whole series from this site, and since these flat coups-de-poing are here associated with side-scrapers and with very well-made cleavers, we have named the industry Nanyukian. There can be no doubt, however, that it is an evolution from the Kenya Acheulean.

The tool is the same as that in photographs Nos. 1 and 2 on Plate IX. The field catalogue number is M.217, 1929.

Material: lava (not determinable).

(Drawings by Mrs Burkitt)

FIGURE 9

0 — Inches

1

2

3

75

FIGURE 10

No. 1. A well-made cleaver from the Forest Station site, Nanyuki. This type of well-made cleaver is associated at this site with large, flat coups-de-poing and with side-scrapers, and we have named the industry Nanyukian.

This tool is the same as in photograph No. 7 on Plate IX. The field catalogue number is M.216, 1929.

Material: lava (not determinable).

Nos. 2 and 3. Two triangular flakes from the Forest Station site, Nanyuki. In some ways they suggest the Mousterian technique. The field catalogue numbers are No. 2, 218a, 1929; No. 3, 218, 1929.

Material: lava (not determinable).

(Drawings by Mrs Burkitt)

FIGURE 10

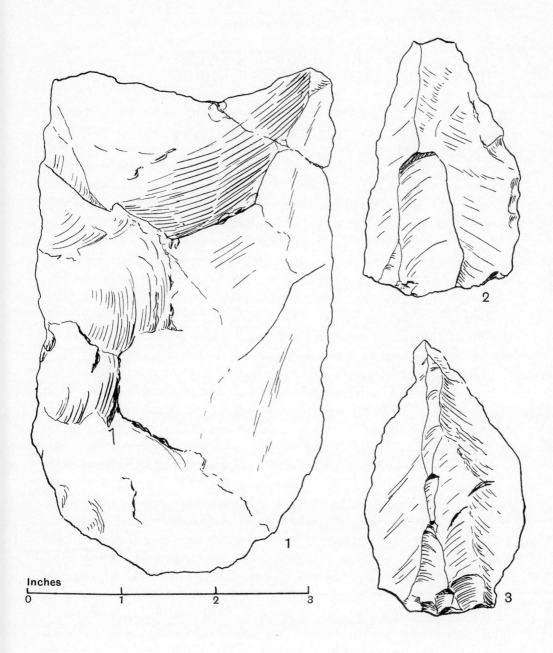

Inches
0   1   2   3

1

2

3

77

CHAPTER VI

THE KENYA MOUSTERIAN AND
THE KENYA STILLBAY

WE have already seen that the Nanyukian culture has certain re-semblances to an early form of Mousterian, especially in its inclusion of side-scrapers with heavy step-flaking. It is at present not possible to decide whether this was due to a fusion of an early Kenya Mousterian influence with a late Kenya Acheulean, or whether it represents an evolution of the Kenya Acheulean towards a more Mousterian type. I am inclined to regard it as an evolution of the Acheulean into the Kenya Mousterian. Whether this theory be true or not only further discoveries can prove, but it is certain that by the beginning of the second major pluvial period, the Gamblian, a Mousterian type of culture which we call Kenya Mousterian was present in Kenya, and this culture became more and more perfect and evolved throughout the period of the Gamblian, and eventually during the decline of the second maximum it developed into an industry closely re-sembling the Stillbay of South Africa, which we call the Kenya Stillbay.

Up to the present no definite occupation level of the makers of the Kenya Mousterian culture has been found, but in Gamble's Cave II in the level described in my field reports as the "2nd occupation level" we have traces of an occasional occupation by men of the tribe who made the Kenya Stillbay. Derived as the Stillbay is from the upper Kenya Mous-terian, its unfinished tools and flakes have a very distinctly Mousterian appearance, and for a long time we regarded the "2nd occupation level" of Gamble's Cave as of upper Kenya Mousterian period owing to the presence of flakes with typically Mousterian type faceted butts (see Fig. 36). Recently, however, I have very carefully re-examined all the flakes and fragments from this level and have discovered among them broken and unfinished pieces which in the light of our now much greater acquaintance with the Kenya Stillbay I have no hesitation in placing as of that culture. From Figure 15 it will be seen that this 2nd occupation level comes only a little before the lower aeolian sand (bed 8) which represents the dry period at the close of the Gamblian. Thus here in Gamble's Cave—as elsewhere in the silts and gravels of the Malewa—is clear evidence that the Kenya Stillbay belongs to the very end of the Gamblian pluvial period.

It is very unfortunate that so far no true occupation site of the real Kenya Mousterian culture, either in its lower or upper form, has been found, for it may be doubted whether the series of tools found in the silts and gravels of the various phases of the Gamblian pluvial period really give us a true picture of the Kenya form of the Mousterian culture. The nearest approach to an occupation site for a travel of Kenya Mousterian is at Wetherell's site on the Kinangop. This is an open station site, but since it cannot at present be fitted with certainty into the stratigraphical sequence, it will not be considered in this book.

The whole development from the lower Kenya Mousterian through the upper Kenya Mousterian to the Kenya Stillbay is a gradual process and all the stages can be found in the series of gravels and silts exposed in the Malewa Valley, Naivasha, where that river cuts through the deposits of the Gamblian pluvial.

In places the exposures have a vertical height of well over one hundred feet, and as the river is very winding in this area, miles of gravels and silts are exposed which have yielded us very many tools.

Careful collecting shows that the tools from the lower exposures are more crude than those from the middle levels, whilst those from the highest levels are of very advanced type, in fact there is evidence of a definite evolution from the bottom to the top of the series. Comparatively few tools have been found in the lowest levels, but there are sufficient to show that a type of Mousterian point with faceted striking platform and typical secondary working was already present. The tools from the lower part of the exposures we call lower Kenya Mousterian.

The middle and higher levels also include some of these more crude forms, which are doubtless derived from earlier beds, but these levels are characterised by a more advanced type of tool which we call upper Kenya Mousterian. Little or no working on the main flake surface occurs up to this point. The uppermost levels contain a very advanced industry in which many of the points are trimmed all over both surfaces and the bulbs and striking platform trimmed right away. This evolution of the Kenya Mousterian into a highly developed industry of Stillbay type, in which the tools are worked very delicately all over both surfaces, is most interesting.

It is exactly paralleled in South Africa and in Rhodesia, where from a culture of general Mousterian form there gradually develops an industry known as Stillbay or Bambata.

Mr M. C. Burkitt and others attribute this rather special development of the Mousterian in Africa to the contact of the makers of the Mousterian culture with a race of neo-anthropic type who had more advanced methods of working stone. Mr Burkitt even suggests that the European Solutrean[1] (to which the South African Stillbay has at least a superficial resemblance) may also be the outcome of such a contact. In Kenya the maker of the Kenya Mousterian tools was certainly living in the same area and at the same time as the Kenya Aurignacian race, so that this theory receives support although not yet proved. So far there is no indication of the physical characters of the race responsible for making the Kenya Mousterian culture, or indeed any of the African Mousterian types of culture. It must not be thought that in describing this industry as Kenya Mousterian there is any intended implication that the race which made the culture was of Neanderthal type.

As already indicated, I believe that the various African Mousterian cultures were developed from the African Acheulean or even the African Chellean and are not directly connected with the European Mousterian, which I regard as one of the lines of evolution from a European Chellean which developed in Europe side by side with the Acheulean which also evolved from the Chellean, but from another branch of it. This view is borne out to a certain extent by M. Péyrony's recent work at Le Moustier.[2] It would not be surprising to find that the early Kenya Mousterian was made by a race somewhat resembling *Homo rhodesiensis*, that is to say a type of man who was not *Homo sapiens*, and who had resemblances to the Neanderthal race, but was nevertheless a distinct species.

The question of the physical characters of the makers of Kenya Stillbay industry is probably different. It seems likely that this industry is the result of the fusion of the Mousterian and Neo-anthropic influences, but this does not necessarily mean that we shall find the racial type is a cross between the two human types. This is in fact improbable, and it is more likely that it was made either by a degenerate off-shoot of the Neo-anthropic group, or else by a very advanced group of the Mousterian folk. The evidence of the skull found by Mr Peers in South Africa, associated with a Stillbay industry, seems to point to the former alternative.[1]

We have already seen that in the Nakuru-Naivasha district the makers of the Kenya Mousterian culture were living contemporaneously with the Kenya Aurignacians. This fact is of considerable importance, and must be kept in mind if an occupation site of the makers of the Mousterian peoples is found and excavated later. We know from the Aurignacian levels excavated in Gamble's Cave II that these more advanced people did not borrow anything from the more primitive folk. It is more than likely, however, that if we discover a proper occupation site of the makers of the Mousterian industry, we shall not only find Mousterian types of tool made by the people themselves, but we shall probably also find a certain number of Aurignacian tool types in the same deposit. This will not necessarily imply the crossing or mixing of the two races, but rather that the more primitive folk, though they could not make long flakes and Chatelperron points themselves, were by no means averse to picking up and using tools thrown away or lost by the Aurignacians, or even to stealing such tools if opportunity occurred. So far all the discoveries of tools of the Kenya Mousterian type *in situ* have been in silts and gravels, and not in cave sites, and this probably accounts for the absence of typical side-scrapers in any numbers which is at first surprising. It may be that the Kenya Mousterian culture differs materially in this respect from the Mousterian of Europe; but it is equally probable that when we find an occupation site we shall find the side-scrapers, which are essentially domestic implements, and were probably used by the women in the homes, and because of this would be less frequently found in gravels or silts.

The tools of the earliest Mousterian levels of the exposures at the old Government Farm at Naivasha consist for the most part of large rolled flakes with faceted striking platforms and little or no secondary working (see No. 1, Fig. 11). Beautiful points with secondary trimming up both edges do however also occur (see No. 2), and there are also discs (see No. 5, Fig. 11). These tools are sometimes of obsidian, and sometimes of amber-coloured or white chert. Besides the tools which are definitely of Mousterian type there are many very crude tools of chert which may be part of the same culture series, or which may be derived tools of some earlier industry at present unknown to us.

In the middle levels of the deposits of Gamblian date at the old Government Farm, the Mousterian points tend to be more finely made, and the secondary working is often very fine. Many of the tools are heavily rolled when found in the gravels, but some from the silts are quite unrolled. Many flakes, with faceted butts but with no secondary trimming, also occur. Examples are shown in Fig. 12 which illustrates the upper Kenya Mousterian. Sometimes a little flaking on the lower surface occurs, but this type of work is not common until the next stage.

The uppermost deposits at the old Government Farm station contain tools of the Kenya Stillbay type. These include small flakes with faceted butts and no secondary work, which are presumably unfinished pieces, and also tools of many shapes and sizes with very fine secondary working on one or both faces (see Fig. 13); sometimes the whole of the lower face is trimmed away so that there is no indication of the butt or bulb. The trimming on many of these Stillbay points resembles the so-called Solutrean retouch of Europe, or perhaps even more the working on the arrowheads of the early Neolithic periods. Some of the work has certainly been done by the process of pressure flaking. But the use of this technique and the practice of working over both surfaces of a tool with fine flakes is insufficient evidence to postulate any Solutrean influence. It seems to be more probable that the resemblance is due to a similar line of evolution in both continents, namely that it is the final result of contact of Neo-anthropic man with a Mousterian culture as has already been suggested.

REFERENCES

1. *South Africa's Past in Stone and Paint*, by M. C. Burkitt, pp. 87 and 170.
2. "Le Moustier. Ses Gisements, ses Industries—ses couches géologiques", by D. Péyrony, in *Revue Anthropologique*, 1930, nos. 1–6.

NOTE

In connection with the Kenya Mousterian culture and its derivative, the Kenya Stillbay, it is interesting to note that as a result of the work of Archdeacon Owen in Kavirondo and of Mr J. Rickman at Mombasa, it has been shown that these two areas are very rich in sites with Mousterian tool types, while comparatively few Aurignacian tool types occur. It seems probable therefore that these areas may be expected to yield the cave sites with Mousterian occupations which we need so badly.

FIGURE 11

Tools of lower Kenya Mousterian type from gravels and silts laid down during the first maximum of the Gamblian pluvial period, and now exposed at the bottom of the valley cut by the Malewa River at Naivasha. These tools were found in the neighbourhood of the old Government Farm.

Many of the tools are heavily rolled, but their Mousterian character is unmistakable. All those figured are of obsidian with the exception of No. 4, which is of amber-coloured chert. The field catalogue numbers are:

No. 1. 6224. 1929.   No. 4. 10612. 1928.   No. 7. Y.132. 1929.
No. 2. M.188. 1929.   No. 5. M.199. 1929.   No. 8. M.196. 1929.
No. 3. 6219. 1929.   No. 6. M.193. 1929.   No. 9. Y.133. 1929.

(Drawings by Mrs Burkitt)

FIGURE 11

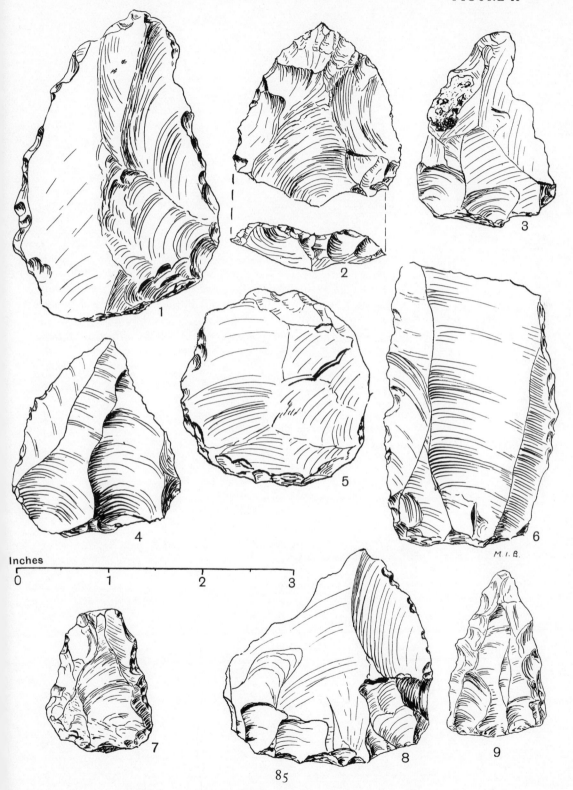

Inches
0   1   2   3

M I B.

FIGURE 12

Tools of upper Kenya Mousterian type from the gravels and silts laid down during the second maximum of the Gamblian pluvial period, and now exposed in the sides of the valley cut by the Malewa River at Naivasha, especially in the neighbourhood of the old Government Farm.

None of them have any signs of work on the lower or main flake surfaces. All the tools figured are of obsidian. The field catalogue numbers are:

No. 1. Y.134. 1929.	No. 4. Y.141. 1929.	No. 7. Y.135. 1929.
No. 2. Y.138. 1929.	No. 5. Y.137. 1929.	No. 8. Y.140. 1929.
No. 3. Y.139. 1929.	No. 6. Y.136. 1929.	

(Drawings by Mrs Burkitt)

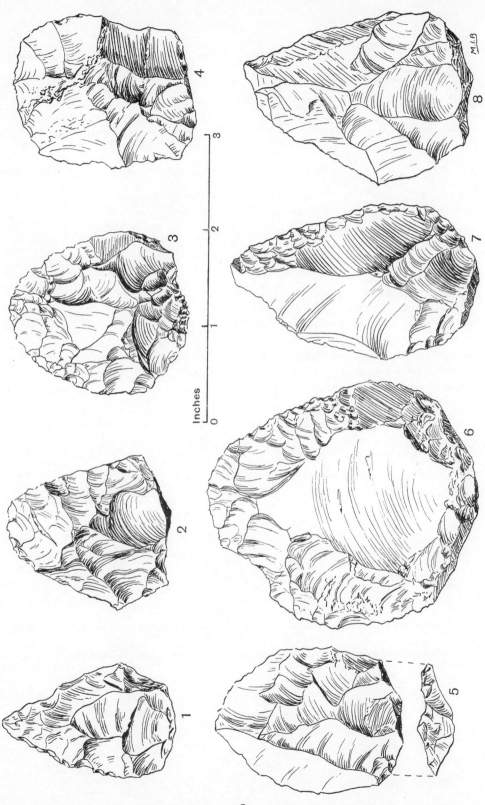

FIGURE 12

Inches

FIGURE 13

Tools of Kenya Stillbay type. This industry belongs to the closing stages of the Gamblian pluvial period. The series of tools in this figure were not collected *in situ*, but the position in which they were found indicated that they were derived from the top levels of the silts which are of late Gamblian date in the Naivasha district, and similar tools, not quite so perfect as those figured, and fragmentary tools of the same type have been found actually *in situ* at this section.

Elsewhere we have found similar tools *in situ* in an old land surface which belongs to the decline of the Gamblian pluvial. This industry is characterised by points with very delicate retouch, frequently on both surfaces of the flake, but numerous cruder tools are often associated with these well-finished examples. The material of the tools figured is obsidian.

The field catalogue numbers are:

No. 1. Y.146. 1929.	No. 4. M.177. 1929.	No. 7. Y.142. 1929.
No. 2. Y.143. 1929.	No. 5. Y.144. 1929.	No. 8. M.168. 1929.
No. 3. M.169. 1920.	No. 6. Y.145. 1929.	

(Drawings by Mrs Burkitt)

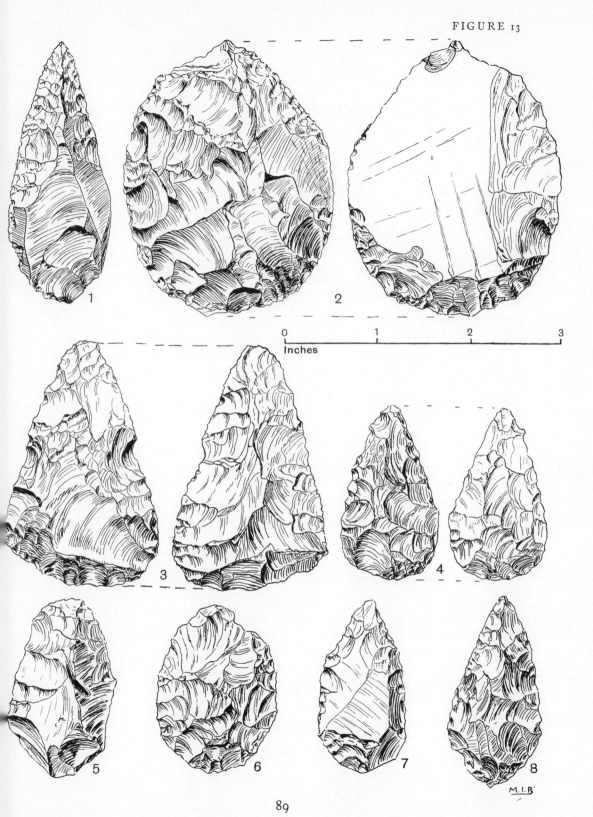

89

CHAPTER VII

THE KENYA AURIGNACIAN

As we saw in Chapter IV, the Kenya Aurignacian goes back to the beginning of the first phase of the Gamblian pluvial period, where it occurs in a primitive form, and it gradually develops right through the Gamblian period, reaching its finest phase during the beginning of the decline after the second Gamblian maximum.

The lower Kenya Aurignacian

At present our knowledge of the lower Kenya Aurignacian is very restricted as no occupation site of the period has as yet been excavated. We know that an early Aurignacian people were in the district as early as the beginning of the Gamblian pluvial, because a certain number of crude but typical tools of Aurignacian type have been found in the lowest levels of silts and gravels of the first maximum of the Gamblian, especially at the exposures of the lake beds in the valley of the Malewa River at the old Government Farm, Naivasha.

We also know that there was a gradual development throughout the Lower Gamblian phase, and the period prior to the maximum of Upper Gamblian, because gravels at the Enderit at Elmenteita, which belong to the very beginning of the Upper Gamblian phase, contain a certain number of rolled Aurignacian tools, while in some places the beach of the lake in the Nakuru basin during the second maximum of the Gamblian phase also contains a few such rolled tools.

We can study the development of the Aurignacian subsequent to the maximum of the Upper Gamblian phase, *i.e.* during its decline, in very great detail from the deposits of the lower levels of Gamble's Cave II which rest immediately upon the beach gravel of the maximum of the Upper Gamblian lake.

For the present we regard the Aurignacian prior to the maximum of the Upper Gamblian phase as lower Kenya Aurignacian, and that which follows the maximum of the Upper Gamblian as upper Kenya Aurignacian. It is likely that the discovery of an occupation site with deposits of the lower Kenya Aurignacian period will necessitate some further sub-division of the culture, but at present this is not necessary.

The Aurignacian types of tool from deposits of known Lower Gamblian date so far consist almost entirely of "*backed blades*". Some of these are very crude while others are of rather better workmanship. Very few end scrapers and no burins have as yet been found, but the development of the lower Kenya Aurignacian into the upper, where burins are common, makes it probable that the lower Kenya Aurignacian had these tools, and that they will be found when a lower Kenya Aurignacian occupation site is eventually discovered. Fig. 14 shows tools representing the lower Kenya Aurignacian as we at present know it.

The upper Kenya Aurignacian

The upper Kenya Aurignacian belongs in time to the period from the maximum of the Upper Gamblian phase, through the decline of this pluvial to a time when the aridity of the inter-pluvial marks its close. The upper Aurignacian can be sub-divided into three phases (*a*), (*b*) and (*c*), based upon the study of the tools of the period, but it must be clearly understood that there is no break between these sub-divisions which are purely arbitrary, and that the evolution of the culture from the beginning to the end was continuous. If a sufficiently big series of tools from any site of upper Kenya Aurignacian date were available, it should be possible to say whether they represented the (*a*), (*b*) or (*c*) phase, but if the series were small it would only be possible to say that it was upper Kenya Aurignacian, without deciding to which phase it belonged.

The type station of the upper Kenya Aurignacian is Gamble's Cave II. In the present book it is not proposed to give any details of the excavation of the site, which will be dealt with in a subsequent publication. But in order that the evidence for the date of the upper Kenya Aurignacian may be clearly understood, and also the relation of the three phases of this upper Aurignacian to each other, and to the later cultures, a brief account of the cave must be given here.

Gamble's Caves I and II are situated on the side of a hill on Mr Gamble's farm at Elmenteita, just above the Enderit River (see Map 2). The hill consists of water-laid tuffaceous material with occasional sandy beds, and is in fact formed by the erosion and weathering of the deposits of the Kamasian pluvial period. A little to the east of the caves is a terrace and a small cliff. We are not at the moment concerned with Gamble's Cave I which yielded little result, but with Gamble's Cave II, where the two lowest occupation levels proved to be upper Kenya Aurignacian.

Plates X and XI show views of the caves. In Plate X the cliff and terrace are clearly seen on the left-hand side on the same level as the caves. Gamble's Cave II is on the right-hand side in the pictures.

Excavations were not only carried out in the deposits lying under the present rock shelter, but were continued a little farther to the west along the cliff face. The lowest occupation level stretched right across the area of both parts, but the overlying strata in the cave were replaced by scree farther to the west. Only the fringe of the lowest occupation level was found under the rock shelter and it was best developed to the west at a point where there was a small lower shelter. The total depth of deposits from the modern floor of the shelter to rock bottom in the first section was twenty-eight feet, and the following table summarises briefly the sequence of the deposits, while Figs. 15 and 16 give the details of the sections below the present-day rock shelter, and to the west along the cliff at a point corresponding to the greatest depth of the fourth occupation level deposits.

Deposits are numbered from *top to bottom* in the order in which they were excavated.

1 and 2. Modern occupation levels containing animal bones in a fairly fresh condition, pottery, and wooden stakes, etc., but no tools of stone, nor any trace of metal. The upper of these deposits is known to be of recent date, as a man was found who remembered living in the rock shelter, and traces of his brushwood fence in front of the shelter were found, and also much sheep dung.

3. A barren grey layer consisting of rock débris derived from the roof of the cave.

4. An aeolian deposit of red colour, consisting of very finely stratified sand.

5. As No. 4.

6. The topmost prehistoric occupation level containing an Elmenteitan industry. Deposit brown to grey black with much ash, hearths, bone débris, etc., also rock rubble from roof of cave.

7. As Nos. 3 and 5.

8. As No. 4.

9. As Nos. 3, 5 and 7.

10. The second prehistoric occupation level. Actually this level consisted almost entirely of rock débris but with very occasional hearths (five in all), around which were

a few flakes of Mousterian type. Associated with these were some typical, but broken, tools of Kenya Stillbay type.

11. A very narrow barren layer of grey débris separating the lowest hearth in No. 11 from the grey black deposit of No. 13. Similar to Nos. 3, 5, 7 and 9.

12. The third prehistoric occupation level in the cave. It contained tools of upper Kenya Aurignacian type, phase (c), and also burials.

13. A barren layer of rock débris from the roof, similar to Nos. 3, 5, 7, 9 and 11.

14. The fourth prehistoric occupation level of very great thickness. There is no break whatever in the deposits of this occupation level, but an arbitrary division half way down shows that the tools from the lower levels are much cruder on the whole than those from the top, and that there is in fact a gradual evolution. This layer consists almost entirely of ash, dust, bone and obsidian.

15. Beach sand and gravel with a few rolled tools and many freshwater shells.

The interpretation of this section is important. Evidence from the other sites shows that the beach (No. 15) is that of the maximum of the Upper Gamblian phase. This beach, both here and elsewhere in the Nakuru basin, stands at about 510 feet* above the level of Lake Nakuru, as fixed on April 10, 1929, which was 5776·84 feet above sea level.

Layer 8, the lower of the two aeolian deposits, represents the period of aridity which marks the very end of the Gamblian and separates it from the Makalian wet phase. This period of aridity can be traced in many exposures separating Gamblian pluvial deposits from those of the Makalian wet phase. Layers 14, 13, 12, 11, 10 and 9, therefore represent the period of the gradual decline of the lake from the 510-foot level to zero, which was in all probability a period of several thousands of years. Layer 14 represents the period immediately following the second maximum of the Gamblian pluvial, and during its deposition the lake edge must have been only a very little distance from the cave. Supporting evidence for this is to be found in the presence of occasional minute and frail freshwater shells in the floor deposits of layer 14, whereas nothing but land snails occur in the higher layers. Fish remains are also very common in layer 14.

The beach gravel contained many freshwater mollusca, some of which are shown in Plate XIV.

Layers 7, 6 and 5 seem to represent the renewed wet conditions which followed upon the desiccation at the end of the Gamblian, and which we call

* The height of the beach ranges from 490 to 530 feet, suggesting slight subsequent tilting. (See Appendix A.)

the Makalian wet phase, and in fact the industry found in the occupation level No. 6 is identical to that found *in situ* in silts of the Makalian wet phase elsewhere. Layer 4, the upper aeolian deposit, thus represents the dry period at the end of the Makalian wet phase. The Nakuran wet phase and its decline is represented by layer 3 which is a deposit of rock débris with no signs of human occupation. This means that after the occupation by the makers of the Elmenteitan culture in Makalian times, the cave was not reoccupied by man until modern times, as represented by layers 2 and 1.

Having thus briefly interpreted the stratigraphical evidence, we must turn to the upper Kenya Aurignacian industry which is found in layers 14 and 12.

In working layer 14, which had a thickness, over its greater extent, of ten feet, it seemed likely that a gradual evolution of the tool types from bottom to top would be found, even though no possible break in the sequence could be detected. Accordingly the deposit was at first worked in six arbitrary divisions of about 1 ft. 8 in., and the tools from each of these arbitrary levels were closely compared. It was found that whereas no difference could be clearly distinguished between the tools from any two adjacent levels, a marked difference was apparent between the tools from the low levels and those from the high ones. It was also noted that on the whole the three upper levels together made a more or less uniform series, and that the three lower levels as a whole were distinguishable from the upper levels by their cruder workmanship, rougher finish, and by the absence of any of the really beautiful tools of the higher levels. The rest of the excavation was therefore carried out by dividing layer 14 into an upper and a lower half; a detailed analysis of the tools from these two arbitrary levels is being prepared and will be published in the later work on Gamble's Caves, meanwhile the analysis has been sufficiently completed to show that such an arbitrary division was in fact fully justified. Bearing in mind the fact that the upper part of the lower levels and the lower part of the upper levels run into each other indistinguishably, and that the division is purely arbitrary, we may consider the lower levels as phase (*a*) of the upper Kenya Aurignacian, and the higher levels as phase (*b*). The difference between the two phases is largely one of size and of workmanship of the tools, and not of the actual types of tools found. In describing the types for the upper Kenya Aurignacian we may group (*a*) and (*b*) phases together.

THE KENYA AURIGNACIAN

The tool types fall under the following main heads:

Blades with blunted backs   Sinew frayers

Scrapers   Blades

Burins   Cores

Fabricators   Sundries

Most of these headings include several sub-divisions, for it is the great variety of the types of tools which Aurignacian man made which distinguishes his culture above all, perhaps, from the more primitive cultures such as the Mousterian.

"Backed blades"

Under this head I class all the tools which have a sharp cutting edge on one side and which are intentionally blunted on the opposite edge. In the upper Kenya Aurignacian in phases (*a*) and (*b*) the following varieties occur:

(1) *Chatelperron types*. The Chatelperron type of backed blade and its derivatives and variations are the commonest of all the backed blade types in the upper Kenya Aurignacian.

There seems at the present day to be some confusion as to what should be called a Chatelperron point, or a derivative of a Chatelperron point, and what should be called a Gravette point.

Judged on the basis of the classification in the Museum of Les Eyzies in the Dordogne, the majority of the backed blades in the upper Kenya Aurignacian belong rather to the Chatelperron class and its derivatives than to the Gravette group. Nos. 20 and 22 in Fig. 19 might perhaps be classed as Gravettes.

(2) *Gravette types*. On the basis of the classification mentioned above, Gravette points are rare in the upper Kenya Aurignacian but occur occasionally, especially in phase (*b*).

(3) *Single-shouldered points*. True single-shouldered points are rare. No. 21 in Fig. 17 and No. 24 in Fig. 20 are the nearest examples we have.

(4) *Lunates*. The larger crescentic tools may be classed among the variations of the Chatelperron point. There are however a number of small crescents ranging in size from about one inch to less than half an inch, and these can only be described as lunates.

(5) *Other microlithic backed blades*. Besides true microlithic crescents there are occasionally very small backed points less than one inch long which

95

are best described as miniature examples of the Gravette or Chatelperron types.

(6) *Notched crescents and backed blades.* A certain number of crescents and backed blades of about one to two inches in size occur, in which a notch has been made at one end of the cutting edge. A number of these are figured; for example, Fig. 18, Nos. 30, 31 and 32, and Fig. 20, Nos. 33, 34, 35 and 36.

(7) *Atypical points.* A number of backed blades occur which do not conveniently fall into any of the above categories, and these are classed as atypical.

Scrapers

The chief scrapers of the Kenya Aurignacian period are:

    (*a*) Round-ended scrapers on blades.
    (*b*) Double-ended scrapers.
    (*c*) Straight-ended scrapers.
    (*d*) Short, stumpy scrapers.
    (*e*) Small double-ended scrapers.
    (*f*) Nosed scrapers.
    (*g*) Hollow scrapers.

The commonest of the scrapers are the ordinary round-ended scrapers on blades, and the rarest are the nosed scrapers. Examples of all the above types from the upper Kenya Aurignacian in Gamble's Cave II are shown in Figs. 21, 22, 23 and 24. Those in Figs. 21 and 22 are from the lowest part of the deposit and are typical of phase (*a*), while those in Figs. 23 and 24 represent the typical scrapers of phase (*b*).

It will be noticed that the latter are on the whole smaller and better made than those in the lower level.

Burins

The burin is usually looked upon as the *sine qua non* of an Aurignacian deposit. The phases (*a*) and (*b*) of the upper Kenya Aurignacian have a great abundance of these tools, including examples of practically every recorded type of burin. The commonest ones which occur are:

    (1) Angle burins of all kinds. (Burins d'angle.)
    (2) Single-blow burins. (Burins simples.)
    (3) Double-blow burins. (Becs de flûte.)
    (4) Atypical burins. (Burins atypiques.)
    (5) Burins on backed blades. (Burins appointés.)

The following types also occur, but they are not common:

Bec-de-perroquet	Plan
Busqué	Polyhedric

Burins are shown in Figs. 25, 26, 27 and 28.

Pseudo "Tardenoisian burins"

Among the finds in the deposits of upper Kenya Aurignacian age are a certain number of flakes that might well be described as "Tardenoisian burins". I do not, however, regard these as intentionally made, but rather as the result of accidental fracture. This point will be discussed in detail below.

Aurignacian fabricators

In many descriptions of Aurignacian sites in France or in North Africa one finds such references as these:

Lames sans retouche—Elles sont au nombre de plusieurs centaines, de longueur variant entre 3 et 15 centimètres. Plus de 200 à section triangulaire ont la crête médiane écrasée plutôt que retouchée: était-ce là le résultat d'une utilisation, une retaille voulue, la crête du nucléus primitif, il est bien difficile de se prononcer. En tous cas ces lames sont particulièrement nombreuses. On les retrouve dans bien d'autres gisements.[1]

or again

Blades, triangular in cross section and retouched on the median ridge. This group contains over 300 pieces. The blades are long, narrow, thick, and in cross section they are triangular. The median ridge bears the retouch. This is really coarse battering and usually of the splintery fracture type, etc.[2]

It is quite evident that the tools being referred to are common in most Aurignacian sites, and one or two tentative suggestions as to their use have been made, but they have not been named, nor are they apparently regarded as an essential tool of the Aurignacian period.

Very large numbers of flakes which fit in with the above descriptions occur in the upper Kenya Aurignacian of phases (a) and (b), and accordingly I determined to try to discover their possible use. Careful sorting showed that two principal forms occur. In the one type only one of the edges of the tool has any evidence of usage, and this edge is always opposed to a flake surface which shows a bulb of percussion. In the other type two or even three of the edges show signs of usage instead of only the one which is opposite the bulb of percussion. It is obvious that the second type must have received the usage on its edges after it was detached from the main core or flake, but the first type may have received its usage either before or after

97

it was detached. Having sub-divided these two main types, my next object was to find out how the signs of usage on these tools had been caused. I reviewed the tools of the upper Aurignacian and was struck by the fact that at a site such as the fourth occupation of Gamble's Cave II there were several thousands of backed blades and scrapers, and abundant evidence in the débris that they were made on the spot, and I began to wonder how they could all have been made. I had been educated on the theory that the secondary working on backed blades and scrapers was the result of *striking* small, delicate trimming blows with a hammer stone, but experiment showed that tools which I made by this process (and a very slow process it had to be if the tool which was being backed was not to be broken) were not in the least like those made by the Aurignacians as regards the retouch. I also noted the absence of any small hammer stones which the percussion theory must have necessitated. I next took a fairly thick flake with a tri-angular section, but with no trace of secondary working on it. I held it in my right hand and with a small, untrimmed flat flake in my left hand I pro-ceeded to try and make the latter into a "backed blade" by the process of pressing with the thick angular edge of the former. I found that I could make a very fine "backed blade" in less than a minute. I continued the experiment and after making some four "backed blades" I examined my triangular section flake, and I found that the edge with which I had been working showed just such an *écrasée* condition as that on the "lames à section triangulaire à crêtes médianes écrasées". By the same process I found that ordinary end scrapers and lunates, etc., could be made at great speed.

When one is working with a flake with triangular section one naturally makes use of all three angle edges one after the other if they are suitable, with the result that one gets a fabricator of my second type.

But many of the "fabricators", as I now classed them, were only used on the edge opposite the flake surface which shows a bulb of percussion, and this suggested that many of them were not used in the form in which they were found.

I next tried making backed blades and scrapers with a rather thick-edged flake, and the result was that along the one edge of this flake I got the usage effect. If I used this much, the used edge would get too worn to be a satisfactory fabricator. Unfortunately I cannot detach this edge, but could I do so (and the Aurignacians certainly could, for that is what the burin technique consists of), I should then have a flake with triangular section, and one ridge (that opposite the flake surface with the bulb of percussion) would show signs of usage, in fact it would be a fabricator of my first type. If this flake came off sufficiently thick and strong for its other two edges to be used as fabricators, I should then use them, but if it came off as a rather fragile flake I could not conveniently use it but would have to discard it, and instead I should continue to use the flake from which I had detached it, and which now would have a nice fresh edge for further use as a fabricator.

This leads on to another consideration. Whereas there can be no question that many burins are in fact tools for working wood and bone, I am inclined to think that some of those that we describe as single-blow burins were not designed as burins but are really flakes which have been used as fabricators, and from which a small flake has been struck when the fabricating edge was too battered to be of any further use. As a result of my investigations I propose the name Aurignacian fabricator for these "lames à section tri-angulaire avec la crête médiane écrasée", but I should emphasise that those with signs of usage on one edge only are probably not the tool, but rather the used edge of a tool struck off when it was too rough for further satis-factory use. Whereas these Aurignacian fabricators are certainly the tools used for making ordinary backed blades of all kinds and also ordinary scrapers, they cannot be used for removing the narrow parallel flakes so typical of the work on middle Aurignacian keeled scrapers in Europe. Nor do I hold, of course, that backed blades and scrapers were not ever made by other tools and other methods, but where they occur in the same deposit as Aurignacian fabricators, one may surely conclude they were made with them.

Fig. 30 and part of Fig. 32 illustrate these fabricators, while Plate XVII shows some backed blades and scrapers made by me, and the fabricator used in making them.

"Sinew frayers"

Among the tool types found in the upper Kenya Aurignacian is one which I propose to name "sinew frayer". The essential characters of this tool are as follows—it is made on a blade, and the direction of the working edge is more or less at right angles to the length of the blade, and the secondary trimming is towards the lower or main flake surface of the imple-

99

ment and forming a wide angle with it. The working edge of the tool is always somewhat rough and irregular, and frequently, after the tool has been made, one or more small flakes have been struck from the working-edge end of the tool on the multi-flake side, with the apparent intention of roughening the working edge. Examples of these tools are shown in Fig. 31 and part of Fig. 32.

At first I regarded these tools as "sundries" and not as a type tool, but the large number found and their similarity one to another forced me to regard them as a type tool of the upper Kenya Aurignacian. I have several reasons for naming this tool "sinew frayer". Among some native tribes in Africa to-day, sinew from the legs and backs of animals is taken and is placed upon a piece of wood, and is then scratched with a jagged piece of metal or bone, and it is frayed so that threads can be pulled off. This same method is also frequently applied to sisal and sansevieria by natives who wish to get the fibre from these plants for making thread and string.

We do not of course know whether early man used vegetable fibre or animal sinew, or both, but it is certain that he used some such material for sewing his animal skins, for making snares, and as strings for his bows. We may therefore suppose that he had some tool for the purpose of fraying his raw material. Further, it was very noticeable, although it may have been merely coincidence, that these tools which I will call "frayers" occurred in the largest quantities in the same part of the cave floors as the bone awls, suggesting, though not in any way proving, some connection between the two.

In August 1929 at Johannesburg during the British Association meeting I showed some of these "frayers" to M. l'Abbé Breuil and he told me that similar tools certainly occur in some at least of the European Aurignacian sites, but they have not been described as a definite type tool.

Blades

Many irregular long flakes with considerable signs of usage and sometimes of secondary trimming occur in the upper Kenya Aurignacian, and more especially in phase (*a*). Many of them are not worth especial mention, but one definite type with secondary retouch along one or both edges on the lower main flake surface seems to be distinctly typical. See Fig. 33, No. 2.

Cores

One of the strange things about the upper Kenya Aurignacian sites is that whereas there are many long flakes, blades, and big tools made on flakes, none of the cores are of any size, or show the removal of any but fairly small flakes. The explanation seems to be that every lump of obsidian was used up to its utmost limit, and that all the larger flakes struck off in the earlier stages were utilised for making large scrapers, blades, and the big Chatelperron points, while the smaller flakes removed from the ever-decreasing core were used for the small scrapers, the small "backed blades" and for the lunates.

Hammer stones

Although the men who lived during the formation of the lowest occupation levels of Gamble's Cave II were certainly making all their tools there, as evidenced by the hundreds of thousands of waste flakes, and by the cores, very few hammer stones have been found, and those found seem hardly to be big enough for the work of detaching the larger flakes from the cores. This fact is not easily explained, but possibly the large cores and also the hammer stones may be in some of the unexcavated parts of the deposit.

Red ochre

Many fragments of red ochre were found all through the deposit. We also found one very nice large lava pebble in which a depression has been worn by constant rubbing with another pebble, which was also found. Both these stones are stained with red ochre, and there seems little doubt that they were used for reducing it to powder. These objects are illustrated in Plate XIII.

Awls of bone and of obsidian

Some delicate bone awls were found. These usually consist of small bird bones, one end of which has been polished to a point. Sometimes, however, the awl is made of a splinter of mammal bone polished at one or both ends. Three awls are figured in Plate XIV. Awls of obsidian, in the common use of the word awl, were absent, but I am inclined to consider all the so-called "Tardenoisian burins" as broken piercing tools. Many of the pseudo "Tardenoisian burins" in my series are characterised by a fairly large base with ordinary backed-blade trimming up one side, but with a marked notch towards the pointed end. At the top of the notch where the width between the backed edge and the sharp edge is very small, one finds the so-called "Tardenoisian burin" facet, always in the direction from the thick-backed edge to the fine sharp cutting edge. In addition to these so-called "Tardenoisian burins" I have many small fine points which show just the reverse type of flake to that of the Tardenoisian burin, and which are the ends of these tools. The crucial question is whether these points were intentionally struck off or broken off accidentally.

Among the group classed as backed blades I have a few tools which have the same wide base and blunt back and notch as the pseudo "Tardenoisian burin", but which, unlike them, continue up to a fine point. I am inclined to believe that the "Tardenoisian burins" are merely broken tools, and that the peculiar kind of fracture typical of them is the result of using these notched points for some such purpose as piercing holes in hard leather. See Fig. 29. It is interesting to note that M. Vignard in his work on the Sébilien[3] describes "Tardenoisian burins" as "mèches à percer", and shows in *his* Plate XXIII innumerable shapes of these tools. I gather that he regards the Tardenoisian burins as tools, while I regard them as broken tools. A further discussion of this question will be found in Chapter XI.

Striking platforms

A faceted striking platform is one of the characteristics of the Mousterian type of flake, and these Mousterian prepared platforms are a common and distinctive feature of the Kenya Mousterian. But in the upper Aurignacian in Kenya many typically Aurignacian flakes show a prepared striking platform, and I thought at first that these indicated Mousterian influence, especially as we know from other evidence that the two races were living in the same district contemporaneously. However, as the result of a careful study of very large numbers of the Aurignacian platforms, and by comparing them with the typical Mousterian type of faceted platform, it is clear that the two are quite distinct, and no connection need be postulated. Fig. 33, Nos. 6, 7, 8 and 9 are a series of four typical upper Kenya Aurignacian platforms, which may be compared and contrasted with the Mousterian ones in Figs. 11 and 12. Apart from the actual platforms the type of flake is quite distinct.

Beads and pendants

The upper Kenya Aurignacian levels of phases (*a*) and (*b*) are characterised by a large number of beads and shell pendants. The beads are small perforated discs of egg-shell, and occasionally hippo ivory. The drilling is sometimes from one side only, sometimes from both. Most of the beads are very irregular in shape, and show no signs of having been rounded by polishing in a grooved stone, very few of them are exactly the same in size and shape. Many of the beads seem to have been threaded, for they show signs of rubbing on both sides; but others which are always of a dark colour* cannot have been threaded, for they are rough and unpolished on one surface and are highly rubbed and polished on the other. This suggests that they were used as ornaments sewn on to the leather skins.

The pendants are made of the shells of freshwater mollusca, and they vary considerably in size and shape. Some of them are ornamented with a little row of dots. Examples are shown in Plate XIV.

Pottery

The question of the existence of pottery in Palaeolithic times has always been a vexed one, but there can be no doubt whatever of the presence of two pieces of pottery in the upper Kenya Aurignacian deposits in Gamble's Cave II. I found one piece myself on February 12, 1929, and on August 27, 1929, Professor Fleure was present at Gamble's Cave when I was digging for a small sample of the deposit from the lower levels of the fourth occupation of the cave for him to examine and another piece was found. Besides these two pieces which were actually found *in situ* in the fourth occupation level, several pieces were found in the riddles on different occasions when deposits of the fourth occupation were being worked; but as none of these was found *in situ* and there was just a possibility of their having fallen from an exposed section of one of the higher deposits, they cannot be taken as evidence. Of the two pieces found *in situ*, that found in the presence of Professor Fleure shows quite unmistakable signs of having been made by smearing clay on the *inside* of a basket, and the impression of the basketwork can be clearly seen in the photograph in Plate XII. The second piece is thicker and is very rough. On being placed in water for cleaning purposes it started to disintegrate, and had to be taken out at once and treated with shellac. This fact probably explains why only two pieces were found.

* These black beads were at first thought to be stone, but Beck reports that they are shell stained in some way.

Both pieces are figured, see Plate XII. There can be no question of this pottery having been carried down from the higher levels by rodents, for it is quite unlike any of the pottery which occurs in the other (higher) levels containing pottery. As we shall see in the next chapter, pottery had reached an advanced stage by the time of the Elmenteitan industry in Makalian times, and it is therefore only reasonable to expect to find crude pottery in these earlier times. One question immediately arises. If these Kenya Aurignacians had pottery, and if they are derived from the same cradle as the European Aurignacian folk, why did the latter have no pottery? To me the absence of pottery in the European Aurignacian has always been a matter of great surprise, for one would expect that a race who were capable of the fine paintings which are found in their caves and of making the wide range of tools which we connect with the Cromagnon people would early have discovered the valuable properties of clay for making baskets water-tight, and thus have discovered pottery, especially as we know that they used clay to model animals, as proved by the clay bisons at Tuc D'Audoubert. To me, the presence of pottery in the time of the upper Aurignacians in East Africa seems less surprising than its absence in the upper Aurignacian sites in Europe. I am even inclined to believe that one day authenticated pottery will be found in some Aurignacian sites in Europe. On the other hand our earliest pottery is only in the upper Kenya Aurignacian, and it may well be that they discovered the use of clay themselves, and that when the Aurignacian stock arrived in Kenya in the lower Kenya Aurignacian stage of development they had no pottery.

From the foregoing description of the culture objects of the upper Kenya Aurignacian it will be seen that it was very different from the more primitive Chellean, Acheulean and Mousterian cultures, in that it had a very wide range of tool types. I have already tried to indicate the probable uses of the Aurignacian fabricators and the sinew frayers and the so-called "Tardenoisian burins", but a few notes on experiments made with some of the other tools may be of interest.

Possible uses of Chatelperron and Gravette points

Chatelperron and Gravette points with their sharp cutting edge and blunted backs closely resemble pen-knife blades, although some of them are very small. On May 6, 1929, I made an experiment of skinning and disembowelling a Thompson's gazelle, which is about the size of a goat, with a single "backed blade" about one and a half inches long. I finished the job easily in twenty minutes unaided, and the backed blade used was still quite sharp at the end of the process. On May 18, 1930, I cut, stripped and did all the preliminary preparation of an arrow-shaft of wood with a single Chatelperron point, but by the end of the operation its edges were considerably blunted and splintered. These two experiments showed that even quite small "backed blades" were perfectly effective as knives for ordinary purposes, and as knives they were undoubtedly principally used.

The enormous variation in size and shape which one finds among the Chatelperron and Gravette points, and which is illustrated in Figs. 17, 18, 19 and 20, seems most probably simply to be due to the shape of the flake selected for the making of any particular tool, and also to the individual whim of the maker, in consideration of the object for which he was making it. One would naturally expect that the Aurignacian hunter whose day's bag consisted of hares and cane rats would sit down and make a small Gravette point with which to skin them, whereas on another occasion, if he had bagged a water-buck or an aard-vark, he would use the very biggest flake that he could obtain and make it into a large Chatelperron point strong enough to cut through the tough hide.

The use of large crescents and lunates

On June 14, 1927, in the upper occupation level of Gamble's Cave II, and again in August 1927, in soil on a hill to the south-west of Kikuyu station, I found lunates in such a position as to leave me in no further doubt at all that they had been hafted as barbs of an arrow-head in the manner shown in Plate XVII. A study of this figure will show clearly how efficient the lunate is for such a purpose. It has a sharp cutting edge and a curved blunt back. When it is set as a barb in a groove, the whole of the sharp cutting edge is facing forwards at an angle which is extremely useful for cutting into the skin and flesh of an animal; while one-half of the blunt back forms the back of the barb so that it does not easily pull out, the other half of the blunt back is let into the wooden shaft of the arrow, and being blunt does not cut its way farther into the wood. We may suppose that these barbs were held in position in the grooves by natural gum of some sort, and that they were poisoned. They would thus be a most deadly weapon, for when the arrow had penetrated deep into the flesh, the heat of the blood would soon soften the resin and the weight of the arrow-shaft would cause it to fall away, leaving the poisoned barbs in the wound. In this connection it is interesting to note that the vast majority of the crescents and lunates were found in the ashes of the hearths, and one can conjecture that this is not purely accidental. It seems possible that this is what would happen:

A hunter, having shot, let us say, an antelope, would follow up the trail of the wounded animal; the blood would melt the resin and the shaft would fall off, leaving the poisoned barbs in the wound; the hunter would pick up his shaft, and he might rebarb it later; the wounded animal would eventually be found dead or dying from the poison, and the hunter would carry it back to the home cave where it would be skinned and cut up, and the meat round the wound and the barbs would be thrown into the fire, possibly because there was some taboo against using the barbs a second time. This would explain the enormous number of crescents and lunates which we find, and also the fact that they are commonest in the ashes of the fires. Nor is a hypothetical reason for such a taboo hard to find if we want one. Probably some individual in trying to extricate barbs from the wound of an animal once cut his finger, and died from the effect of the poison, and the taboo came into existence, especially as it was so easy to make new barbs.

The range in size of the barbs from crescents one and a half inches long to minute lunates less than half an inch, is easily explained by the range in the size of the game which was hunted. The bones found in the ash and hearths of Gamble's Cave II, in the fourth occupation, represent animals ranging from lion and buffalo to cane rats and hyrax. Of course arrow barbs may not have been the only use for the crescents, but it was surely one, and it is this use of the bow and arrow which to my mind explains the fact that the Aurignacians were such superior hunters to the Mousterians.

The use of burins

In French Aurignacian deposits the association of the burins with engraved bones and stones, and also with engravings upon the walls of the caves, has resulted in the general view that the burin is essentially an engraving tool. While accepting this as one of its uses, I am inclined to think that that was not its original or principal use. Burins are frequently found in deposits where there is no trace of engraving of any kind, and we must therefore postulate some other use for them. Wood must certainly have been used by prehistoric man, but as it is seldom preserved we know little of his method of using it. We have seen that in East Africa he almost certainly used crescents as barbs for arrows, and this implies that the wooden arrow-shafts were grooved to take the barbs. In May 1929 I set myself to make an arrow with barbs, using only Aurignacian tools, and I found that the trimming and smoothing of the wooden shaft and point could be done with backed blades and hollow scrapers, but when it came to cutting the grooves for the barbs I attempted to do this with the fine edge of the backed blade, whereupon I simply splintered the edge of my tool and made little effect on the wood. I then took a burin of the double-blow or *bec de flûte* type (Fig. 27, No. 8 is the one which I used) and with this as my tool the grooving was a simple matter, and I am satisfied that this was one of the common uses of true burins.

The resulting barbed arrow is that shown in Plate XVII.

Whereas many burins are what I call true burins and were definite tools, there are a number of tools which, thanks to the presence of the burin facet and burin technique, are classed as burins, but which I am convinced are not really burins at all.

In dealing with Aurignacian fabricators I have already indicated my belief that one of the types, that with the used edge opposite the flake surface showing the bulb of percussion, is in fact but half the tool. I believe that a large flake with a fairly thick edge was used as a fabricator, and that when the edge became too jagged through use, a blow was struck which detached a flake with the damaged edge. To detach such a flake the burin blow technique would have to be employed, and the result would be a burin facet on the original main flake, while the minor flake would show a flake side with a bulb of percussion, and opposite this a ridge with much usage. The main original flake could now be easily classified as a single-blow burin, in fact I believe that many single-blow burins are nothing more than half of an Aurignacian fabricator.

Use of scrapers

Under the general term scraper it is usual to class round-ended scrapers, hollow scrapers, square-ended scrapers, and core scrapers. Frequent experiment has shown that the round-ended ones are exceedingly efficient tools for braying and dressing hides in order to make them soft and supple for wear. They are especially suitable for this purpose if held more or less perpendicular to the skin and used with a pulling action. The range in size of these round-ended scrapers from tools three inches long and an inch or more in width, to tools the size of one's thumb nail, is probably due to the different sizes of the skins which were dressed. The upper Aurignacian folk in Kenya certainly killed anything from large antelopes to hares and hyrax, and we may conclude that they used all skins for clothing, for hunting-bags, etc.

Hollow scrapers seem certainly to have been principally used for rubbing down arrow-shafts and other wooden tools, and they are quite efficient for the purpose. At present I can find no really adequate use for core scrapers or for square-ended scrapers, though following Mr Van Reit Lowe of South Africa I incline to class the former not as scrapers at all, but as fabricators used for detaching the flakes from cores and for making scrapers and burins.

Use of awls of bone and stone

Although no eyed needles are known in the upper Kenya Aurignacian, this does not mean that the people did not know how to sew skins, for the sewing of leather is more easily done with an awl than with a needle, and nearly all the skin sewing done by African races to-day, some of which is very fine work indeed, is done without eyed needles. Whereas the bone awls were probably all used for this purpose, we may suppose that some of the obsidian pointed tools were used for piercing the shell pendants and the beads.

Human remains

Although for purposes of description phases (*a*) and (*b*) of the upper Kenya Aurignacian have been classed together, as already said it should be possible to distinguish them from each other if a sufficiently big series is available. In Figs. 17 to 32 inclusive series of tools from phases (*a*) and (*b*) are shown, and by making a study of these it can be seen clearly that certain of the more finely made types of backed blades are absent in (*a*) while common in (*b*). Similarly the scrapers of phase (*b*) are on the whole smaller and finer, and in the earlier series there is a feeling of cruder workmanship than that found in the later series.

So far the human remains from the phases (*a*) and (*b*) of the upper Kenya Aurignacian are confined to three human teeth, and it is not until phase (*c*) that skeletons have been found.

THE KENYA AURIGNACIAN

Phase (c)

We have examined the evidence for the lower Kenya Aurignacian, and we have also discussed the lower divisions of the upper Kenya Aurignacian in some detail. The third division of the upper Kenya Aurignacian belongs in time to a period about mid-way between the second maximum of the Gamblian pluvial (*i.e.* Upper Gamblian) and the complete desiccation which marks the end of the Gamblian. In Gamble's Cave II the deposits of the third phase of the upper Kenya Aurignacian are in part separated from the earlier phases by a sterile layer (due to rock fall) and in part lie directly on the earlier deposits. This third phase is unfortunately only represented by a comparatively small series of tools, which are perhaps not sufficient by which to judge it fairly. It would seem, however, that the finest period of the upper Kenya Aurignacian had passed, and that the culture was degenerating somewhat. A series of tools is shown in Fig. 35. The whole group shows close resemblances to the preceding phase (*b*), and with only a small series available, it would not be possible to distinguish it with any certainty from that phase, but for its stratigraphical position. It should be noted that this level yielded three or four fragments of pottery, similar in type to the crude piece from the level of phase (*b*).

To this period belong the human remains known as Gamble's Cave II skeletons, Nos. 1, 2, 3, 4 and 5. The first three were very fragmentary, but the last two were in good condition. These remains have not yet been fully studied, and a detailed description is reserved for a later publication. They certainly do not represent a modern negro type, and they seem to have considerable resemblances to the Oldoway skeleton found by Professor Reck in 1913 in North Tanganyika Territory. They were buried in the ultra-contracted position, males lying on the right side, females on the left, and were freely sprinkled with red ochre. Photographs of skeletons Nos. 4 and 5 *in situ* and of the reconstructed skull of No. 5 are shown in Plates XV and XVI.

REFERENCES

1. *Stations Préhistoriques de Château de Bassaler près Brive. I. La Grotte de la Fort Robert*, by Abbés Bardon and A. and J. Bouyssonie, pp. 8, 9.
2. "A contribution to the study of Prehistoric man in Algeria, N. Africa", by A. W. Pond, in *Bulletin of the Beloit College*, vol. xxvi, no. 5.
3. *Une nouvelle Industrie Lithique. Le Sébilien*, by E. Vignard, 1923.

FIGURE 14

"Backed blades" and other tools of lower Kenya Aurignacian type. Nos. 1 and 2 are rolled backed blades from the beach gravel in Gamble's Cave II beneath the upper Kenya Aurignacian deposits. Nos. 3–12 came from the silts and gravels of the first maximum of the Gamblian pluvial, where they are exposed in the Naivasha area by the Malewa River valley. Nos. 3–8 are crude "backed blades". No. 11 is simply a flake with a little irregular retouch. No. 9 is an end-scraper, and No. 10 is a hollow scraper. No. 12 has all the appearance of the "Aurignacian fabricators" so common in the upper Kenya Aurignacian.

Except for No. 10, which is chert, all these tools are of obsidian. The field numbers are:

No. 1. Y.6. 1929.   No. 5. M.389. 1929.   No. 9. Y.71. 1929.
No. 2. L.481. 1929.   No. 6. 6212. 1929.   No. 10. M.390. 1929.
No. 3. 6215. 1929.   No. 7. 6214. 1929.   No. 11. Y.73. 1929.
No. 4. 6218. 1929.   No. 8. Y.72. 1929.   No. 12. Y.70. 1929.

Note. These tools are from the same deposits as the lower Kenya Mousterian tools shown in Figure 11.

FIGURE 14

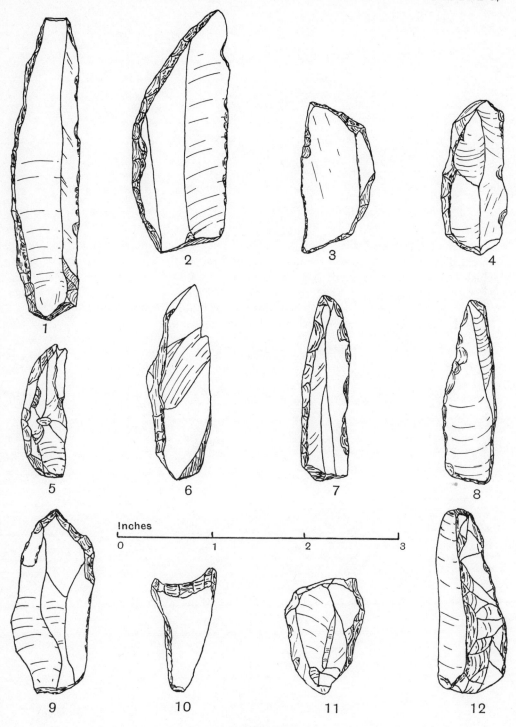

Inches
0   1   2   3

III

View of Gamble's Caves from the opposite hill. The positions of the caves are indicated by arrows. Note also the line of the terrace on the same level as the caves which marks the beach of Lake Nakuru during the second maximum of the Gamblian pluvial.

The caves were cut by the waters of this lake, and the lowest stratum in them is a beach sand and gravel containing many freshwater mollusca.

(Photograph by Mr J. H. Braunholtz)

PLATE X

PLATE XI

1. A close view of Gamble's Caves taken from the tree which can be seen to the left of Gamble's Cave I in Plate X. The arrows indicate the approximate positions of the two sections through the deposits which are shown in Figures 15 and 16.

2. Gamble's Cave II. A dotted line shows the level of the cave floor when excavations were begun; to the right is seen the level of the scree which was banked against the cliff at that point.

The bottom of the cave is nowhere visible.

Note. Gamble's Caves are, strictly speaking, only rock shelters.

PLATE XI

1

2

FIGURE 15

Note. This is a section of the deposits in Gamble's Cave II at the middle point of the cave or rock shelter. Read from bottom to top.

Layer 1. Modern occupation level composed of sheep dung, soil, hearths, bones of domestic animals etc. (Kikuyu.)

Layer 2. Modern occupation level composed of hearths, wild animal bones, some pottery, but no stone tools. (Probably Wandorobo.)

Layer 3. Sterile layer of dust and rock débris derived from the roof. This represents a fairly long period without any occupation. It probably represents the Nakuran wet phase.

Layer 4. Aeolian sand (red) representing dry period at the end of the Makalian wet phase.

Layer 5. Rock débris (sterile).

Layer 6. Prehistoric occupation level with Elmenteitan culture, tools, pottery and many animal bones.

Layer 7. Rock débris (sterile). Layers 5, 6 and 7 together represent the Makalian wet phase.

Layer 8. Aeolian sand (red) representing period of desiccation at the close of the Gamblian pluvial.

Layer 9. Rock débris (sterile).

Layer 10. Mainly rock débris derived from roof, but with occasional prehistoric hearths, some animal bones, and a few flakes, and broken tools, of Kenya Stillbay type.

Layer 11. A level characterised by burials. In this part of the cave there were three skeletons at this level, resting on the "third occupation level" and covered roughly with large blocks of stone, which were overlain immediately by the deposit No. 10.

Layer 12. Prehistoric occupation level with hearths, animal bones, crude pottery and tools of the upper Kenya Aurignacian type (phase (*c*)).

Layer 13. Fallen blocks of stone from the roof and rock débris. At this part of the excavation this level separated the upper Kenya Aurignacian of phase (*c*) from that of phase (*b*).

Layer 14. Prehistoric occupation level with tools of upper Kenya Aurignacian type. An arbitrary division was made (see dotted line), and classification shows a distinct evolution in the tools from lower to higher levels. Phase (*b*) is at the top, phase (*a*) below. Layers 14, 13, 12, 11, 10 and 9 represent the gradual decline of the Gamblian pluvial after the second maximum.

Layer 15. Beach sand and gravel containing very many freshwater shells, chiefly *Corbicula africana*, *Melanoides tuberculata*; also a few rolled tools of lower Kenya Aurignacian type. This represents the level of Lake Nakuru at the second maximum of the Gamblian pluvial, and is approximately 500 feet above present lake level.

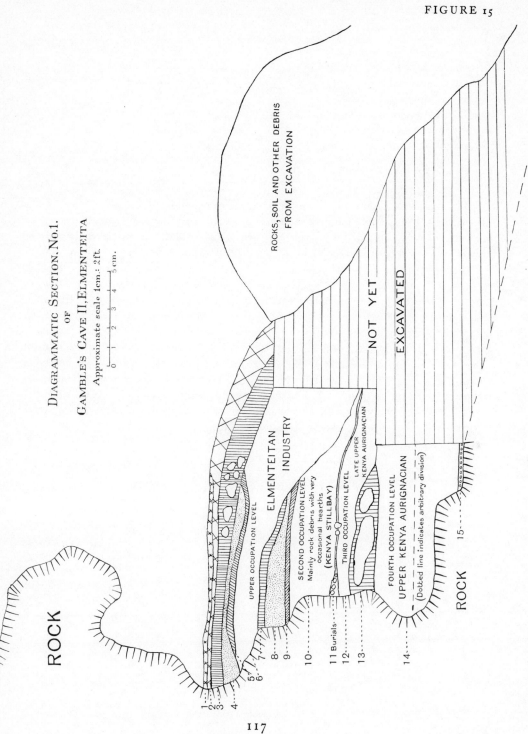

FIGURE 15

DIAGRAMMATIC SECTION. No.1.
OF
GAMBLE'S CAVE II, ELMENTEITA
Approximate scale 1cm.: 2ft.

0 1 2 3 4 5 cm.

ROCK

ROCKS, SOIL AND OTHER DEBRIS FROM EXCAVATION

NOT YET EXCAVATED

ELMENTEITAN INDUSTRY

UPPER OCCUPATION LEVEL

SECOND OCCUPATION LEVEL
Mainly rock debris with very occasional hearths
(KENYA STILLBAY)

THIRD OCCUPATION LEVEL

LATE UPPER KENYA AURIGNACIAN

FOURTH OCCUPATION LEVEL
UPPER KENYA AURIGNACIAN
(Dotted line indicates arbitrary division)

ROCK

1
2
3
4
5
6
7
8
9
10
11 Burials
12
13
14
15

117

FIGURE 16

The section in Figure 15 shows the sequence of deposits in Gamble's Cave II on a line through the middle of the rock shelter. The section in Figure 16 shows the sequence of deposits to the west of the upper rock shelter on a line through the middle of the lower "cave" which was completely filled with deposits.

Layers 1 to 7 were replaced by scree. Layers 9 and 10 were entirely missing, this being due to the absence of rock shelter at this point, since the lower shelter was now completely filled up, and the upper shelter did not extend so far west; for the same reason layer 12 is here not a true occupation level, but rather a grey-black débris with occasional tools and bones, outliers from the occupation level proper which was concentrated farther to the east under the over-hang of the upper shelter. In this grey-black débris were two more skeletons, overlain by blocks of stone and in every way comparable to those which lay on layer 12 farther to the east. Layer 14 was here very rich, and was concentrated in and in front of the lower rock shelter, filling it to within two feet of the roof. The dotted line shows the arbitrary division of the upper Kenya Aurignacian level into phases (a) and (b). Phase (a) rests immediately upon the beach gravel and sand which is a continuation of layer 15 of the other section.

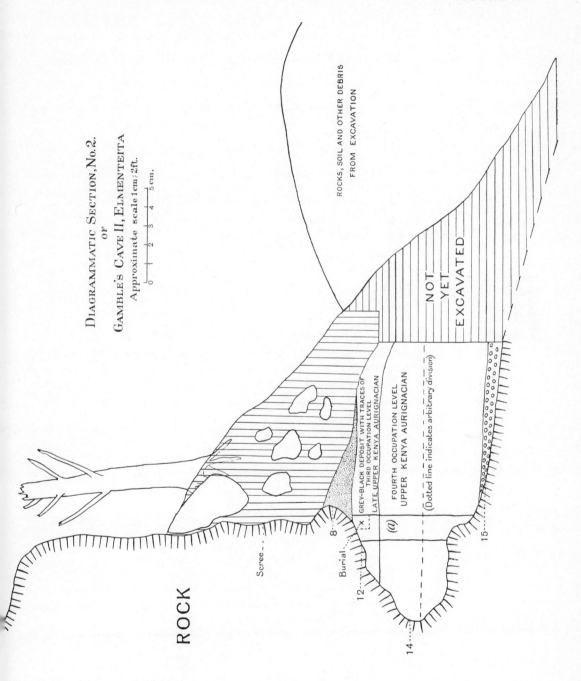

DIAGRAMMATIC SECTION, No.2.
OF
GAMBLE'S CAVE II, ELMENTEITA
Approximate scale 1cm:2ft.

0 1 2 3 4 5 cm.

FIGURE 16

ROCKS, SOIL AND OTHER DEBRIS
FROM EXCAVATION

NOT
YET
EXCAVATED

GREY-BLACK DEPOSIT WITH TRACES OF
THIRD OCCUPATION LEVEL
LATE UPPER KENYA AURIGNACIAN

FOURTH OCCUPATION LEVEL
UPPER KENYA AURIGNACIAN

(Dotted line indicates arbitrary division)

ROCK

Scree

Burial

(a)

8

12

14

15

x

119

PLATE XII

Two fragments of pottery from the fourth occupation level (upper Kenya Aurignacian) in Gamble's Cave II, Elmenteita. The period is the decline of the Gamblian pluvial after the second maximum.

No. 1. This fragment is 58 mm. in its greatest horizontal length, 49 mm. in its greatest width, and 8·5 mm. thick. It was found in the lower half of the upper Kenya Aurignacian occupation level in the presence of Professor J. H. Fleure, F.R.S. on August 27th, 1929. It consists of a part of a lump of clay which had been plastered on to the inside of a basket. The basket must then have been burnt either intentionally or by accident. The impress of the basket is clearly seen in the photograph.

No. 2. The only other fragment of pottery found *in situ* in the upper Kenya Aurignacian levels in Gamble's Cave II. It came from the upper part of the Aurignacian occupation level, and is therefore slightly later in time than the other piece. It is very poorly baked and when it was put into water to be washed it began to disintegrate. It is 100 mm. long, 61·5 mm. wide, and 11 mm. thick.

Note. No. 1 was found with the tools of phase (*a*) and No. 2 with tools of phase (*b*) of the upper Kenya Aurignacian.

PLATE XII

1

2

PLATE XIII

1. A large lump of lava 205 mm. long, 178 mm. wide, and 89·5 mm. thick. It has been utilised for grinding ochre. As a result of this usage it has a deep trough worn in it. It was found in the lower levels of the fourth occupation level (upper Kenya Aurignacian) in Gamble's Cave II, i.e. with tools of phase (c).

2. A pebble of lava found near Number 1. The lower half of the pebble has been much worn through use, and as it fits well into the trough of Number 1, it is presumed to be the stone which was used in grinding the ochre. It is 67 mm. long, 56 mm. in greatest diameter, and 53·5 mm. measured at right angles to the greatest diameter.

(Period—decline of the Gamblian pluvial after the second maximum.)

PLATE XIII

1

2

PLATE XIV

Beads, shell pendants, bone awls from the lower part of the "fourth occupation level" (upper Kenya Aurignacian) of Gamble's Cave II, Elmenteita. Similar objects occurred throughout the whole of the "fourth occupation level," i.e. phases (*a*) and (*b*) of the upper Kenya Aurignacian.

The shells at the right-hand top corner came from the beach sand at the very base of the deposits in Gamble's Cave II.

(Period—just after the second maximum of the Gamblian pluvial.)

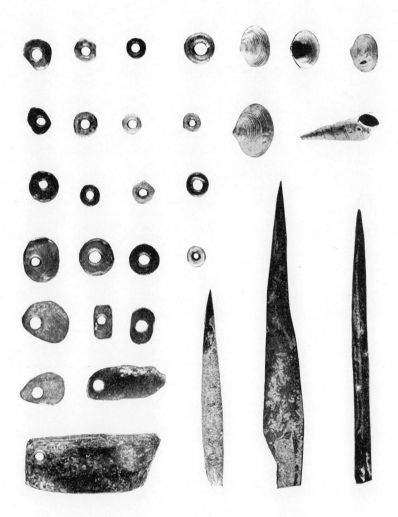

PLATE XIV

PLATE XV

View of the skeleton Number 4 from the third occupation level of Gamble's Cave II, Elmenteita, during the process of excavation. The third occupation level represents the very close of the upper Kenya Aurignacian occupation of Gamble's Caves.

The period of the third occupation is during the decline of the Gamblian pluvial after the second maximum, and the tools at this level are of phase (c) of the upper Kenya Aurignacian.

This skeleton is in the ultra-contracted position and was freely covered with red ochre. No ornaments were found with it.

PLATE XV

127

No. 1. View of the skull of skeleton Number 5 from the third occupation level of Gamble's Cave II, Elmenteita, during the process of excavation.

This skeleton is of the same date as Number 4 shown in Plate XV. It is probably that of a woman, and was freely covered with red ochre, but no ornaments were found with it.

No. 2. Full-face and profile views of the skull Number 5. The left-hand side of the skull is unfortunately warped in the region of the face.

PLATE XVI

1

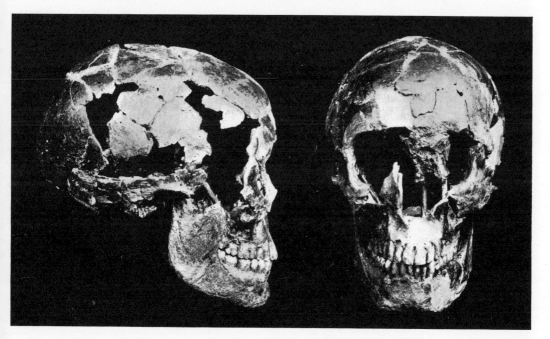

2

PLATE XVII

Nos. 1–8. A series of obsidian tools to illustrate the author's theory concerning the making of "backed blades" and scrapers. No. 1 is a thick, angular piece of obsidian which I used as a fabricator to produce the blunt backs of Nos. 2, 3, and 4, all of which are fairly typical "backed blades" made by me. No. 2 is mounted to show only the bluntened back. No. 3 is a very thin blade on which the blunt curved back was produced in less than one minute. No. 4 is a large "backed blade". No. 1 had no signs of retouch or battering on it when selected to make "backed blades", but it now has all the characteristic "écrasée" appearance so typical of the "Aurignacian fabricators." No. 7 is an end-scraper which was also made by using No. 1 as fabricator. No. 8 is an end-scraper which was made with No. 5. When selected to be used as a trial fabricator No. 5 had no trace of secondary flaking on its lower or main flake surface. After making the scraper No. 8 and several lunates, it had achieved the appearance seen in the plate. It is now a typical "lame écaillée" and may be compared with No. 6 which is a genuine "lame écaillée" from the Elmenteitan industry. (See page 174.)

No. 9. Five lunates hafted in the manner suggested in the text, to form barbs for an arrow. The wooden foreshaft was made with stone tools—to wit—a "backed blade" and a hollow scraper, and the grooves for mounting the barbs were cut with a burin.

PLATE XVII

FIGURE 17

"Backed blades" from phase (*a*) of the upper Kenya Aurignacian levels (fourth occupation level) in Gamble's Cave II, Elmenteita. The period is just after the second maximum of the Gamblian pluvial.

There is a wide range of "backed blade" types in this level, and this series has been chosen as illustrating the main types of large blades, while on Figure 18 the smaller ones are illustrated. All these tools are of obsidian, and the field catalogue numbers are given below:

No. 1. Y.31. 1929.	No. 8. Y.27. 1929.	No. 15. Y.32. 1929.
No. 2. F.155. 1929.	No. 9. F.571. 1929.	No. 16. H.424. 1929.
No. 3. A.367. 1929.	No. 10. Y.30. 1929.	No. 17. L.499. 1929.
No. 4. Y.24. 1929.	No. 11. Y.28. 1929.	No. 18. E.343. 1929.
No. 5. H.280. 1929.	No. 12. Y.46. 1929.	No. 19. Y.26. 1929.
No. 6. Y.21. 1929.	No. 13. Y.22. 1929.	No. 20. Y.23. 1929.
No. 7. Y.25. 1929.	No. 14. Y.29. 1929.	No. 21. L.485. 1929.

FIGURE 17

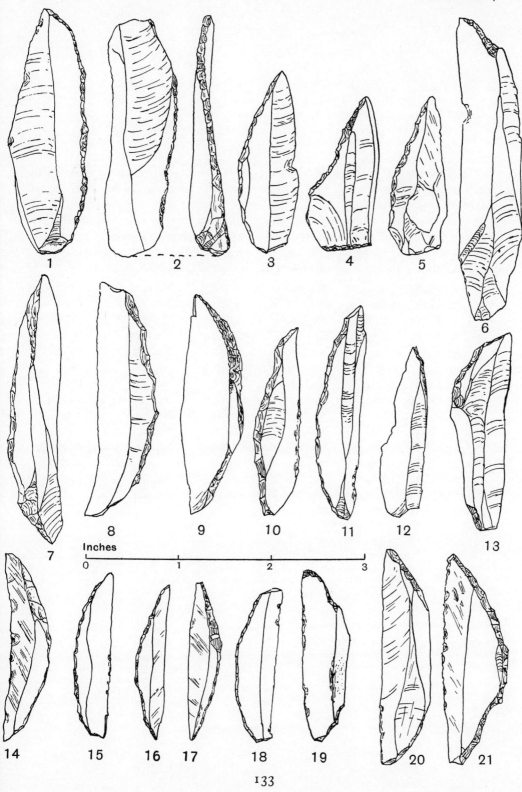

Inches
0   1   2   3

FIGURE 18

"Backed blades" from phase (*a*) of the upper Kenya Aurignacian levels (fourth occupation level), Gamble's Cave II, Elmenteita. The period is just after the second maximum of the Gamblian pluvial. This series, together with the preceding figure, indicates the range of the tools which fall into the general category of "backed blades". The percentage of small tools to large is fairly low in the lower part of the upper Kenya Aurignacian, and fine, narrow tools like Nos. 13 and 14 are rare in this level. All these tools are of obsidian, and the field catalogue numbers are:

No. 1. L.489. 1929.	No. 16. Z.36. 1929.	No. 31. G.940. 1929.
No. 2. Z.12. 1929.	No. 17. Z.22. 1929.	No. 32. Z.24. 1929.
No. 3. L.556. 1929.	No. 18. Z.28. 1929.	No. 33. Z.15. 1929.
No. 4. Z.16. 1929.	No. 19. H.755. 1929.	No. 34. Z.35. 1929.
No. 5. Z.11. 1929.	No. 20. E.741. 1929.	No. 35. Z.25. 1929.
No. 6. Z.7. 1929.	No. 21. H.701. 1929.	No. 36. Z.26. 1929.
No. 7. L.484. 1929.	No. 22. Z.27. 1929.	No. 37. Z.29. 1929.
No. 8. G.696. 1929.	No. 23. G.973. 1929.	No. 38. G.432. 1929.
No. 9. Z.8. 1929.	No. 24. G.465. 1929.	No. 39. 538. 1929.
No. 10. Z.30. 1929.	No. 25. Z.32. 1929.	No. 40. Z.31. 1929.
No. 11. Z.18. 1929.	No. 26. Z.14. 1929.	No. 41. (lost after being
No. 12. Z.10. 1929.	No. 27. Z.12. 1929.	drawn)
No. 13. Z.20. 1929.	No. 28. Z.9. 1929.	No. 42. G.560. 1929.
No. 14. Z.13. 1929.	No. 29. G.86. 1929.	No. 43. Z.34. 1929.
No. 15. Z.19. 1929.	No. 30. Z.33. 1929.	

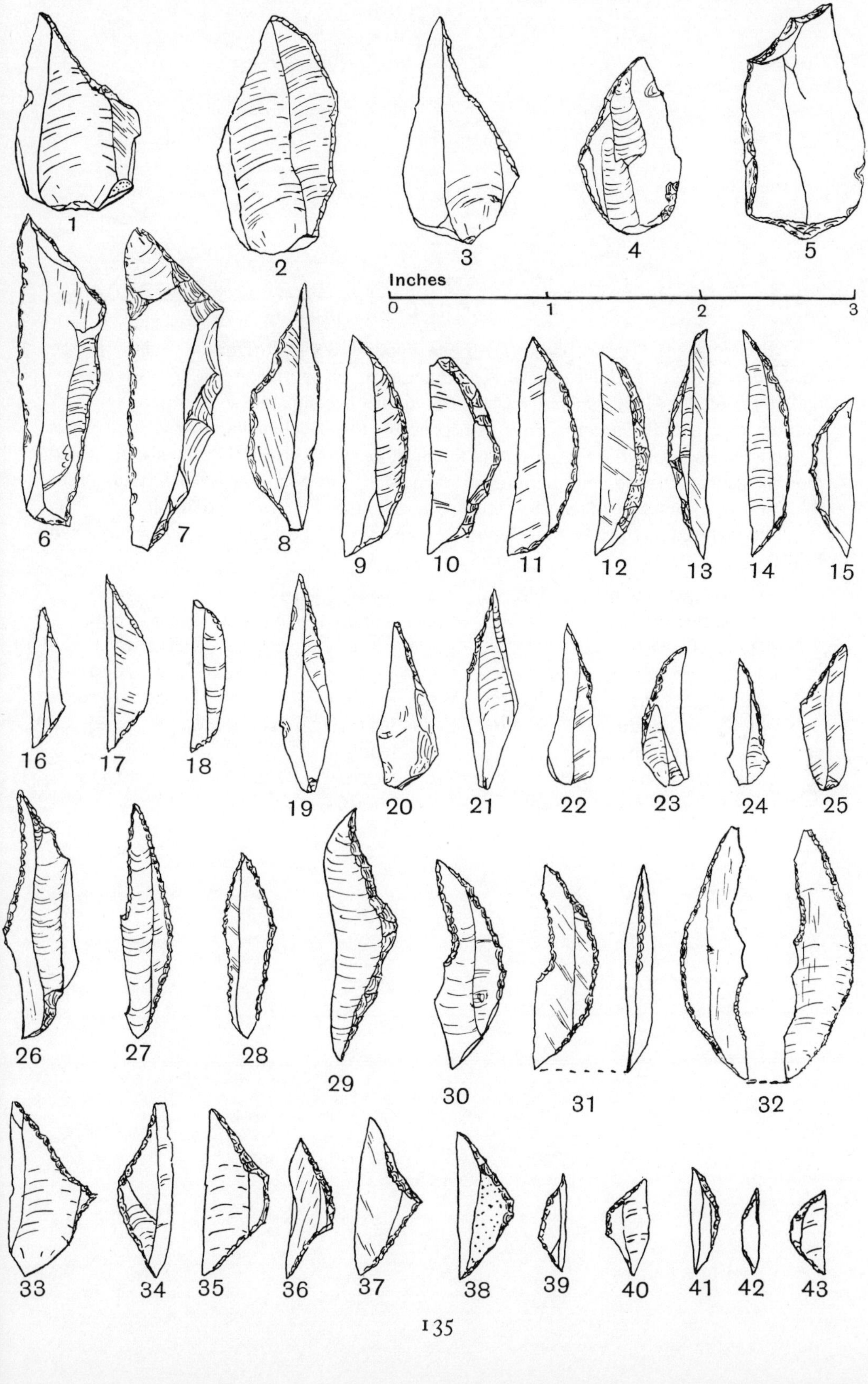

FIGURE 18

Inches

0   1   2   3

1 2 3 4 5
6 7 8 9 10 11 12 13 14 15
16 17 18 19 20 21 22 23 24 25
26 27 28 29 30 31 32
33 34 35 36 37 38 39 40 41 42 43

FIGURE 19

"Backed blades" from phase (*b*) of the upper Kenya Aurignacian levels (fourth occupation level) in Gamble's Cave II, Elmenteita. The period is just after the second maximum of the Gamblian pluvial. If this figure is compared with Figure 17 from the lower part of the upper Kenya Aurignacian, the development of the industry is clearly seen. Most of the tools are now much more symmetrical, they are also finer and more delicately finished, and the number of tools such as Nos. 1–4 is small, while tools like Nos. 5, 6, 7, 12, 13, 14, 18, 20, 21, 22, 25, and 26 are very common.

The material of all these tools is obsidian, and the field catalogue numbers are given below:

No. 1. L.744. 1929.	No. 11. Y.47. 1929.	No. 21. Y.52. 1929.
No. 2. L.201. 1929.	No. 12. Y.41. 1929.	No. 22. Y.53. 1929.
No. 3. C.667. 1929.	No. 13. Y.51. 1929.	No. 23. Y.45. 1929.
No. 4. C.192. 1929.	No. 14. Y.40. 1929.	No. 24. Y.42. 1929.
No. 5. Y.50. 1929.	No. 15. Y.35. 1929.	No. 25. D.129. 1929.
No. 6. Y.33. 1929.	No. 16. Y.48. 1929.	No. 26. Y.38. 1929.
No. 7. D.324. 1929.	No. 17. Y.49. 1929.	No. 27. Y.34. 1929.
No. 8. Y.36. 1929.	No. 18. Y.67. 1929.	No. 28. L.761. 1929.
No. 9. Y.44. 1929.	No. 19. Y.39. 1929.	
No. 10. Y.37. 1929.	No. 20. Y.43. 1929.	

FIGURE 19

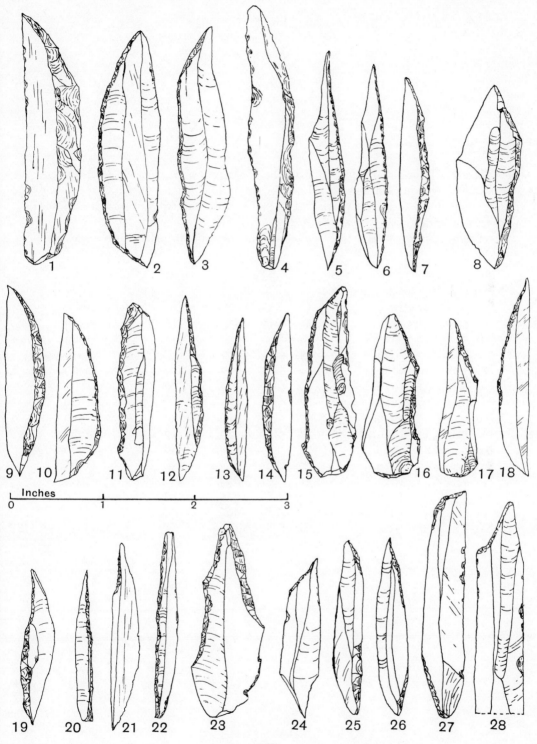

Inches
0   1   2   3

137

FIGURE 20

"Backed blades" from phase (*b*) of the upper Kenya Aurignacian levels (fourth occupation level) in Gamble's Cave II, Elmenteita. The period is just after the second maximum of the Gamblian pluvial. This series shows the types of smaller "backed blades" associated with those shown in Figure 19.

The material of all these tools is obsidian, and the field catalogue numbers are given below:

No. 1. I.286. 1929.	No. 18. Z.63. 1929.	No. 35. Z.65. 1929.
No. 2. Z.55. 1929.	No. 19. Z.56. 1929.	No. 36. Z.66. 1929.
No. 3. D.302. 1929.	No. 20. Z.51. 1929.	No. 37. Z.86. 1929.
No. 4. Z.62. 1929.	No. 21. Z.46. 1929.	No. 38. Z.58. 1929.
No. 5. C.218. 1929.	No. 22. Z.60. 1929.	No. 39. Z.83. 1929.
No. 6. L.797. 1929.	No. 23. Z.69. 1929.	No. 40. Z.78. 1929.
No. 7. Z.57. 1929.	No. 24. Z.45. 1929.	No. 41. Z.81. 1929.
No. 8. C.631. 1929.	No. 25. Z.70. 1929.	No. 42. Z.52. 1929.
No. 9. C.660. 1929.	No. 26. Z.50. 1929.	No. 43. Z.64. 1929.
No. 10. Z.74. 1929.	No. 27. Z.61. 1929.	No. 44. Z.82. 1929.
No. 11. Z.43. 1929.	No. 28. Z.54. 1929.	No. 45. Z.72. 1929.
No. 12. Z.48. 1929.	No. 29. Z.67. 1929.	No. 46. Z.87. 1929.
No. 13. Z.49. 1929.	No. 30. D.268. 1929.	No. 47. Z.88. 1929.
No. 14. Z.44. 1929.	No. 31. Z.77. 1929.	No. 48. Z.75. 1929.
No. 15. Z.73. 1929.	No. 32. Z.84. 1929.	No. 49. Z.59. 1929.
No. 16. Z.47. 1929.	No. 33. Z.53. 1929.	
No. 17. Z.80. 1929.	No. 34. L.815. 1929.	

FIGURE 20

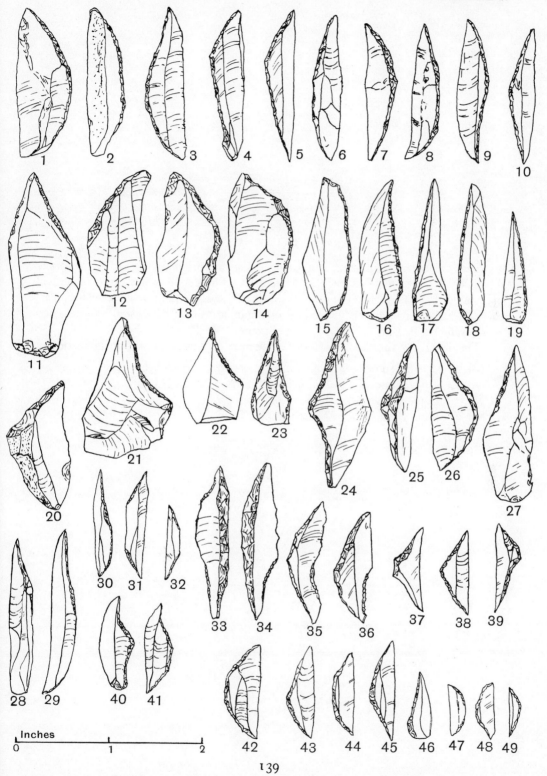

Inches
0   1   2

FIGURE 21

End-scrapers from phase *(a)* of the upper Kenya Aurignacian levels (fourth occupation level) of Gamble's Cave II, Elmenteita. The period is just after the second maximum of the Gamblian pluvial. In this level a certain number of the end-scrapers show a tendency towards the type known in France as "Gratoir à museau". Nos. 7 and 8 are examples of these.

The material of these tools is obsidian. The field catalogue numbers are given below:

No. 1. L.391. 1929.   No. 5. Y.75. 1929.   No. 9. Z.98. 1929.
No. 2. Z.95. 1929.   No. 6. Y.2. 1929.   No. 10. Y.6. 1929.
No. 3. L.398. 1929.   No. 7. Z.96. 1929.
No. 4. Y.4. 1929.   No. 8. Z.99. 1929.

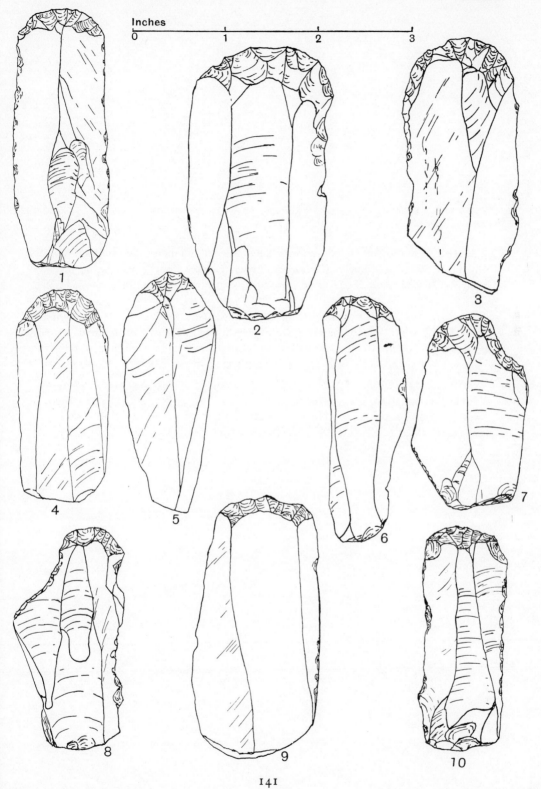

FIGURE 21

Inches

0   1   2   3

1

2

3

4

5

6

7

8

9

10

FIGURE 22

End-scrapers, double-ended scrapers, square-ended scrapers, and hollow scrapers from phase (*a*) of the upper Kenya Aurignacian levels (fourth occupation level) of Gamble's Cave II, Elmenteita. The period is just after the maximum of the Gamblian pluvial.

Number 3 is about the smallest of the end-scrapers from phase (*a*) of the upper Kenya Aurignacian, but in phase (*b*), see Figures 23 and 24, many of the small scrapers are found. The hollow scrapers are all on very irregular fragments. The material of all these tools is obsidian. The field catalogue numbers are given below:

No. 1. L.401. 1929.	No. 5. Z.97. 1929.	No. 9. Y.5. 1929.
No. 2. Z.94. 1929.	No. 6. Y.3. 1929.	No. 10. L.420. 1929.
No. 3. Y.6a. 1929.	No. 7. F.110. 1929.	No. 11. Y.9. 1929.
No. 4. F.108. 1929.	No. 8. Y.7. 1929.	No. 12. Y.8. 1929.

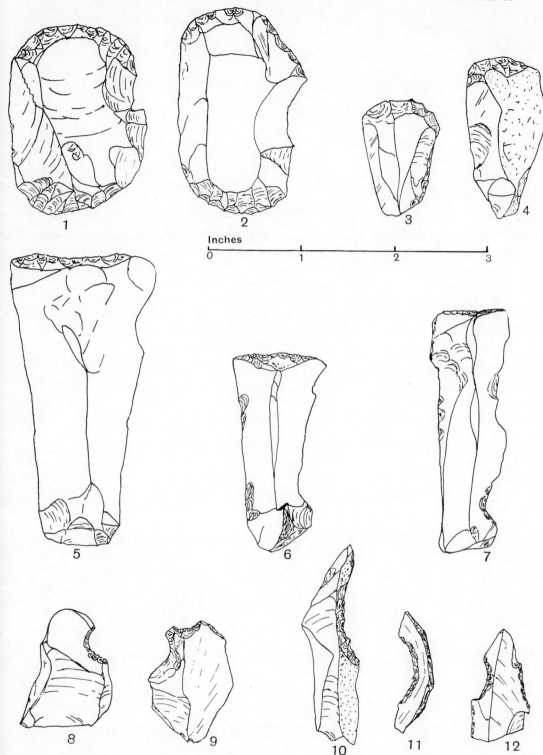

FIGURE 22

Inches

1

2

3

4

5

6

7

8

9

10

11

12

0   1   2   3

FIGURE 23

End-scrapers from phase (*b*) of the upper Kenya Aurignacian levels (fourth occupation level) of Gamble's Cave II, Elmenteita. The period is just after the second maximum of the Gamblian pluvial.

Although individual examples from this level match those from phase (*a*) in size and poorness of workmanship, when a series is taken from each level those from the phase (*b*) are as a whole smaller and better finished. Compare this series with those in Figure 21. The material of these tools is obsidian. The field catalogue numbers are given below:

No. 1. Y.58. 1929.	No. 5. J.550. 1929.	No. 9. Y.61. 1929.
No. 2. C.117. 1929.	No. 6. J.590. 1929.	No. 10. L.620. 1929.
No. 3. J.490. 1929.	No. 7. K.499. 1929.	No. 11. J.440. 1929.
No. 4. Y.60. 1929.	No. 8. L.637. 1929.	

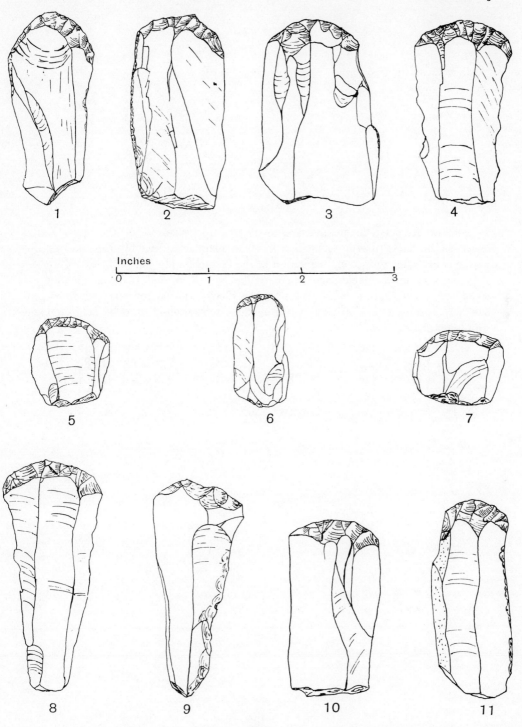

FIGURE 23

Inches

0   1   2   3

1   2   3   4

5   6   7

8   9   10   11

145

FIGURE 24

Hollow scrapers, double-ended scrapers etc. from phase (*b*) of the upper Kenya Aurignacian levels (fourth occupation level) in Gamble's Cave II, Elmenteita. The period is just after the second maximum of the Gamblian pluvial.

The very small double-ended scrapers like Nos. 8, 9, and 10 recall to mind the small scrapers that are so very typical of the Kenya Wilton industry, which is considerably later in date. The material of all these tools is obsidian. The field catalogue numbers are given below:

No. 1. L.613. 1929.	No. 6. L.621. 1929.	No. 11. K.492. 1929.
No. 2. J.981. 1929.	No. 7. L.634. 1929.	No. 12. D.889. 1929.
No. 3. L.647. 1929.	No. 8. L.616. 1929.	No. 13. J.4. 1929.
No. 4. Y.59. 1929.	No. 9. J.558. 1929.	
No. 5. D.909. 1929.	No. 10. Y.62. 1929.	

FIGURE 24

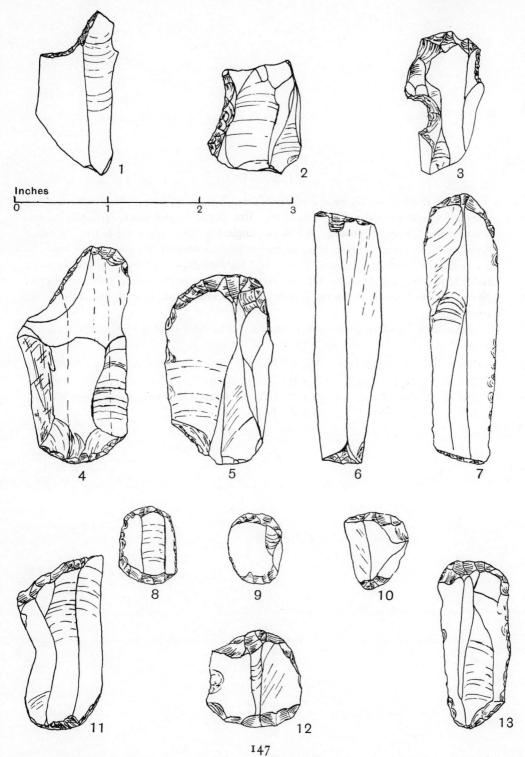

FIGURE 25

Burins from phase (*a*) of the upper Kenya Aurignacian levels (fourth occupation level) of Gamble's Cave II, Elmenteita. The period is just after the second maximum of the Gamblian pluvial. All the tools in this figure are angle burins. Some of them, as Nos. 1 and 2, show signs of having been re-sharpened two or three times by the removal of fresh burin facets. Nos. 7 and 8 are double-ended angle burins. Nos. 10 and 11 are angle burins at the top end and single blow burins at the lower end, while No. 9 is an angle burin at the top end and an atypical form of burin busqué at the lower end.

The material of all these tools is obsidian. The field catalogue numbers are given below:

No. 1. Y.13. 1929. No. 5. H.913. 1929. No. 9. Y.17. 1929.
No. 2. H.217. 1929. No. 6. Y.16. 1929. No. 10. L.917. 1929.
No. 3. Y.11. 1929. No. 7. G.494. 1929. No. 11. G.498. 1929.
No. 4. Y.10. 1929. No. 8. L.924. 1929.

FIGURE 25

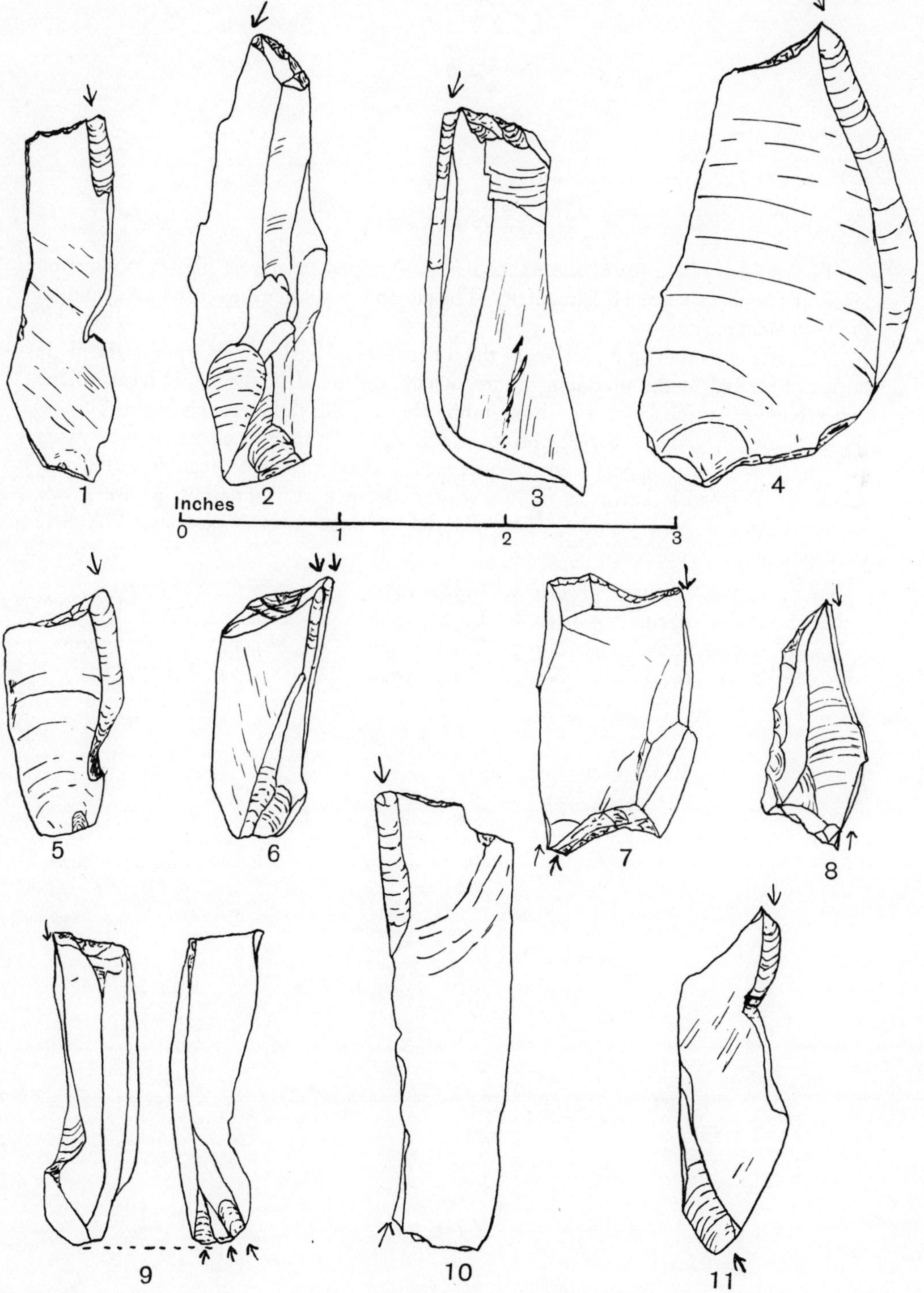

Inches

| 0 | 1 | 2 | 3 |

1 2 3 4

5 6 7 8

9 10 11

FIGURE 26

Burins from phase (*a*) of the upper Kenya Aurignacian levels (fourth occupation level) of Gamble's Cave II, Elmenteita. The period is just after the second maximum of the Gamblian pluvial.

The burins in this figure represent the other types of burins in addition to the angle burins illustrated in the preceding figure, which are found in the lower levels of the upper Kenya Aurignacian. The most interesting are the rather rough burins busqués (Nos. 2 and 3), and the bec-de-perroquet (No. 4). Although neither of these types are common in the upper Kenya Aurignacian, they cannot be regarded simply as accidents. Polyhedric burins as in Nos. 8 and 9 are fairly numerous, as are burins appointés such as Nos. 5 and 6. The material of these tools is obsidian. The field catalogue numbers are given below:

No. 1. L.916. 1929.	No. 5. L.58. 1929.	No. 9. Y.15. 1929.
No. 2. H.81. 1929.	No. 6. L.927. 1929.	No. 10. Y.12. 1929.
No. 3. Y.74. 1929.	No. 7. Y.20. 1929.	No. 11. Y.18. 1929.
No. 4. Y.14. 1929.	No. 8. Y.19. 1929.	No. 12. L.917. 1929.

FIGURE 26

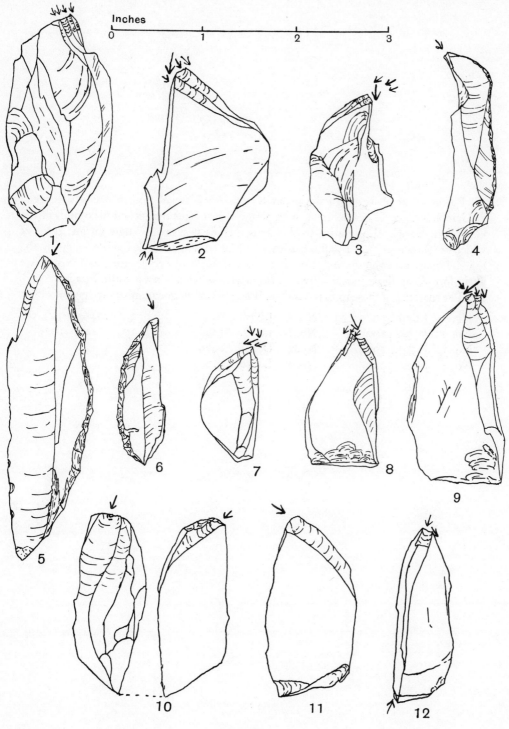

Inches

0   1   2   3

FIGURE 27

Burins from phase (*b*) of the upper Kenya Aurignacian (fourth occupation level) of Gamble's Cave II, Elmenteita. The period is just after the second maximum of the Gamblian pluvial. The burins in this level include very many angle burins, types of which are shown in Nos. 1 to 6 inclusive, and No. 10 which is a double-ended burin, the top end being an angle burin. Nos. 8 and 9 are forms of bec-de-flute, and No. 7 is a burin formed by the removal of two burin facets backed against a natural fracture.

The material of these tools is obsidian. The field catalogue numbers are given below:

No. 1. J.679. 1929.	No. 5. J.636. 1929.	No. 9. L.945. 1929.
No. 2. J.782. 1929.	No. 6. J.357. 1929.	No. 10. C.144. 1929.
No. 3. J.330. 1929.	No. 7. D.798. 1929.	
No. 4. J.97. 1929.	No. 8. L.929. 1929.	

FIGURE 27

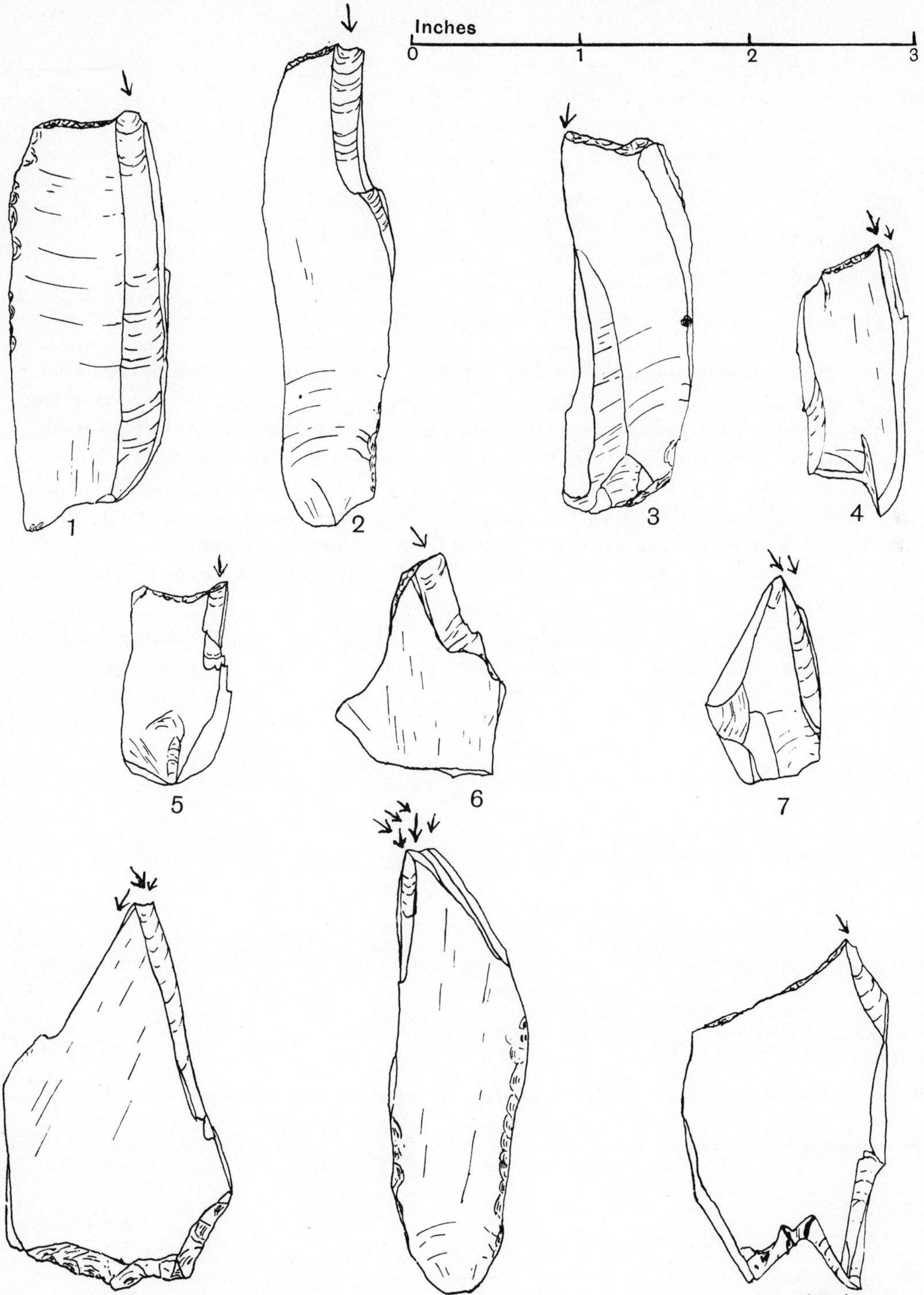

Inches
0   1   2   3

1

2

3

4

5

6

7

8

9

10

153

FIGURE 28

Burins from phase (*b*) of the upper Kenya Aurignacian levels (fourth occupation level) of Gamble's Cave II, Elmenteita. The series shown here, together with those in the preceding figure, represent the types of burins found in this level. No bec-de-perroquet were found, but the types of burin busqué were better made, see Nos. 4, 7 and 8. Nos. 1 and 2 are typical of the burins appointés, that is of burins made against "backed blades". No. 3 is a double-ended angle burin, and No. 6 is a single blow burin. No. 5 is a small bec-de-flute, and No. 9 is of the type known as burin plan.

The material of all these tools is obsidian. The field catalogue numbers are given below:

No. 1. L.757. 1929.	No. 4. L.931. 1929.	No. 7. L.948. 1929.
No. 2. C.988. 1929.	No. 5. D.841. 1929.	No. 8. J.702. 1929.
No. 3. C.143. 1929.	No. 6. C.151. 1929.	No. 9. J.82. 1929.

FIGURE 28

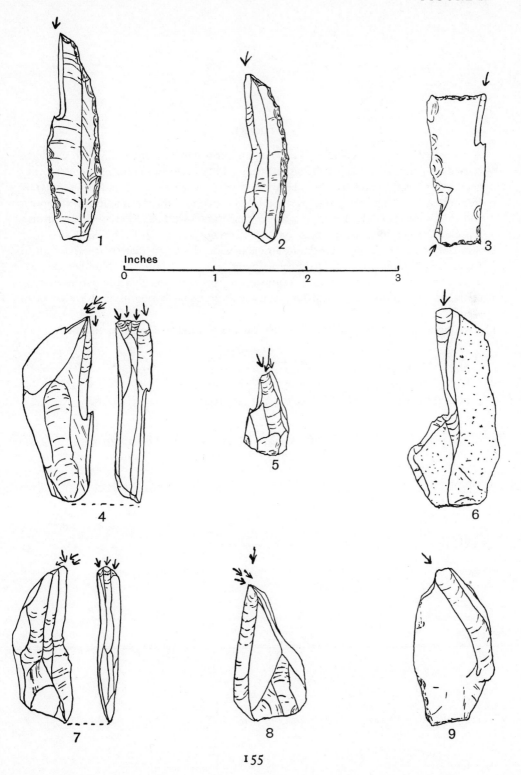

Inches

0   1   2   3

FIGURE 29

Tools showing the so-called Tardenoisian burin type of facet, and which would be classed by many writers as Tardenoisian burins. They occur in the upper Kenya Aurignacian of phases (*a*) and (*b*). Numbers 1 to 7 are from phase (*a*). Numbers 8 to 11 are from phase (*b*). Numbers 4 and 5 are slightly twisted to show the retouch of the notch, and so do not show the facet. I consider that these so-called "Tardenoisian burins" represent broken tools, the peculiar type of "Tardenoisian burin facet" being the direct result of breakage through use in a particular way. I suggest that the tools shown in Figure 18, Numbers 1, 3, 8, 36 (inverted), and 37, or in Figure 20, Numbers 21, 22, 23, 40 and 41, represent the unbroken forms of this tool, and that the particular type of fracture is due to using them for some such purpose as boring in hard leather or in wood.

These tools are of obsidian. The field catalogue numbers are given below:

Phase (a)

No. 1. Y.169. 1929.   No. 4. Y.171. 1929.   No. 7. Y.172. 1929.
No. 2. Y.170. 1929.   No. 5. Y.175. 1929.
No. 3. Y.173. 1929.   No. 6. Y.174. 1929.

Phase (b)

No. 8. Y.176. 1929.   No. 10. Y.178. 1929.
No. 9. Y.177. 1929.   No. 11. K.3. 1929.

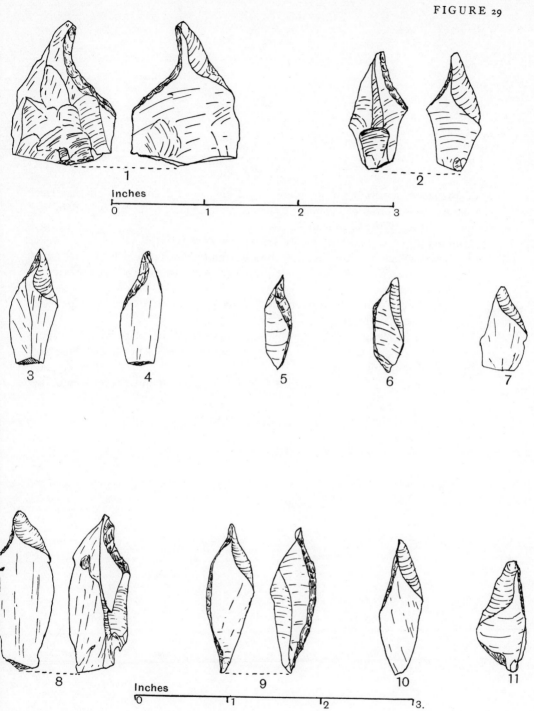

FIGURE 29

Inches
0   1   2   3

1

2

3   4   5   6   7

8   9   10   11

Inches
0   1   2   3.

157

FIGURE 30

Aurignacian fabricators from phase (*a*) of the upper Kenya Aurignacian levels (fourth occupation level) of Gamble's Cave II, Elmenteita. The period is just after the second maximum of the Gamblian pluvial.

Aurignacian fabricators may be divided into two classes:

(*a*) Those which have been used as fabricators in the form in which they are found.

(*b*) Those which really only represent the detached "worn edge" of a fabricator-core, or of a fabricator-flake.

Nos. 1, 2, 4 and 6 in this figure belong to class (*a*), since more than one edge shows signs of usage as a fabricator.

Nos. 3, 5 and 7 belong to class (*b*), since the only edge which shows signs of usage as a fabricator is that opposite the bulb of percussion, which was made by the detaching blow struck to remove the worn edge.

The material of these tools is obsidian. The field catalogue numbers are given below:

No. 1. Z.38. 1929.   No. 4. Z.39. 1929.   No. 7. Z.42. 1929.
No. 2. 3597. 1928.   No. 5. Z.41. 1929.
No. 3. M.392. 1929. No. 6. L.451. 1929.

FIGURE 30

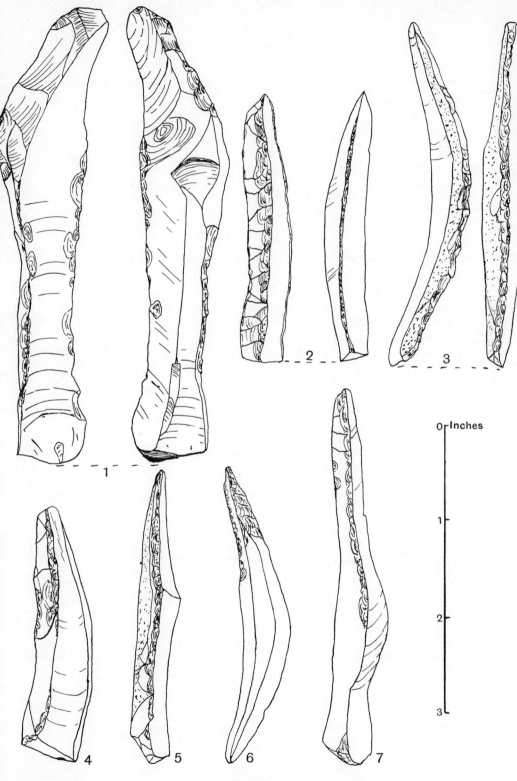

0 Inches

1

2

3

1

2

3

4

5

6

7

FIGURE 31

"Sinew frayers" from phase (*a*) of the upper Kenya Aurignacian levels (fourth occupation level) of Gamble's Cave II, Elmenteita. The period is just after the second maximum of the Gamblian pluvial.

These "sinew frayers", of which many hundreds were found, are characterised by a special type of retouch across the end of a flake, more or less at right angles to the main flake, and always towards the main flake surface.

The material of these tools is obsidian. The field catalogue numbers are given below:

No. 1. L.440. 1929. No. 4. Z.92. 1929. No. 7. E.572. 1929.
No. 2. Z.89. 1929. No. 5. Z.91. 1929. No. 8. Z.90. 1929.
No. 3. L.441. 1929. No. 6. G.562. 1929.

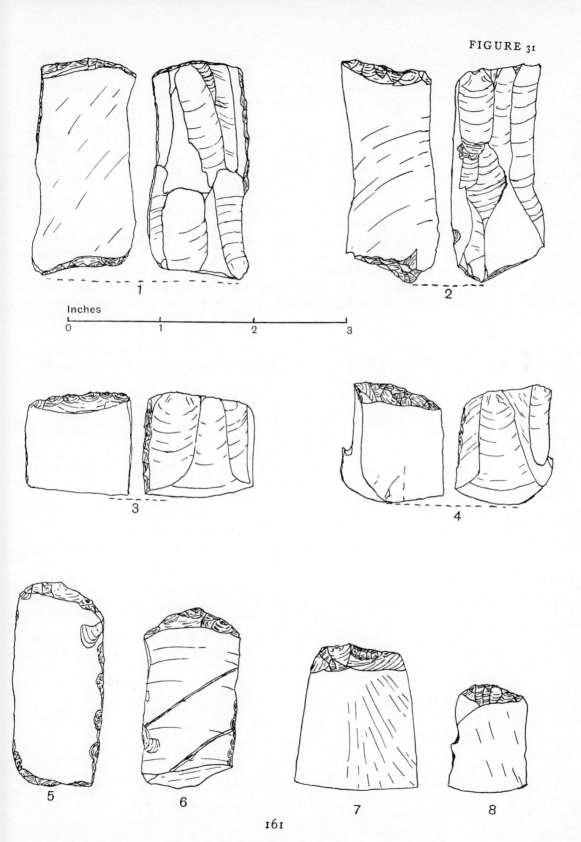

FIGURE 31

Inches

0   1   2   3

1

2

3

4

5

6

7

8

FIGURE 32

"Sinew frayers" and Aurignacian fabricators from phase (*b*) of the upper Kenya Aurignacian levels (fourth occupation level) in Gamble's Cave II, Elmenteita. The period is just after the second maximum of the Gamblian pluvial.

Nos. 1 to 8 inclusive are forms of "sinew frayer" which in phase (*b*) of the upper Aurignacian tend to be smaller than in phase (*a*). Nos. 9 to 15 inclusive are forms of the "Aurignacian fabricator". Nos. 10, 11, and 15 are of class (*a*) type, having more than one edge which has been used as a fabricator, or, as in No. 15, having only one edge used as a fabricator, but that edge being the one which was only made by the removal of the piece from the core, so that it cannot have been used while on a core. Nos. 9, 12, 13 and 14 belong to class (*b*).

The material is obsidian. The field catalogue numbers are given below:

No. 1. L.972. 1929.	No. 6. Z.5. 1929.	No. 11. Z.2. 1929.
No. 2. Z.6. 1929.	No. 7. J.643. 1929.	No. 12. Z.3. 1929.
No. 3. J.655. 1929.	No. 8. K.18. 1929.	No. 13. J.190. 1929.
No. 4. Z.4. 1929.	No. 9. L.704. 1929.	No. 14. E.79. 1929.
No. 5. K.453. 1929.	No. 10. D.989. 1929.	No. 15. Z.1. 1929.

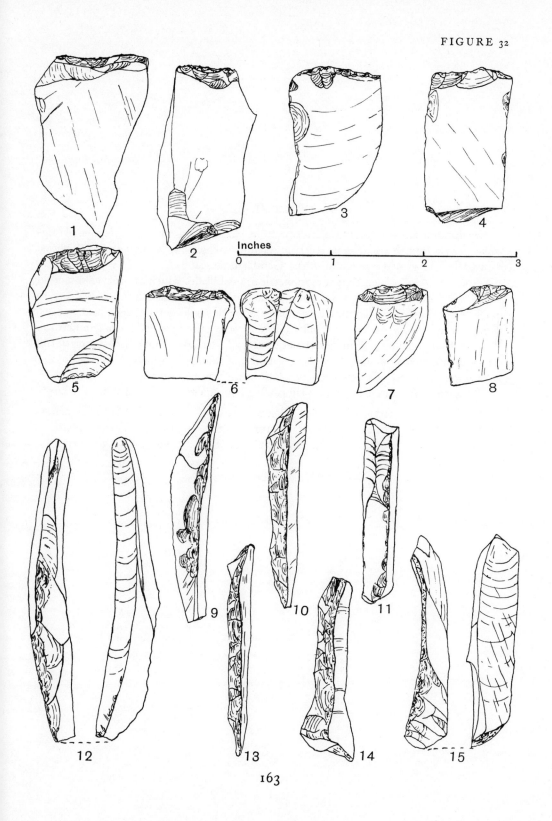

FIGURE 32

Inches
0   1   2   3

1
2
3
4
5
6
7
8
9
10
11
12
13
14
15

FIGURE 33

Blades and faceted striking platforms from phase (*a*) of the upper Kenya Aurignacian levels (fourth occupation level) in Gamble's Cave II, Elmenteita. The period is just after the second maximum of the Gamblian pluvial.

Nos. 1 to 5 inclusive. Large, asymmetrical, used blades which are very common in phase (*a*) of the upper Kenya Aurignacian, and which occur also in phase (*b*), but in much fewer numbers. They should be compared with the long two-edged blades of the Elmenteitan industry, see Figs. 37 and 38. The latter are far finer and more symmetrical.

Nos. 6 to 9 inclusive. Four examples of faceted platforms. Such striking platforms are by no means uncommon on the larger blades of the upper Kenya Aurignacian, and must not be confused with the striking platforms of the Mousterian.

The material is obsidian. The field catalogue numbers are given below:

No. 1. Y.125. 1929.	No. 4. Y.123. 1929.	No. 7. Y.124. 1929.
No. 2. Y.128. 1929.	No. 5. V.126. 1929.	No. 8. Y.131. 1929.
No. 3. Y.127. 1929.	No. 6. 2022. 1929.	No. 9. Y.130. 1929.

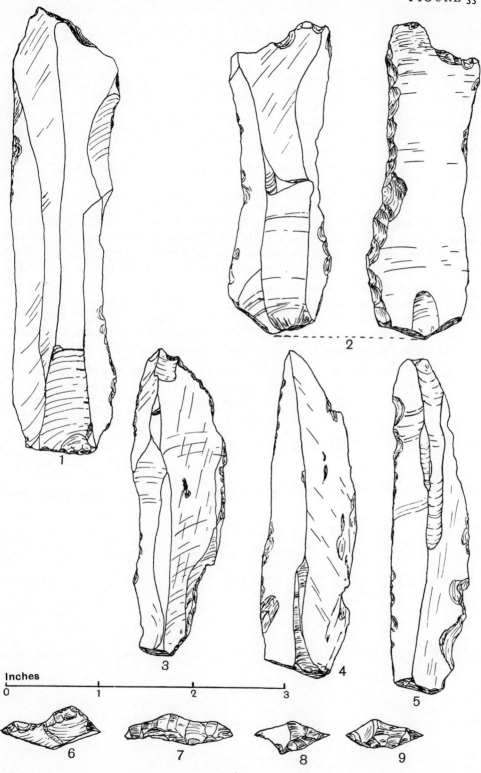

FIGURE 33

Inches

0   1   2   3

1

2

3

4

5

6

7

8

9

165

FIGURE 34

Tools of upper Kenya Aurignacian type found *in situ* in the gravels and silts of the second part of the Gamblian pluvial at the old Government Farm, Naivasha, exposed in the Malewa River Valley. This series is interesting for it corroborates the dating of the upper Kenya Aurignacian levels in Gamble's Cave II as just after the maximum of the second part of the Gamblian pluvial.

This series of upper Kenya Aurignacian tools comes from the same horizon in the silts and gravels as do the upper Kenya Mousterian tools in Fig. 12, thus also corroborating the contemporaneity of the Kenya Aurignacian and the Kenya Mousterian.

The tools figured are of obsidian. The field catalogue numbers are given below:

No. 1. Y.156. 1929.	No. 6. Y.159. 1929.	No. 11. Y.164. 1929.
No. 2. Y.154. 1929.	No. 7. Y.165. 1929.	No. 12. Y.161. 1929.
No. 3. Y.155. 1929.	No. 8. Y.166. 1929.	No. 13. Y.163. 1929.
No. 4. Y.157. 1929.	No. 9. Y.168. 1929.	No. 14. Y.160. 1929.
No. 5. Y.158. 1929.	No. 10. Y.167. 1929.	No. 15. Y.162. 1929.

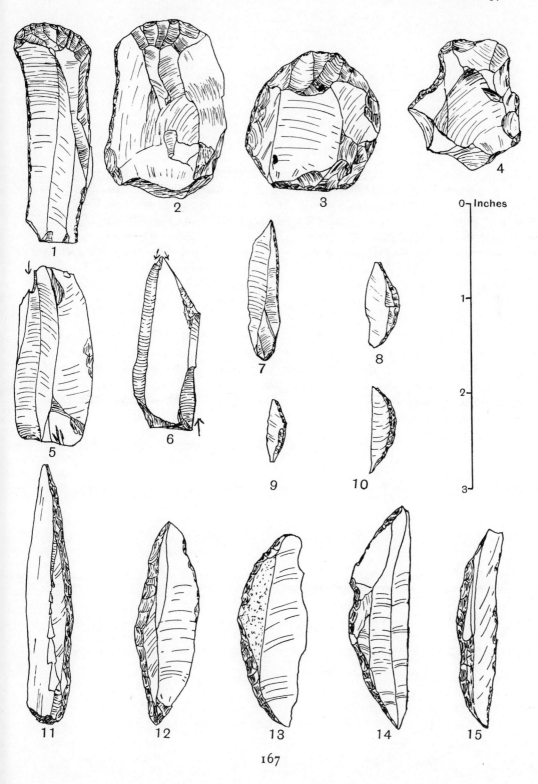

FIGURE 34

0 ⌐ Inches

1

2

3

1

2

3

4

5

6

7

8

9

10

11

12

13

14

15

FIGURE 35

Tools from the third occupation level in Gamble's Cave II, Elmenteita. The period is the decline of the Gamblian pluvial. In the section in Gamble's Cave II under the rock shelter proper, this occupation floor was separated from the fourth occupation by a sterile layer of fallen rock. But farther to the west, in the section that was worked later, this layer of fallen rock was absent and the third occupation rested immediately upon the fourth occupation level, but differed from it somewhat in colour and in texture. The third occupation, in fact, represents phase (c) of the upper Kenya Aurignacian in Gamble's Cave II. Very few tools were found, but this figure is representative of the level. It was to this level that the Gamble's Cave skeletons belong.

The material of the tools is obsidian. The field catalogue numbers are given below:

No. 1. L.286. 1929.   No. 7. 5369. 1929.   No. 13. 5360. 1929.
No. 2. Y.151. 1929.   No. 8. 5372. 1929.   No. 14. 5365. 1929.
No. 3. 5376. 1929.   No. 9. 5366. 1929.   No. 15. 5364. 1929.
No. 4. L.283. 1929   No. 10. 5371. 1929.   No. 16. Y.152. 1929.
No. 5. Y.153. 1929.   No. 11. 5362. 1929.
No. 6. L.279. 1929.   No. 12. L.276. 1929.

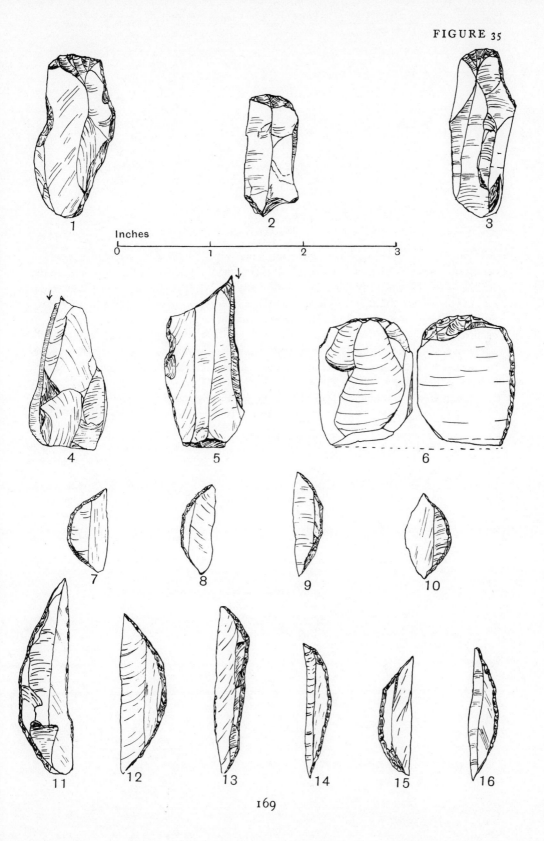

FIGURE 35

Inches

0   1   2   3

1

2

3

4

5

6

7

8

9

10

11

12

13

14

15

16

169

FIGURE 36

Three of the flakes with marked striking platforms which were found in the second occupation level in Gamble's Cave II, Elmenteita. The period is the very end of the decline of the Gamblian pluvial. No signs of any Kenya Aurignacian or of Elmenteitan types of tools were found in this level, and these flakes seem to be referable to the Kenya Stillbay. The very occasional hearths found in this level seem to represent not so much an occupation of the rock shelter, as an occasional visit to it during a storm. As a result only a few flakes and broken tools were left to give any information concerning the people responsible for these fires, and such flakes and tools as we have certainly suggest the Kenya Stillbay rather than a Kenya Aurignacian derivative.

The material is obsidian. The field catalogue numbers are given below:

1. G.II.b.1.E.   2. G.II.b.3.E.   3. G.II.b.4.E.

(Drawings by Mrs Burkitt)

FIGURE 36

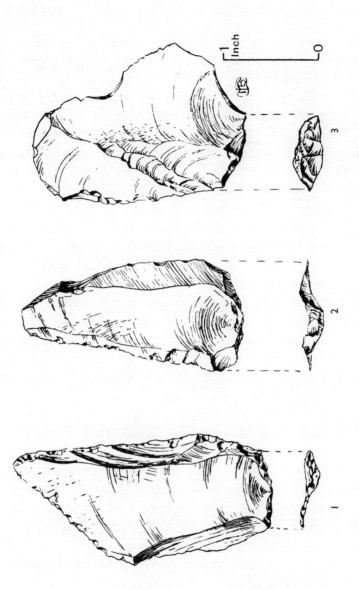

CHAPTER VIII

THE MESOLITHIC CULTURES IN KENYA

IN the present state of our knowledge there is a big hiatus between the phase (*c*) of the upper Kenya Aurignacian and the Elmenteitan culture which belongs to the maximum of the Makalian wet phase. The Elmenteitan culture certainly represents a very late and aberrant development of the upper Kenya Aurignacian culture, but whereas in the latter we have the very beginnings of pottery of a crude form—probably discovered as the result of lining a basket with clay and burning the basket—by the time of the Elmenteitan culture we have very well-developed pottery with a wide range in the size of the pots and shapes of rim and some decoration and even polishing. This means that somewhere away from the Rift Valley area, which became desiccated during the dry period which separated the end of the Gamblian pluvial from the Makalian wet phase, and was therefore not suitable for man, we ought to find the stage which represents the development from the crude pottery and the fine Aurignacian lithic culture to the developed pottery and somewhat cruder lithic culture of the Elmenteitan folk. Meanwhile we must examine the Elmenteitan culture. The type station may be taken as the upper occupation level of Gamble's Cave II, which lies between the lower aeolian sand which represents the arid period at the end of the Gamblian and the upper aeolian sand which marks the very end of the Makalian period, see Fig. 15. Separating the occupation level from these aeolian deposits, above and below, were barren layers of rock débris from the roof, indicating that the people whose deposits form the upper occupation level did not come there immediately the dry period ended, nor did they continue to use the cave to the very end of the Makalian wet phase. In fact the upper occupation level represents the period just prior to, during, and after the maximum of the Makalian phase.

The principal stone tools of the Elmenteitan industry are:

(1) Regular two-edged blades.
(2) (*a*) Backed blades. (*b*) Microliths and lunates.
(3) Scrapers.
(4) Lames écaillées.
(5) Cores.

A very few burins are also found.

THE MESOLITHIC CULTURES IN KENYA

The two-edged blades

These blades range in size from six inches long and about one and a quarter inches wide, to three inches long and barely half an inch wide. Many, but not all of them, show much abrasion of the cutting edges due to long use, and occasionally there is just an indication of re-touch, as though there was an attempt to re-sharpen an edge blunted by much use. On many of the flakes there is a suggestion of trimming on the upper or many-flake surface at the bulb end with a view to reducing the thickness of the blade at this end for hafting. By the analogy of the long obsidian blades from the Admiralty Islands which are hafted, we may conclude that that was the method of use of these Elmenteitan blades. If hafted, some would serve admirably as spear points, and others as two-edged knives and daggers. Besides the complete blades, hundreds of broken sections of long blades were found, indicating that they were the commonest type of tool in the Elmenteitan series. (See Figs. 37, 38.)

"Backed blades"

In the Elmenteitan culture, "backed blades" of any size are far from common, and the range of size and shape of the few found shows that this was no longer the type tool of the industry, as it certainly was in upper Kenya Aurignacian times. The series illustrated in Fig. 39 shows the range of the tools of this type; the workmanship is on the whole very degenerate when compared with that of the upper Kenya Aurignacian.

Microliths and lunates

Of the "backed blade" group the only type which is at all common is the lunate. These if found individually could not be distinguished from the lunates of the upper Kenya Aurignacian, but when a whole series from the two periods is compared, there is a distinct difference. Those of the Elmenteitan period, considered as a group, are more symmetrical and a large proportion have no ridge flake on either surface, and they are generally better made. In fact the lunate seems to reach its finest development at this period, for those of the Kenya Wilton a little later tend to be thicker and less well made.

Scrapers

There are comparatively few scrapers in the Elmenteitan at the type station, but those which occur are not very distinct from the scrapers of the

173

upper Kenya Aurignacian. There are round-ended and square-ended scrapers, and scrapers on long blades occur, but no thumb-nail scrapers were found.

Lames écaillées

These tools have been described and figured by various French writers who have shown that they occur in the upper Aurignacian levels in France and in the Magdalenian. In Kenya not a single example of the lames écaillées is known from among the thousands of tools of the upper Kenya Aurignacian, but it is a common, in fact a type tool of the Elmenteitan culture. A typical series is shown in Fig. 40. The possible uses of this tool have not been much discussed, but I believe that a view has been expressed in France that it represents a chisel, and that the peculiar flaking at both ends of the tool is the result, on the one end, of the impact of the hammer stone with which the chisel was struck, and at the other end, of the repercussion of the blow from the object which was being struck by the chisel. I myself cannot subscribe to this view. It is very noticeable in Kenya that the lames écaillées occur in the Elmenteitan culture where there is no trace of any Aurignacian fabricators, and experiments show that by using the end of a blade as a fabricator for making lunates or backed blades and scrapers, with a rather different action from that which is used when these tools are being made with an Aurignacian fabricator, the lames écaillées effect is produced. I am therefore inclined to regard them as nothing but an alternative type of fabricator which in Kenya happens to characterise the Elmenteitan. In Plate XVII, Nos. 5 and 6, an example of a lame écaillée from the Elmenteitan (No. 6) and one which was the result of my using the ends of a flake as a fabricator (No. 5) are compared. The scraper (No. 8) was made with No. 5.

Burins

Burins are rare in the Elmenteitan, but a few atypical ones have been found. This scarcity of burins is surprising, as the presence of lunates which were undoubtedly hafted as arrow barbs suggests that burins ought to occur. Some other tool was possibly used for grooving wood at this date.

Cores

It is again a very noticeable fact that, despite the large size of many of the blades in the Elmenteitan industry, no large cores are found. The few cores present are barely large enough to produce flakes for the making of the lunates. This indicates the using of the material to its limit, and this was probably because the source of raw material was some miles away from the site which we are considering as our type station.

Bone tools

Several bone awls were found, but they are not common. No trace of barbed harpoons or of similar tools occurs.

Pottery

Enormous quantities of sherds occur at the type station, and a large variety of rim types can be detected. The size of the pots ranged from small bowls with a diameter of about four and a half inches to immense jars with an estimated diameter at the neck of over a foot. The shapes of the pots also varied considerably, some having pointed bases and others rounded, others again are more or less flat at the base.

In some cases rivet holes, drilled through the pot from both directions, occur, and there is also evidence that holes in pots were used for attaching string handles for carrying them, for cases occur of holes being made in the moist pottery before baking.

A more detailed study of the pottery will be made in a later publication or in a special paper.

The complete pot in Plate XVIII is from the Elmenteitan deposit at Bromhead's site. Fig. 41 gives a few sections through some of the larger pieces of rim from the Elmenteitan level in Gamble's Cave II.

The human type

Although no skeletons were found in the upper occupation level of Gamble's Cave II, a site called Bromhead's site which yielded an identical industry with the same tool types and pottery, and which is, on geological evidence, of Makalian date, gave us a large number of human remains. There is a certain range of variation in the skull types which will be investigated and dealt with in detail in a special publication on the human remains from prehistoric sites in Kenya.

In the present book no attempt will therefore be made to discuss these human remains. Photographs of some of the chief skulls from Bromhead's site, Elmenteita, are given in Plates XIX and XX, and the non-negro character of the skulls is illustrated in the top photograph in Plate XIX where Elmenteita A is compared with two Bantu skulls.

The Kenya Wilton

The type station for this culture is in a drift known as Long's Drift on the lower reaches of the Enderit River, Elmenteita.

Here the more typical Makalian deposits which overlie the Gamblian deposits unconformably at the Enderit Drift are in turn overlain, but with a slight unconformity, by shallow beds of stratified brown muds and silts. These beds at the point in question are some 185 feet above present lake level, and are being continually cut through during the rainy season by flood action, and many tools were found washing out. Excavations were therefore carried out at undisturbed parts of the beds, and a large series of tools and some pottery were recovered.

The height of these deposits above the present lake level shows that they cannot have been deposited during the Nakuran wet phase, and, moreover, they overlie the more typical beds of the Makalian period without any very marked unconformity. There can be little doubt, therefore, that they represent a stage in the regression of the Makalian lake. The explanation of the presence of a large series of tools at the site would seem to be as follows. During the retreat of the lake the makers of the Kenya Wilton culture were living near the shore line, and a small temporary rise in the lake level swamped the camp site, burying the débris of the site in muds and silts.

The industry

The typical tools of the Kenya Wilton series fall into two groups both of which are microlithic: (1) lunates, (2) thumb-nail scrapers. A few larger tools occur but are not typical; they include cores and core scrapers, and larger crude end-scrapers, and occasional burins. The lunates and the thumb-nail scrapers resemble so closely the corresponding tools in the Wilton of Rhodesia that the two industries may well prove to be allied.

Variations of the lunates include triangles and trapezes. The most common type of microlithic scraper is a double-ended scraper with the curves at the opposite ends dissimilar, one end being very much arched, and the other a very low curve. A type series of these Kenya Wilton tools is shown in Figs. 42 and 43.

The pottery found at this site is all very fragmentary, but includes several rims which recall those of the Elmenteitan. Only one fragment with decoration on it was found; it is shown in Plate XXI, No. 1, and is worth special attention.

While writing my field reports during the season 1928–9 I inclined to the view that this industry from Long's Drift was of the same date and period as that at Willey's Kopje, Eburru, found in 1927, and as the deposits at the Makalia Burial Site (1929).

Detailed examination of all the evidence, however, shows that the Long's Drift site belongs in fact to the closing stages of the Makalian wet phase, a date which is certainly too early for the Willey's Kopje site, while the pottery and tools also differentiate the industry found at Long's Drift from that of the other two sites, which in all probability date from the time of the next wet phase, the Nakuran (see Chapter IX). There are no human remains which we can at present assign to the Kenya Wilton.

FIGURE 37

Long two-edged blades with chipped edges due to usage, from the Elmenteitan level (first occupation level (1)) in Gamble's Cave II, Elmenteita. The period is the Makalian wet phase. The long blades are very typical of the Elmenteitan industry and occur in large numbers in this level. They are very frequently found broken. They are usually better made and more symmetrical than the long used blades which are found in the lower levels of the upper Kenya Aurignacian (see Figure 33).

The material of these tools is obsidian. The field catalogue numbers are given below:

No. 1. Y.120. 1929.   No. 3. L. 298. 1929.
No. 2. L.288. 1929.   No. 4. L.292. 1929.

Note. In the field reports the occupation levels were numbered from the top downwards as found, thus the uppermost or latest occupation level in the cave was called "first", and the lowest one found called "fourth".

FIGURE 37

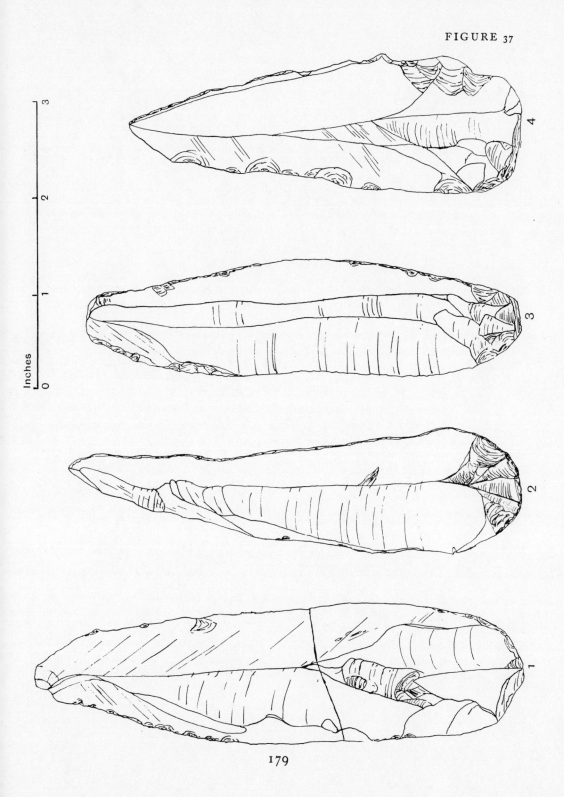

Inches

0 1 2 3

179

FIGURE 38

Long two-edged blades with chipped edges due to usage, from the Elmenteitan level (first occupation level) in Gamble's Cave II, Elmenteita. The period is the Makalian wet phase.

These blades are further examples of the type figured in Fig. 37.

The material is obsidian. The field catalogue numbers are given below:

No. 1. G.II.3.   No. 3. G.II.112.   No. 5. G.II.103.
No. 2. G.II.104.   No. 4. L.291. 1929.

Note. In the field reports the occupation levels were numbered from the top downwards as found, thus the uppermost or latest occupation level in the cave was called "first", and the lowest one found was called "fourth".

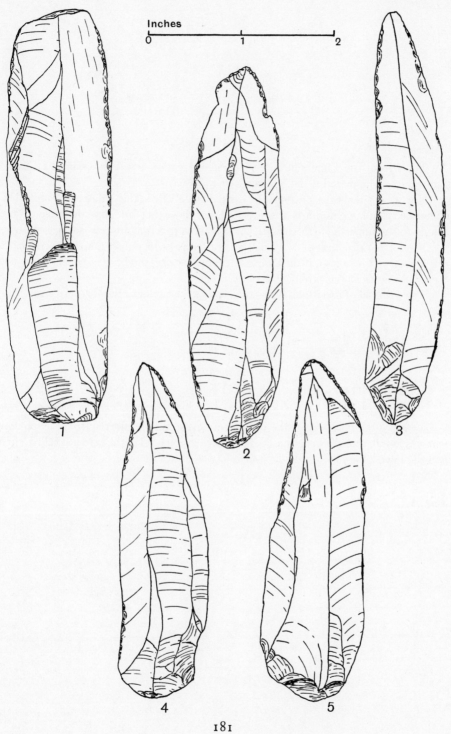

FIGURE 38

Inches

0   1   2

1

2

3

4

5

FIGURE 39

Tools from the Elmenteitan level (first occupation level) in Gamble's Cave II, Elmenteita. The period is the Makalian wet phase.

Nos. 1 to 5 inclusive. Forms of "backed blade" from this industry. Backed blades do not occur in large numbers at this period, but those that are found might equally well belong to the upper Kenya Aurignacian if they were found alone as surface tools.

Nos. 6 to 11 inclusive. Various types of scrapers, including a hollow scraper from this industry. These also, if they were not found *in situ*, might well belong to an upper Kenya Aurignacian culture.

The material of these tools is obsidian. The field catalogue numbers are given below:

Backed Blades

No. 1. G.II.1.E.	No. 3. Y.54. 1929.	No. 5. G.II.43.
No. 2. G.II.8.E.	No. 4. G.II.41.	

Scrapers

No. 6. G.II.14.E.	No. 8. G.II.17.	No. 10. G.II.25.
No. 7. G.II.29.	No. 9. G.II.4.E.	No. 11. L.266. 1929.

Note. In the field reports the occupation levels were numbered from the top downwards as found, thus the uppermost or latest occupation level in the cave was called "first", and the lowest found was called "fourth".

FIGURE 39

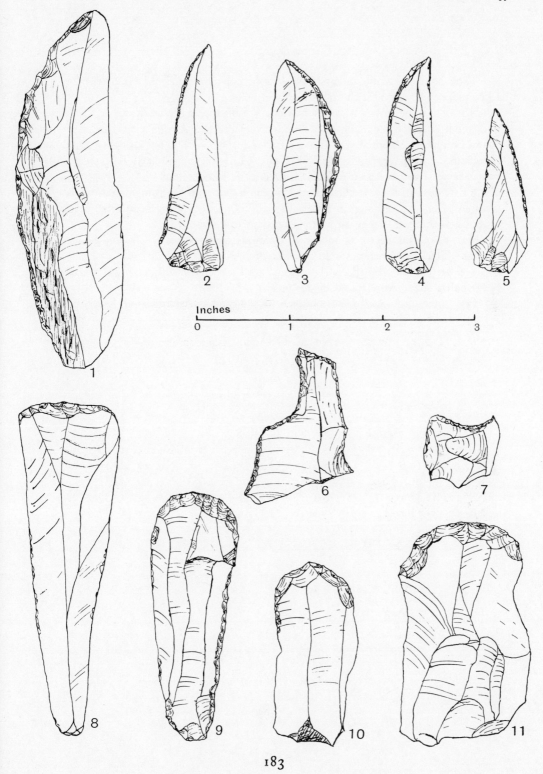

Inches
0   1   2   3

FIGURE 40

Tools from the Elmenteitan level (first occupation level) of Gamble's Cave II, Elmenteita. The period is the Makalian wet phase.

Nos. 1 to 6 inclusive. "Lames écaillées." This tool is the fabricator of the Elmenteitan industry, and seems entirely to have replaced the Aurignacian fabricator. The "lame écaillée" is essentially an Elmenteitan industry tool, and not a single example was found among some 57,000 tools in the Kenya Aurignacian, similarly no typical Aurignacian fabricators have been noted as yet from the Elmenteitan.

No. 7. One of the few burins that has been found with the Elmenteitan industry. It is an angle burin. Although a few burins are found, they are certainly not a type tool in the Elementeitan as they are in the Kenya Aurignacian.

Nos. 8, 9, and 12 to 25 inclusive. Various forms of small "backed blades" and lunates which are very common in the Elmenteitan industry.

Nos. 10 and 11. Small tools trimmed up both edges with very steep trimming. Some half a dozen were found in this level.

The material of these tools is obsidian. Field catalogue numbers are given below:

Lames écaillées

No. 1. L.242. 1929.	No. 3. G.II.89.	No. 5. Y.55. 1929.
No. 2. 1001. 1928.	No. 4. L.244. 1929.	No. 6. G.II.7.

Burin

No. 7. Y.56. 1929.

Crescents, etc.

No. 8. Y.57. 1929.	No. 14. G.II.282.	No. 20. G.II.160.
No. 9. G.II.149.	No. 15. G.II.9.E.	No. 21. G.II.139.
No. 10. G.II.61.	No. 16. G.II.186.	No. 22. Y.123. 1929.
No. 11. Y.66. 1929.	No. 17. G.II.12.E.	No. 23. G.II.171.
No. 12. G.II.168.	No. 18. G.II.285.	No. 24. G.II.283.
No. 13. G.II.10.E.	No. 19. G.II.145.	No. 25. G.II.227.

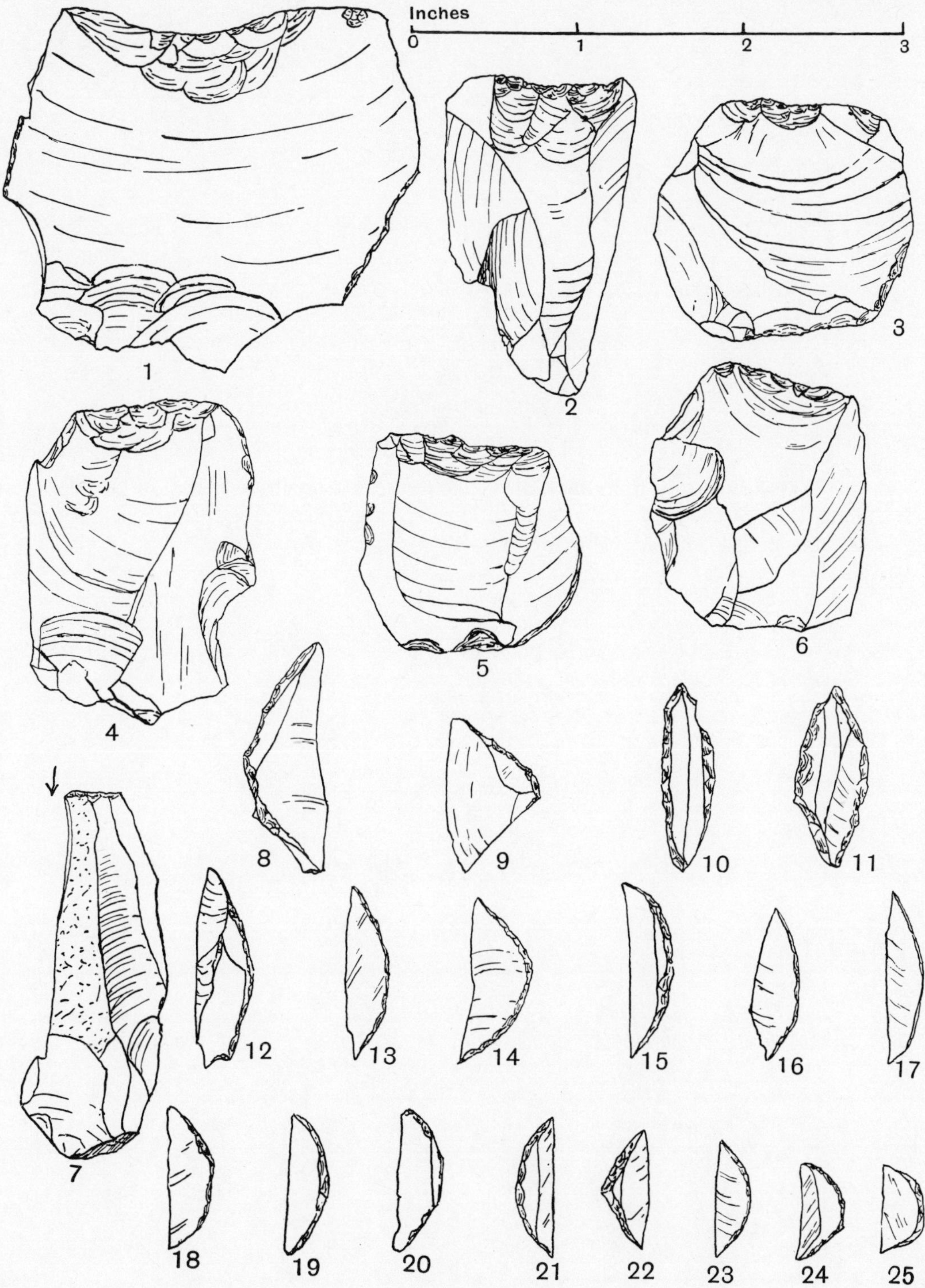

FIGURE 40

Inches

0   1   2   3

FIGURE 41

Types of pot rims from the Elmenteitan level (first occupation level) in Gamble's Cave II, Elmenteita.

The period is the Makalian wet phase.

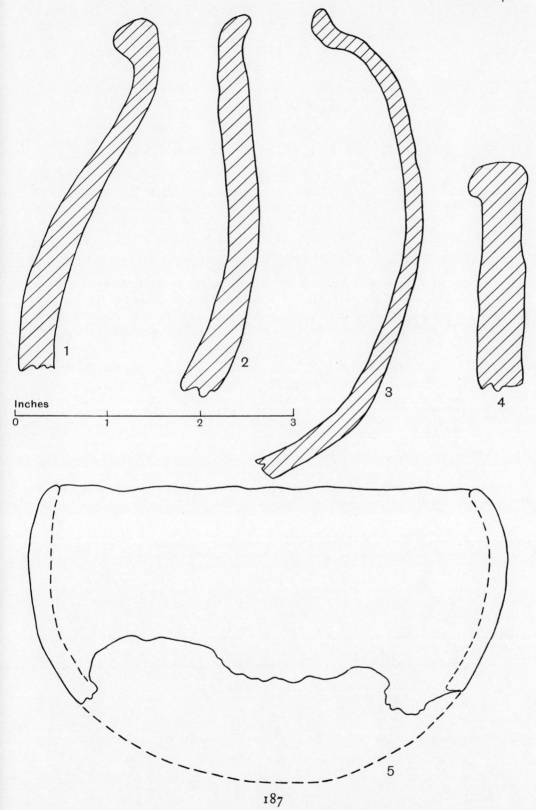

Inches

0   1   2   3

1

2

3

4

5

187

PLATE XVIII

A pot from Bromhead's site, Elmenteita. This site can be accurately dated as being after the beginning of the Makalian wet phase and before its maximum. The pot was with a typical Elmenteitan industry, and closely resembles pottery from other sites found with an Elmenteitan industry. Other types of rim were also common during this period.

PLATE XVIII

189

PLATE XIX

No. 1. The skull Elmenteita 'A' (on right) contrasted with two modern native skulls. That in the centre is of a Uganda native, that on the left of a Kikuyu.

Nos. 2 and 3. Full-face and profile views of the skull Elmenteita 'A'. This is the type skull of the males from Bromhead's site, Elmenteita, and belongs in time to the period of the rise of the Makalian wet phase. It is associated with an Elmenteitan industry.

PLATE XIX

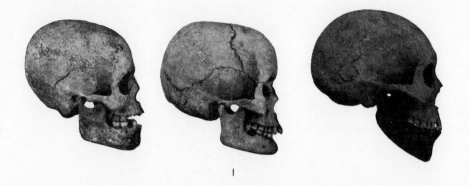

1

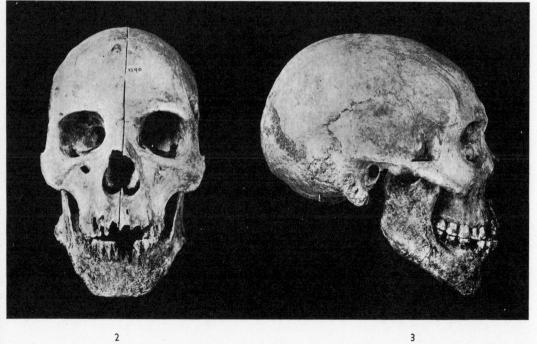

2   3

PLATE XX

Nos. 1 and 2. Full-face and profile views of the skull Elmenteita 'D'. This is the type skull of the females from Bromhead's site. Its close resemblance to the male type Elmenteita 'A' is easily seen.

Nos. 3 and 4. Full-face and profile views of the skull Elmenteita 'F 1.' which represents another female type found at Bromhead's site.

Both these skulls belong to the rise of the Makalian wet phase, and were associated with an Elmenteitan industry.

PLATE XX

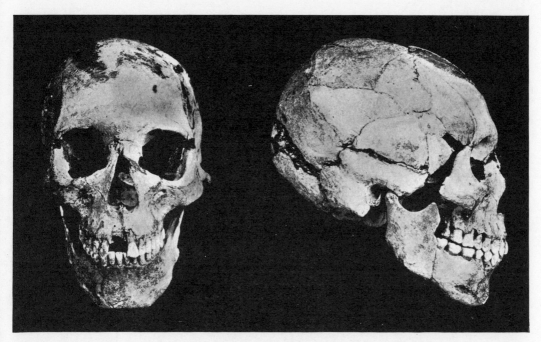

1   2

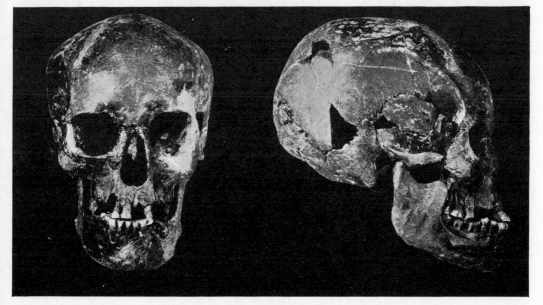

3   4

FIGURE 42

Tools of Kenya Wilton type from Long's Drift site, Enderit River, Elmenteita. The period is the decline of the Makalian wet phase. The Kenya Wilton is characterised by the association of large numbers of small scrapers and lunates. A few larger "backed blades" occur, but they are poorly made and do not seem to be typical. Nos. 1 to 12 inclusive and Nos. 14 to 17 inclusive show the types of small scraper which abound, while Nos. 13, 18, and 19 to 40 inclusive represent the lunates.

The material of these tools is obsidian. The field catalogue numbers are given below:

No. 1. 1477. 1928.	No. 15. 4605. 1928.	No. 29. 4520. 1928.
No. 2. 1906. 1928.	No. 16. 4657. 1928.	No. 30. 4454. 1928.
No. 3. 4594. 1928.	No. 17. 5708. 1928.	No. 31. 1667. 1928.
No. 4. 5920. 1928.	No. 18. 1776. 1928.	No. 32. Y.64. 1929.
No. 5. 1870. 1928.	No. 19. 5979. 1928.	No. 33. 4487. 1928.
No. 6. 1742. 1928.	No. 20. 4457. 1928.	No. 34. 1402. 1928.
No. 7. 1184. 1928.	No. 21. 5762. 1928.	No. 35. 5827. 1928.
No. 8. 1590. 1928.	No. 22. 1640. 1928.	No. 36. 1783. 1928.
No. 9. 4634. 1928.	No. 23. 5982. 1928.	No. 37. 1696. 1928.
No. 10. 4603. 1928.	No. 24. 5761. 1928.	No. 38. 4491. 1928.
No. 11. 4636. 1928.	No. 25. 5822. 1928.	No. 39. 1836. 1928.
No. 12. 5731. 1928.	No. 26. 5998. 1928.	No. 40. 1632. 1928.
No. 13. 4463. 1928.	No. 27. 6027. 1928.	
No. 14. 1450. 1928.	No. 28. 5801. 1928.	

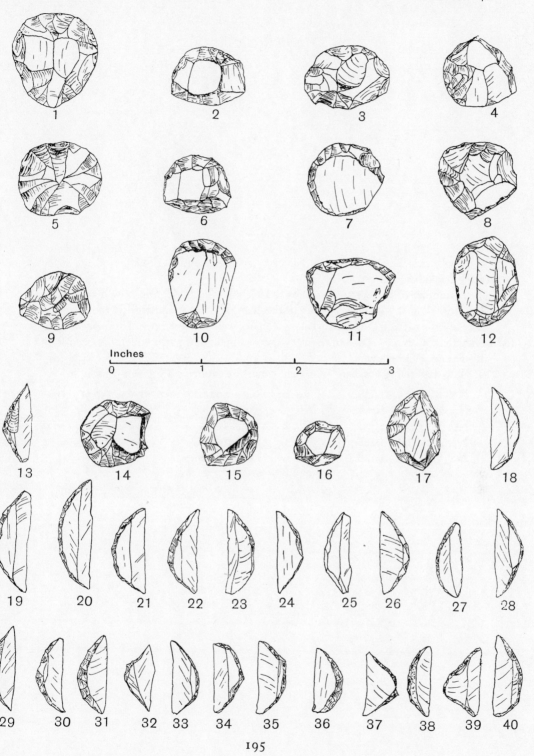

FIGURE 42

Inches
0   1   2   3

FIGURE 43

Tools from Long's Drift site, Enderit River, Elmenteita. The period is the decline of the Makalian wet phase.

A number of end-scrapers such as those shown in this figure, Nos. 1 to 8 inclusive and Nos. 10 to 13 inclusive, occur in the Kenya Wilton industry. If they were found alone on the surface they might belong equally well to the Kenya Aurignacian or to the Elmenteitan. No. 9 is one of the very few examples of a burin which has been found at this Kenya Wilton site.

The material is obsidian. The field catalogue numbers are given below:

No. 1. 1905. 1928.   No. 6. 7860. 1928.   No. 11. 5931. 1928.
No. 2. 5691. 1928.   No. 7. 1498. 1928.   No. 12. 1808. 1928.
No. 3. 1921. 1928.   No. 8. Y.63. 1929.   No. 13. 5906. 1928.
No. 4. 4598. 1928.   No. 9. 5734. 1928.
No. 5. 1452. 1928.   No. 10. 1806. 1928.

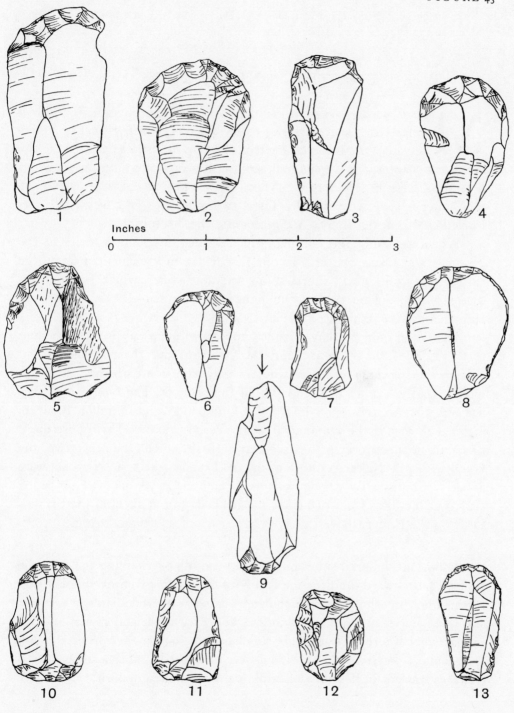

FIGURE 43

Inches

0   1   2   3

197

CHAPTER IX

THE NEOLITHIC CULTURES IN KENYA

MUCH work remains to be done on the Neolithic sites in Kenya before the exact sequence of the various industries can be determined. On geological evidence the two industries described in the foregoing chapter, the Elmenteitan and the Kenya Wilton, can be shown to belong to different stages of the Makalian wet phase, and their relation to each other is also determinable. These two industries may be regarded as transitional from the Kenya Aurignacian to the Neolithic.

When we study the cultures which belong in point of time to the Nakuran wet phase, we find in one of them a new element, namely the existence of stone bowls, mortars and grinding stones, which seems to indicate some sort of agriculture, and in the other polished axes, and I therefore class them as Neolithic.

There seem, on present evidence, to be two main cultures that belong to this period, the Gumban and the Njoroan, but there is insufficient evidence upon which to decide whether they were contemporary, or if not, which was their order of occupation of the country. The Gumban culture has two distinct divisions which I call Gumban A and Gumban B. I am inclined to regard the Gumban A as the earliest, and so I will describe it first, but further work in the area may well show that the other two, the Gumban B (the Nakuru culture of my field reports) and the Njoroan, were as early. Comparatively little work has been done as yet on any Gumban A sites, but the finds from two sites, the Makalia burial site and the Stable's Drift on the Enderit River, give us some idea of its characteristics.

The Gumban A

The Makalia burial site is on a flat-topped hill overlooking the Makalia valley. A backward limit for the dating of the site is given by the fact that it rests upon an ash deposit which can be dated as of Makalian age. At this site three burial mounds were noticed and excavated, and it was also remarked that wherever burrowing animals had dug on the top of the hill fragments of pottery and of obsidian were unearthed, and so a series of trial trenches was cut in the hope of finding a true midden deposit.

In this we were disappointed, but at the same time the trial trenches yielded numerous pottery fragments and obsidian flakes beneath the humus. The pottery is very fragmentary, but a careful study of it shows a few pieces which are *identical* to some very curious pottery from a deposit in Stable's Drift on the Enderit River. This pottery is so unlike anything from any other sites and is so curious, that it seems safe to consider that the two sites were roughly contemporary. At the latter site the pottery was found in a bank of stratified mud which, by its level, seems to represent the upper limit of the lake during the Nakuran wet phase, and we may provisionally regard the Gumban A as belonging to about the period of the maximum of the Nakuran wet phase.

So far very few finished tools have been found at either of these sites, but the pottery is very distinctive indeed. A few fragments of crude stone bowls have also been found. The obsidian tools found include crude scrapers and a few lunates.

The pottery is of a type which has never been found before as far as I am aware. The Stable's Drift site yielded a very large number of pieces which are in course of being put together as I write, and which seem likely to give us at least three complete pots and several fairly complete ones. The pottery is characterised by being decorated over the whole of the external surface, and the pattern of decoration is chiefly one which suggests a basket-work motif. But the pottery is, moreover, exceedingly curious in that the whole of the interior of the pots was heavily scratched with deep irregular lines while the clay was still wet. A detailed study of this pottery must be held over for a later publication, but the photographs on Plates XXII and XXIII give an excellent idea of its characteristics.

The burials

The three burials at Makalia burial site have yielded interesting skeletons which will be dealt with in detail in the publication, now in course of preparation, in which the human remains from the various prehistoric sites in Kenya will be described.

It may, however, be noted here that each burial was in a shallow grave overlain by a pile of large stones, and that each skeleton was in a semi-crouched position.

All three skulls are characterised by the removal of the two central lower incisors. The skull—No. I—from this site in some ways resembles the type found with the Elmenteitan culture and may be regarded as a derivative of that type. The other two are quite distinct and resemble closely the skulls from Willey's Kopje.

In Plate XXIV one of the skulls from Willey's Kopje is shown (which seems to be the normal type for this period) and also the skull No. I from the Makalia burial site which recalls the earlier Elmenteitan skulls, although it is of later date and has the two central lower incisors missing, as have the other skulls of this later period.

The Gumban B

In 1923 Major J. A. Macdonald of Nakuru found a most interesting burial site on his farm, some two or three miles outside Nakuru just off the Nakuru-Nairobi road. The letter sent by Major Macdonald to the local press recording the site is quoted in full in Appendix G. I got into touch with Major Macdonald at once, and although I was not able to excavate the site until 1926, he kindly left it undisturbed.

The Nakuru site consists of a small lava cliff facing the west. Against this cliff was a large banked pile of rocks, many of which showed by their material that they had been artificially brought there, and were not simply scree fallen from the cliff. Minor excavations by Major Macdonald brought to light a number of stone bowls and mortars, much bone débris, and a white powdery earth which he described as "Fuller's earth".

When I started excavations I imagined that I was dealing with débris and rock which was blocking up the mouth of a rock shelter, but this was not in fact the case, although it was not until the excavation was nearly completed that its true nature was understood. The soil filling the gaps between the boulders and rocks was full of fragmentary animal remains and also of obsidian fragments, including a fairly large percentage of tools. At intervals in the mass of boulders, fragmentary remains of human skeletons, in a very bad state of preservation, were found, and these were at first taken to be casual burials. Altogether the remains of eight such fragmentary skeletons were found. Throughout the deposit broken fragments of stone bowls, mortars, and querns occurred, while in a crevice of the cliff face near the top of the mound of stones a complete and perfect bowl was found, and a smaller circular stone dish. The stone bowls found by Major Macdonald also came from comparatively high levels in the deposit.

Subsequently, at the lowest level in the mound, very carefully buried in the ultra-crouched position and with red ochre around the bones, we found a complete and perfect skull and skeleton, Nakuru No. IX. Near this skeleton were two beads, one of faïence and one of agate, and also an unfinished stone bowl and the tool with which it was being made.

In the neighbourhood of the Nakuru site or burial mound are the remains of many stone hut circles, pits, etc., which have yet to be worked and mapped, but which clearly were the home sites of the people responsible for the burial mound.

The true explanation of the burial mound with its scattered fragmentary human skeletons, and its one perfect skeleton at the bottom, seems to be as follows: the skeleton at the bottom, Nakuru No. IX, represents an important personage, probably a chief, who was buried with considerable ceremonial, and the skeletons among the burial mound boulders seem to indicate human beings sacrificed at the grave and thrown upon the mound at intervals during the process of building up the pile of rocks. The bone débris and obsidian flakes found among the boulders of the burial are hard to explain, but the whole material resembled midden material, and we can only postulate some custom whereby rubbish-heap material was used to help to build up the grave mound. The tools of obsidian and bone and the stone pots, bowls, etc., presumably represent gifts to the dead for use in the next world.

It is interesting to note that this discovery is not unparalleled, and that the custom of burying an important person in a large mound with human sacrifices, stone bowls and beads, and to fill up the burial with rubbish, including bones and obsidian flakes, was apparently typical of the Gumban B folk, for in the year 1913 Doctors Reck and Arning discovered just such a burial in the Ngorongoro Crater in North Tanganyika Territory.* Unfortunately owing to the war the skulls and most of the objects excavated were lost, but the beads and stone bowls and the whole description of the burial mound tallies so well with that of the Nakuru site that there can be no doubt that their site was a burial mound of the Gumban B folk.

* See references at end of Chapter I.

The industry

The obsidian tools found at the Nakuru site fall into the following chief types:

Small backed blades.   Lunates.   Scrapers.

A very few crude burins also occur.

A single example of a fine double-ended sinew-frayer was found, but it is made of a different obsidian from that of which all the other tools are made, and I think it represents a tool of an earlier period, picked up and carried to the site. All the obsidian tools from the site with the single exception of the sinew-frayer mentioned above are, on the whole, of crude workmanship. That they are in some way derived from or connected with the earlier Aurignacian is suggested by their forms, but they are a very degenerate representative of the group. A series of tools is shown in Figs. 44 and 45.

Bone tools

A certain number of rough bone awls occurred, and three of these are figured in Plate XXIX.

Beads

The two beads found have already been mentioned and they are certainly of imported origin, and give a backward date for the site and culture. According to Mr H. C. Beck they are not earlier than 3000 B.C., and might be considerably later. The evidence of the beads will be further discussed in Chapter XI. One of these beads is of agate, barrel-shaped, and drilled from both ends, and the other is of faïence. (See Appendix F.)

Stone bowls and mortars, etc.

The most flourishing and at the same time the most characteristic part of the Gumban B culture is that represented by the bowls, mortars, etc., made of stone. The objects of this group may be divided into the following classes.

(*a*) Bowls.
(*b*) Pestles and mortars.
(*c*) Flat saucers.
(*d*) Querns.
(*e*) Tools for making the bowls.

Bowls

The best of the bowls is shown in Plate XXV, Nos. 3 and 3 *a*. It is a beautifully made bowl with a flat circular base, the sides curve gently upwards and the outer diameter of the top is 194·5 mm. The walls average about one inch only in thickness. The material of this bowl is a lava. The other bowls are less perfect.

Pestles and mortars

The best pestle and mortar is shown in Plate XXV, Nos. 1 and 1 *a*. The mortar has a flat base with a diameter of about 125 mm. and perpendicular sides rising to a height of 93 mm.

Near it was found the pestle shown in it in the Plate. It is made of schist, while the mortar is made of hard volcanic ash.

Flat saucers

Plate XXV, Nos. 2 and 2 *a*, shows one of the typical flat saucer-shaped stones well made, and with a rounded base and curved sides.

Querns

There are several broken querns which have signs of considerable usage before being broken, but only one complete one. The latter is small, and shows much less signs of usage than the large broken ones. The small unbroken one is figured in Plate XXVI, No. 1.

Unfinished bowl

Perhaps the most interesting discovery at the Nakuru site was a partially made stone bowl and the tool with which it was being made. But for this discovery it would have been hard indeed to understand how Neolithic man with no metal weapons contrived to make such beautiful bowls, as for example that in Plate XXV.

The unfinished example is shown in Plate XXVI, No. 2, and the tool with which it was being made is figured in Plate XXVII. The latter consists of a triangular piece of very hard heavy lava with a rather blunt point. With this the softer pumiceous lava was being "picked", in the form of a circular trench round a central core. One presumes that when the trench was a little deeper the central core was to be struck a blow in order to detach it, and the excavation would then be continued. The reverse side of the block shows that the workman had also roughly outlined the base of his bowl.

Crowbar?

Another curious discovery was a large wedge-shaped tool some 500 mm. long and weighing 23 lb. 12 oz., which has evident signs of use at its working end, and which was presumably something in the nature of a crow-bar for quarrying raw material. See Plate XXVIII.

The pottery

The fragments of pottery from the Nakuru site are very small, and it is therefore hard to judge what the pots of this period were like. Several fragments show a corded decoration, and another small fragment suggests the presence of a spout.

It is to be hoped, that when excavations can be carried out in the hut circles at this site or at some other site of this period, more pottery will be found which can be better studied.

The human remains

The detailed description of the human remains is held over for a later publication now in course of preparation, but photographs of the principal skeleton, No. IX, and of the skull are shown in Plate XXX. The skull is remarkable for its length of face and depth of palate; it is in most essentials entirely non-negroid, although the forehead does show the negro characteristic of a single central frontal boss. The nose and face are essentially non-negro.

It should be noted that this Gumban B phase skull has *not* had the central lower incisors extracted.

The Njoroan culture

There are a number of records of polished axes having been found in Kenya, but I am only aware of one having been found in association with other objects in a burial site. The site was found by a foreman named Mr Tough, who was in charge of a gang of natives digging the foundation trenches of a new house for Mr Sewall of Njoro on his farm there. The foundation trenches exposed a series of shallow graves, in one of which a polished stone axe was found. The matter was reported to me by Mr C. J. Oakes, through whose kindness I visited the site on July 1, 1927. Unlike any of the burial sites of other cultures so far found in Kenya, this site consisted of full-length graves for extended burials, and all the graves exposed were parallel to each other. Unfortunately most of the human bones had disintegrated completely and only a few very small fragments were found, but several small pieces of pottery and a number of obsidian flakes were found. No more polished axes could be discovered.

It was impossible to persuade those responsible for the building of the house to change the site, nor was it possible to carry out any extensive work on the day of my visit, and I fear that the site has by now been built over.

For the time being I propose to apply the name Njoroan to this culture, which is characterised by the presence of polished axes and by cemeteries with full-length parallel graves. There is at present no satisfactory indication of the date of this culture, but I have included it in this chapter because of the presence of the polished axe, which I regard as evidence of a Neolithic date. The axe is shown in Plate XXXI.

PLATE XXI

No. 1. Pottery fragment from Long's Drift site, Elmenteita, associated with a lower Kenya Wilton industry. It has a curious wavy line decoration, and is the only decorated piece found at the site.

Nos. 2–7. Fragments of pottery from the Makalia burial site, Elmenteita, associated with a very sparse industry and three burials. Some of these fragments (see Nos. 5 and 6) have all the characters of the pottery from Stable's Drift site, Enderit River, Elmenteita. This latter site was apparently buried in the muds of the Nakuran wet phase, so that the date is probably during that phase.

PLATE XXI

1

2

3

4

5

6

7

PLATE XXII

Two views of a fragment of one of the pots from Stable's Drift site. The whole of the interior surfaces of all the pots are heavily scored with deep lines scratched on while the clay was still wet, before baking.

Compare this piece of pottery with the fragments from the Makalia burial site, Nos. 5 and 6 on Plate XXI. No. 5 is a view of the inside of a fragment, No. 6 is of the outer decoration.

This pottery is typical of the Gumban A culture and belongs to the period of the Nakuran wet phase.

PLATE XXII

209

PLATE XXIII

Two views of one of the reconstructed pots from the Stable's Drift site, Enderit River, Elmenteita. This pottery belongs to the Gumban A culture of which it is typical. The external decoration, as well as the shape of the pot, all suggest that it is an imitation of basket-work. Note especially the very asymmetrical shape of the mouth of the pot.

The Gumban A culture belongs in time to the Nakuran wet phase.

The dimensions of the pot are:

Height $6\frac{1}{2}$ inches.

Maximum diameter of pot $9\frac{5}{8}$ inches.

Maximum diameter of mouth $7\frac{3}{4}$ inches.

PLATE XXIII

0   1   2   3 ins.

211

PLATE XXIV

Nos. 1 and 2. Full-face and profile views of skull No. II from Willey's Kopje, Eburru. There is no positive evidence upon which to date this skull, but several factors suggest that it is of the same period as the Makalia burial site skulls. Two imperfect skulls of this type were found, moreover, at the Makalia burial site itself.

Nos. 3 and 4. Full-face and profile views of skull No. I from the Makalia burial site, Elmenteita. This skull is in many respects unlike the other two skulls from the same site, but resembles them in having had the two central lower incisors removed during life (as also in the case of all the skulls from the Willey's Kopje site).

Both these skulls represent the makers of the Gumban A culture (Neolithic).

PLATE XXIV

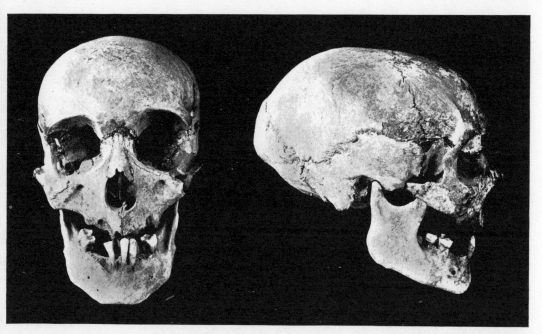

1   2

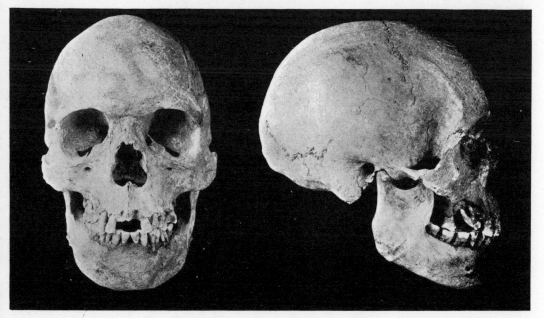

3   4

FIGURE 44

Tools from the Nakuru burial site on Major Macdonald's farm. The tools were found in association with the stone-bowls, etc. which characterise the Gumban B culture (Neolithic). The period of the Gumban B seems to coincide with the Nakuran wet phase.

Gumban B is easily distinguished from the Kenya Wilton by the absence of the typical small "thumb-nail" scrapers and by the presence of well-made stone-bowls, mortars, etc.

Nos. 2 to 12 inclusive are "backed blades" which if found on the surface might equally well be classed as of Kenya Aurignacian age. No. 1 is the largest blade found in the site. It has no secondary work on it.

The material of these tools is obsidian. The field catalogue numbers are given below:

No. 1. Y.76. 1929.	No. 5. Y.79. 1929.	No. 9. Y.84. 1929.
No. 2. Y.78. 1929.	No. 6. Y.121. 1929.	No. 10. Y.83. 1929.
No. 3. Y.80. 1929.	No. 7. Y.81. 1929.	No. 11. Y.87. 1929.
No. 4. Y.77. 1929.	No. 8. Y.85. 1929.	No. 12. Y.86. 1929.

FIGURE 44

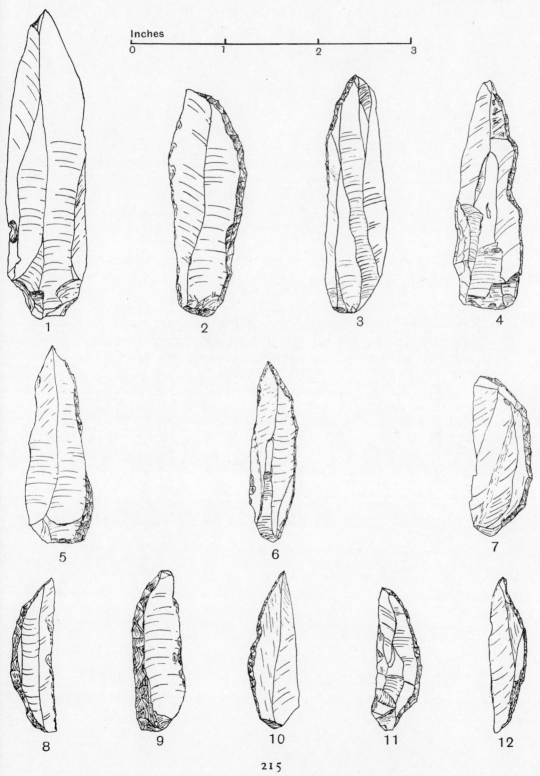

Inches
0   1   2   3

1   2   3   4

5   6   7

8   9   10   11   12

FIGURE 45

Tools from the Nakuru burial site on Major Macdonald's farm; they were found in association with the stone bowls, etc. which characterise the Gumban B culture (Neolithic). The period is the Nakuran wet phase.

No. 1. A double-ended "sinew frayer", the only one from the site, and as it is made of quite different obsidian from the other tools, it is almost certainly a tool of the Kenya Aurignacian period which was picked up and taken to the site.

Nos. 2 and 3. Examples of burins found with the Gumban B culture. They are not numerous at this period but occasional ones occur, as indeed they do in Neolithic Europe.

No. 4. A hollow scraper.

Nos. 6 and 7. End-scrapers.

Nos. 8 to 38 inclusive. These represent the rather crudely made lunates which are very common in the Gumban B culture.

The material of these tools is obsidian. Field catalogue numbers are given below:

No. 1. N.B.1.	No. 14. Y.89. 1929.	No. 27. Y.95. 1929.
No. 2. Y.118. 1929.	No. 15. Y.92. 1929.	No. 28. Y.98. 1929.
No. 3. Y.82. 1929.	No. 16. Y.94. 1929.	No. 29. Y.97. 1929.
No. 4. Y.117. 1929.	No. 17. Y.100. 1929.	No. 30. Y.99. 1929.
No. 5. Y.119. 1929.	No. 18. Y.110. 1929.	No. 31. Y.96. 1929.
No. 6. N.B.3.	No. 19. Y.102. 1929.	No. 32. Y.103. 1929.
No. 7. N.B.2.	No. 20. Y.104. 1929.	No. 33. Y.105. 1929.
No. 8. Y.90. 1929.	No. 21. Y.109. 1929.	No. 34. Y.106. 1929.
No. 9. N.B.10.	No. 22. Y.114. 1929.	No. 35. Y.101. 1929.
No. 10. Y.93. 1929.	No. 23. Y.113. 1929.	No. 36. Y.108. 1929.
No. 11. Y.88. 1929.	No. 24. Y.115. 1929.	No. 37. Y.112. 1929.
No. 12. N.B.13.	No. 25. Y.111. 1929.	No. 38. Y.107. 1929.
No. 13. Y.91. 1929.	No. 26. Y.116. 1929.	

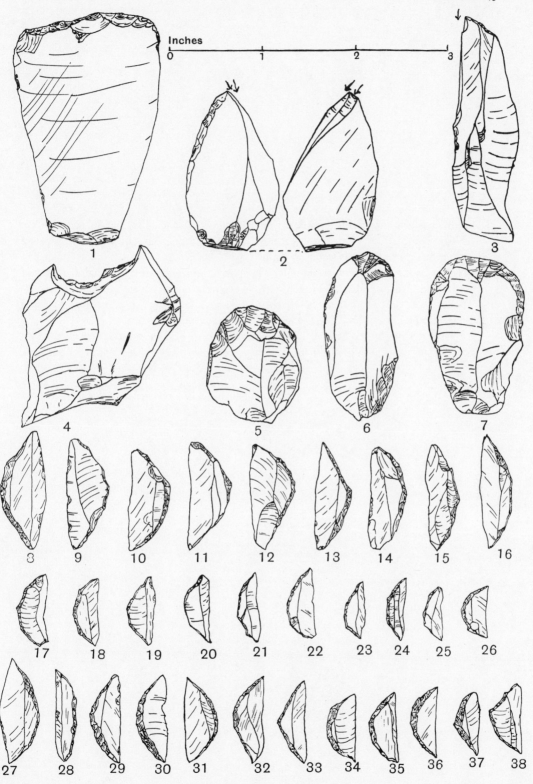

FIGURE 45

Inches

0   1   2   3

1   2   3

4   5   6   7

8   9   10   11   12   13   14   15   16

17   18   19   20   21   22   23   24   25   26

27   28   29   30   31   32   33   34   35   36   37   38

217

PLATE XXV

Stone utensils found at the Nakuru burial site on Major Macdonald's farm.

Nos. 1 and 1 *a*. Flat bottomed mortar with pestle. Height 93 mm., greatest diameter 129 mm., least diameter 125 mm.

Nos. 2 and 2 *a*. Shallow stone bowl. Height 80 mm., greatest external diameter at rim 193 mm., least external diameter at rim 190 mm.

Nos. 3 and 3 *a*. Deep stone bowl with flat base. Height 131 mm., greatest external diameter at rim 194·5 mm., least external diameter at rim 193 mm.

These utensils are typical of the Gumban B culture and are associated with a rather degenerate series of tools of obsidian. The period of this culture is the Nakuru wet phase.

PLATE XXV

1   2   3

1*a*   2*a*   3*a*

PLATE XXVI

Objects in stone found at the Nakuru burial site on Major Macdonald's farm. They are associated with a Gumban B culture.

No. 1. Lower stone of a saddle quern. Length 354 mm., width 255 mm., thickness 65 mm.

No. 2. Unfinished stone bowl. Greatest width 296 mm., width at right angles to greatest width 258 mm., height 185 mm. (all approximate measurements).

Near this was found the tool with which the bowl was being made. (See Plate XXVII.)

Period—Nakuran wet phase.

PLATE XXVI

1

2

PLATE XXVII

Two views of the triangular tool which was found near the unfinished bowl at the Nakuru burial site on Major Macdonald's farm, and which had certainly been used in making the bowl. Its length is 191 mm., width 120 mm. and thickness 62·5 mm. It was found with a Gumban B culture.

Period—Nakuran wet phase.

PLATE XXVII

PLATE XXVIII

Two views of a very large stone tool found at the Nakuru burial site on Major Macdonald's farm, associated with a Gumban B culture.

This tool seems to have been used as a crowbar for detaching blocks of rock which were to be made into bowls, etc. Its length is 496 mm., breadth 170 mm., and greatest thickness 145·5 mm.

Period—Nakuran wet phase.

PLATE XXVIII

PLATE XXIX

Bone awls found at the Nakuru burial site on Major Macdonald's farm, associated with the other objects of the Gumban B culture.

The period is the Nakuran wet phase.

PLATE XXIX

PLATE XXX

No. 1. The skeleton known as Nakuru IX *in situ* in the Nakuru burial site on Major Macdonald's farm.

This skeleton was the primary burial and was found at the very bottom of the large burial mound. The skeleton was lying on its left side in the ultra-contracted position, and was freely covered with red ocre.

Nos. 2 and 3. Full-face and profile views of the skull Nakuru IX (male). This skeleton was associated with the stone bowls etc. and represents the makers of the Gumban B culture.

PLATE XXX

1

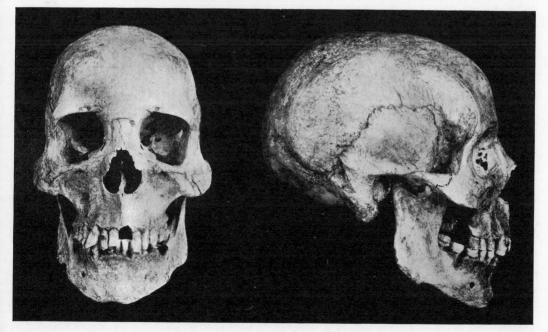

2   3

PLATE XXXI

Two views of the polished axe from the burial site on Mr Sewall's farm at Njoro. The measurements of the tool are: length 131 mm., greatest width, 76 mm., width of butt, 43·5 mm.

This polished axe culture is tentatively named Njoroan.

PLATE XXXI

231

THE RELATION OF THE KENYA CULTURES TO THOSE OF EUROPE AND OF SOUTH AFRICA

THE Kenya Culture Sequence and its relation to the pluvial and post-pluvial climatic sequence has been described in the preceding chapters. The possibilities of correlation of the pluvial periods in East Africa with the glacial periods of Europe have also been indicated.

In Appendix B, Dr C. E. P. Brooks discusses the problem of glacial-pluvial correlation from the point of view of the meteorologist, and states his tentative conclusions. With these I am entirely in agreement. *It cannot be emphasised too strongly that this detailed correlation is only tentative and cannot yet be regarded as proved.*

Before reading the ensuing chapters Appendix B should be studied. For convenience, however, the principal suggested correlations may be tabulated here. The similarity between this table and that of Blanckenhorne for Palestine, which was noted at the end of Chapter II, is significant.

Nakuran wet phase	Wet period *circa* 850 B.C.
Dry period	Climatic optimum
Makalian wet phase	Bühl stadium, etc., to climatic optimum
Dry period	Achen retreat, etc.
Gamblian pluvial. The sub-divisions are Lower Gamblian and Upper Gamblian with a mid-Gamblian pause	{ Würm glacial Riss-Würm inter-glacial Riss glacial
Long break with periods of faulting and volcanic activity	Mindel-Riss inter-glacial
Kamasian pluvial. Sub-divisions unknown but may include Mr Wayland's Kafuan and Sangoan	{ Mindel glacial Günz-Mindel inter-glacial Günz glacial

Since there is no general agreement between European Archaeologists as to the exact relation of some of the earlier cultures in Europe to the glacial and inter-glacial sequence, it is not possible in some cases to say whether a given culture is earlier or later in Europe than in Kenya, even if our tentative glacial-pluvial correlation is correct.

Moreover, recent discoveries in Europe have caused considerable modifications, which have not yet been published. In view of these facts I do not propose to discuss the comparative dating of the East African and European cultures in detail at present. In the following pages I propose rather to discuss the problems of the relationship of the Kenya cultures to those of Europe and South Africa, and I shall only indicate whether a Kenya culture seems to be earlier or later than a corresponding one in Europe when the question of date is relevant to the argument.

Unfortunately I have not sufficient details concerning the recent work which has been done in North Africa to make any satisfactory comparison with that area, but I understand that Mr E. Passemard is now preparing a comprehensive study of the North African sequence and of the evidence upon which it is founded, and this will fill a long-felt want.

During the past few years in Europe a considerable amount of new evidence has been found which must materially alter the older conception of the lower Palaeolithic sequence. Unfortunately much of this work is as yet unpublished, but the recent paper by M. Péyrony on Le Moustier[1] is a notable contribution. The old idea that there was a simple progression from the Chellean to the Acheulean and then on to a pure Mousterian must now be laid aside, for Péyrony has shown that a pure Mousterian culture without any traces of coups-de-poing is often earlier than the Acheuleo-Mousterian, or Mousterian with coups-de-poing, which used to be considered as an early phase of the Mousterian. In fact it seems clear from Péyrony's work that two tribes were living simultaneously in the Dordogne valley, the one having a purely Mousterian culture with no coups-de-poing, and the other consisting of a very advanced Acheulean with a fair amount of borrowed Mousterian types.

M. l'Abbé Breuil[2] has further shown that there is every reason to believe that there was an evolution in Europe of a purely flake tool culture at the same time as the Chelleo-Acheulean culture was developing with coups-de-poing as its type tools. The Clacton and the Levalloisian are early stages of this flake culture which culminated in the Mousterian.

The South African culture sequence has been recently described by M. C. Burkitt,[3] and by Goodwin and Lowe,[4] and still more recently l'Abbé Breuil has visited South Africa, and a preliminary note on the result of his tour has been published.[5] In South Africa the lower, middle and upper divisions of the Stellenbosch culture represent the evolution of the coups-de-poing culture from the Chellean to the late Acheulean stages. Apart from the differences of material, this culture in South Africa is identical to the Kenya Chellean and Acheulean and to the European Chellean and Acheulean. Following on the Stellenbosch culture is the Fauresmith culture, which is again divided into lower, middle and upper.5 The lower and upper Fauresmith seem to correspond to the Levalloisian flake industry of Europe, while the middle Fauresmith apparently corresponds to the Nanyukian of Kenya and to one of the Acheuleo-Mousterian mixed industries as found in the Dordogne valley in Europe. Next in South Africa comes a short period when a South African Mousterian flourished in a pure form, only to be interrupted by the arrival of Neoanthropic influences which resulted in industries such as that at Stillbay, Cape Flats and Fishhoek, which have a curious pseudo-Solutrean appearance. In Kenya, as in South Africa, we have at present no trace of an early purely flake culture contemporary with and distinct from the Chellean and Acheulean, which are characterised by coups-de-poing, but such a culture may well exist, and if so it will doubtless be found with further work. Meanwhile it is significant that the Acheulean phase in each of these two African areas is followed by a phase which has a mixture of Acheulean and Mousterian (or Levalloisian) characteristics.

But let us examine the problem of the exactly identical development of the crude Chellean to a very advanced Acheulean which takes place in South Africa, in Kenya and in Europe (and also in Rhodesia, Somaliland, Egypt, Palestine and North Africa, although we cannot discuss these areas here). A combination of the theories of independent evolution and of diffusion seems to be the best explanation; that is to say that there was probably a diffusion of an early hominid stock which took with it the first beginnings of a crude Chellean or even pre-Chellean type of culture, and then in different areas this crude culture gradually developed along independent but comparatively parallel lines through the later Chellean and Acheulean culture phases of each area. Of course in some countries the development may have been slower than in others, so that it cannot, for example, be argued that the finding of an Acheulean culture in a given deposit dates it as con-temporary with another deposit containing a similar culture, and therefore, as we have seen in an earlier chapter, other means must be found for the purposes of correlation. Except that in Europe the flake cultures which lead up to the Mousterian are now shown to have been developing simultaneously with the Chelleo-Acheulean, it would not be difficult to imagine that just as the Acheulean was apparently the natural line of evolution from the Chellean, so the Mousterian was the natural outcome of the Acheulean. Even with the European evidence as it stands, I am inclined to think that it is by no means unlikely that in Africa the flake cultures, such as the lower Fauresmith and lower Kenya Mousterian, represent a natural evolution from the upper Stellenbosch and upper Kenya Acheulean respectively, and that the development was chiefly due to the material which it was often necessary to use in making the coups-de-poing in these areas, and which would certainly tend towards the evolution of a *"tortoise core"* technique.

It is most unfortunate that practically nothing is at present known of the human type which made the Chellean and Acheulean cultures in Europe, and that absolutely nothing is as yet known of the types responsible for these cultures in Africa. Such a discovery would go a long way towards proving or disproving the theory of independent evolution after an early diffusion of common stock. If this theory is true, we should expect the respective human types to be more and more dissimilar with each successive cultural phase, although possibly retaining certain common and characteristic features.

In South Africa, just as in Kenya, we have already seen that the local Mousterian eventually developed into a culture which has many superficial resemblances to the Solutrean, and is apparently the result of a fusion of the Mousterian culture with a Neoanthropic one. This does not necessarily mean that there was an interbreeding of two distinct human species, for in the first place we do not know for certain that the human type responsible for the Mousterian culture in Africa was of *non-Homo sapiens* type. Moreover, even if the Stillbay type of culture in East and South Africa is the result of a culture fusion as suggested, there is no proof that its makers were not a branch of the Neoanthropic stock who borrowed some of the Mousterian technique, rather than that it was a branch of the Mousterian stock who borrowed some of the Neoanthropic ideas. In fact the evidence of the skull found by Messrs Peers in the Fishhoek cave[6] with a Stillbay type of industry definitely favours the former alternative, since this skull is certainly *Homo sapiens*, and is regarded as a proto-Bushman type.[7] Moreover, it has been suggested by Burkitt that the true explanation of the Solutrean culture in Europe, which has definite likenesses to the Stillbay, may be the result of a fusion of Neoanthropic and Mousterian culture influences in Western Europe.[8] Here, too, the makers were certainly of *Homo sapiens* type. In other words, the "Stillbay" types of culture in Africa definitely suggest an independent parallel evolution, and so lend support to the view that the earlier stages were also due to parallel lines of evolution.

So far (with the partial exception of the Stillbay culture) we have been dealing with cultures which are not characterised by a wide range of highly specialised tools, but only by a comparatively short range of tools which fall mainly under the category of "general utility" tools, and this renders it less difficult to believe that they may be due to independent evolution. The restricted range of tool types in the Chellean, Acheulean, and Mousterian types of culture is in Europe usually attributed to the fact that they were not the work of man of the *Homo sapiens* species, but of more primitive races such as the Neanderthal race which was certainly responsible for the Mousterian culture of Europe. It is this paucity of tool types that makes me believe that when we eventually find the skulls of the makers of the African Mousterian they will prove to be of *non-Homo sapiens* type, although probably not of Neanderthal type, but merely an allied race like *Homo rhodesiensis*. The partial exception (mentioned above) of the Stillbay culture group is therefore explicable on the grounds that the *Homo sapiens* influence was already at work.

We must now turn our attention to the Aurignacian cultures. As we have seen, in Kenya the lower Aurignacian makes its appearance at the very beginning of the Gamblian pluvial, at the same time as the earliest pure Mousterian which we have yet found in Kenya, and the two distinct cultures then develop contemporaneously throughout the period of the two maxima of the Gamblian pluvial until finally the Kenya Mousterian develops into the Kenya Stillbay, while the Kenya Aurignacian eventually develops into the Elmenteitan.

I am not aware that in South Africa any true pure lower or even upper Aurignacian has been found, although there is ample evidence of its influence and of the cultures derived from it. The Howieson's Poort[9] industry has certainly a strong Aurignacian "flavour", as has the Saw Mills industry in Rhodesia[10]; but neither is a pure Aurignacian, any more than that claim can be made for the Smithfield or Wilton cultures. In North Africa, especially in Algeria and Morocco, there is a very fine lower Aurignacian (known locally by various names such as lower Capsian and lower Getulian) which develops locally through several stages, which finally diverge into sundry contemporaneous microlithic industries very similar to the Wilton of Kenya or Azilian and Tardenoisian of Europe (see next chapter).

In Western Europe the earliest Aurignacian phase is that known as lower Aurignacian, which is in every way comparable to the lower Capsian, and which in some ways has more resemblance to the lower part (phase *a*) of the upper Kenya Aurignacian than to our lower Kenya Aurignacian. In Europe this lower Aurignacian, which certainly came from North Africa and which is associated with the Combe Capelle and Grimaldi types of skull, is followed by a quite distinct culture which was (unfortunately to my mind) named the middle Aurignacian. Like the lower Aurignacian it was made by men of *Homo sapiens* type, but of the Cromagnon race, and it has certain tool types in common with the lower Aurignacian, yet has many others which distinguish it from that culture. The middle Aurignacian seems to have been brought to Western Europe by the Cromagnon type of man, and as far as the evidence goes, arrived probably from Asia *via* Central Europe. We will return to the evidence for these facts later. The first arrivals of the middle Aurignacians in France seem to have practised full-length burials, but there is evidence that the middle and lower Aurignacian elements soon intermingled, so that in many of the later middle Aurignacian levels the culture has been somewhat modified, and the contracted method of burial also occurs again as an alternative to full-length burial.*

The upper Aurignacian in Western Europe is apparently mainly derived from this mixture of the lower with the middle Aurignacian, but in some parts the middle Aurignacian influence had not penetrated, so that local upper Aurignacian industries occur derived directly from the lower Aurignacian. When one turns to Central and Eastern Europe and to Palestine,[11] as far as I am able to interpret the evidence, no true lower Aurignacian occurs, and the earliest Aurignacian culture is of middle Aurignacian type followed by upper Aurignacian, and the former rests stratigraphically immediately upon Mousterian levels. This seems to point to the conclusion that the middle Aurignacian culture, and that branch of the *Homo sapiens* stock which brought it to Europe, came from Asia, while the bearers of the lower Aurignacian stock came to Europe from North Africa.

The present known distribution of the lower Aurignacian type of culture

---

* The views which I have expressed as to the middle Aurignacian are not orthodox, but are based upon a reconsideration of the subject in the light of recent finds.

is Italy, France and North Spain, North Africa and Kenya, and in all these areas it would seem that even at its first appearance it is already fairly well developed. This indicates that it had already begun to develop somewhere else, and that its arrival in each place was due to migration, very probably connected with climatic changes. It is generally accepted that in North Africa this culture is earlier than in Europe, but I am not aware that any detailed work has been done in the North African area which would show how much earlier this culture was there. It should be possible to ascertain this on the basis of a study of the river terraces and their relation to the raised beaches of the Mediterranean, or even by a study of the past climatic conditions. In Kenya the first presence of the lower Aurignacians is, as far as we know, at the very base of the Gamblian deposits, and if our suggested correlation of the glacial and pluvial periods is accepted, this means that the lower Aurignacian arrived in Kenya fairly early in the time of the Riss glaciation, which is very much earlier than its arrival in Europe, and probably somewhat earlier than its arrival in North Africa, though this cannot be certain.

Two possible explanations emerge from this study of the distribution of the lower Aurignacian (African Aurignacian) and the middle Aurignacian (Euro-Asian Aurignacian). The first view is that the cradle of Modern Man, that is of *Homo sapiens*, lies somewhere in Asia, and that at an early date a number of different branches of this stock moved in various directions, both westwards and eastwards. We are here only concerned with two of these hypothetical waves of migration; one with an early form of middle Aurignacian culture seems to have spread *via* Palestine and the Caucasus to Central and eventually to Western Europe; the other with an early form of the lower Aurignacian culture spread down through Arabia and crossed into Africa at about the Straits of Babel-Mandeb, thence *via* Somaliland and Abyssinia into the Sudan and the Sahara area, and so to North Africa. Of course these movements would not be sudden migrations, but rather in the nature of gradual wandering and expansion in search of new hunting grounds, and small branches of the movement would tend to break off and diverge from the main line of movement. This explanation accounts both for the similarities and differences between the lower and so-called middle Aurignacian branches of the early *Homo sapiens* stock, and also for the fact that the lower Aurignacians in Kenya are so much earlier than in North Africa or in Europe; since the gradual advance from Central East Africa to North West Africa must have taken an immense time if it was simply in the nature of a gradual expansion.

The other view is that the cradle of the Aurignacian races lies hidden somewhere in the Sahara area, probably in the south-east, and that an early wave of movement carried one branch of the stock *via* Somaliland and the Straits of Babel-Mandeb into Arabia, and thence to some unknown secondary centre of distribution in Asia. At this secondary centre it is suggested that the middle Aurignacian culture developed, and then spread *via* Palestine to Europe; while other branches spread westwards to India and to China, others again remaining in the fertile valleys of Mesopotamia where they gradually developed and became eventually the cradle of the Neolithic civilisations.

Meanwhile other movements from the supposed Saharan cradle would have resulted in the arrival of the lower Capsian in North Africa, and on into Europe as the lower Aurignacian, and also in the arrival of the lower Aurignacian in Kenya.

But explanations such as these are only hypothetical and speculative, and although in the past I have held the latter to be the more likely, in the light of a more detailed study of all available evidence, I feel that until further knowledge is forthcoming either view is equally justifiable. One of the keys to the problem would seem to be Somaliland, and I therefore propose to go there for a preliminary survey when I am en route for Kenya in 1931.

REFERENCES

1. "Le Moustier", by D. Péyrony, in *Revue Anthropologique*, nos. 1–6, 1930.
2. "Manuel de Recherches Préhistoriques. Synchronisme des Glaciations et des Industries Humaines", by M. l'Abbé H. Breuil.
3. *South Africa's Past in Stone and Paint*, by M. C. Burkitt.
4. "The Stone Age Cultures of S. Africa", by A. J. Goodwin and C. van Reit Lowe, *Annals of the South African Museum*, vol. XXVII, 1929.
5. "Fresh Light on the Prehistoric Archaeology of S. Africa", by C. van Reit Lowe, in *Bantu Studies*, vol. III, no. 4, 1929.
6. *South Africa's Past in Stone and Paint*, by M. C. Burkitt, p. 87.
7. Supplement to *Nature*, June 21, 1930, p. 935, by Sir A. Keith, F.R.S.
8. *South Africa's Past in Stone and Paint*, by M. C. Burkitt.
9. "Some Stone Implements from a rock shelter at Howieson's Poort", by Rev. P. Stapelton and J. Hewitt, in *South African Journal of Science*, vol. XXIV, p. 574.
10. *The Stone Age in Rhodesia*, by Rev. Neville Jones.
11. "Presidential Address to Prehistoric Society of East Anglia by Dr D. A. E. Garrod, 1927", *Proceedings of P.S.E.A.* vol. v, part III.

CHAPTER XI

THE RELATION OF THE KENYA CULTURES
TO THOSE OF EUROPE AND OF
SOUTH AFRICA (*continued*)

I N the preceding chapter I discussed the Kenya cultures up to the end of the Kenya Aurignacian and outlined their relation to similar cultures elsewhere; in this chapter I shall deal with the subsequent cultures.

We have already seen that the Kenya Aurignacian continued its development after the end of the Gamblian pluvial, so that by the time of the maximum of the Makalian wet phase it was so differentiated as to be considered as a new and distinct culture—the Elmenteitan. Could we discover all the intervening stages, we should probably find that the development was so gradual that it would be difficult to determine at what point in the sequence it ceased to be late Kenya Aurignacian and could be termed Elmenteitan. In fact we may regard the Elmenteitan as a local, advanced development of the Aurignacian. The reason why we have a hiatus between the two is that within the Rift Valley area the break between the Gamblian and the Makalian was marked by a period of intense aridity, so that the development from late Kenya Aurignacian to Elmenteitan must have taken place elsewhere, in an area where the effect of the decrease in rainfall was not disastrous; and when more outlying sites are worked, especially in high altitudes near mountains such as Mount Kenya, the gap should be bridged.

In the classical areas of south-western Europe the position is very similar, only the hiatus between the upper Aurignacian and the Magdalenian which represents its local development is due to the temporary invasion of the Solutrean race. Somewhere in Europe, in an area not affected by the Solutrean invasion, a branch of the upper Aurignacian was surely developing into the more specialised Magdalenian which eventually returned to the south-western areas.

The Elmenteitan in Kenya therefore culturally corresponds to the European Magdalenian, but the two are so distinct from each other that it would be unwise and wrong to call the Elmenteitan by the name of Kenya Magdalenian. The reason for this great difference is that whereas each of these two can be traced back to an Aurignacian phase, the Elmenteitan is the result of a direct evolution from the lower (or African) Aurignacian through an upper Kenya Aurignacian phase, whereas the Magdalenian is the product of the European, upper Aurignacian, which was itself not a pure development from the lower Aurignacian, but rather of a fusion between the lower and middle Aurignacian influences.

As we saw in Chapter x, the Aurignacian culture, properly speaking, does not occur in South Africa, although its influence was felt, as evidenced by such industries as Howieson's Poort and Fishhoek,[1] which were probably made by Neoanthropic man, although a very strong Mousterian culture influence remained. The Elmenteitan also seems to have no corresponding culture in South Africa, but possibly the Smithfield A was its contemporary, though this is by no means certain. But if the Elmenteitan has no true South African equivalent, this is certainly not the case with the Kenya Wilton. In South Africa the Wilton is found in its purest and finest form in Rhodesia,[2] and it seems later to have spread far and wide into South Africa, and probably to have caused considerable modifications in the later stages of the Smithfield. The similarity of the Wilton of Rhodesia and of South Africa to that of Kenya must not be regarded, however, as evidence of contemporaneity. On the contrary it seems that this culture is of more and more recent date the farther south one goes, thus indicating that it was the direct result of a true culture spread over a considerable period of time.

The Wilton is a typical microlithic culture of the type which occurs almost everywhere as the final stage of development of the Aurignacian, in those areas where an Aurignacian has existed. The Wilton certainly occurs in Tanganyika Territory, and it has already been described as a type culture in Kenya, and it would seem that the Magosian in Uganda[3] is also a closely allied culture. All over North Africa similar cultures occur, and also all over western Europe. They are all characterised by small lunates and other geometric tools, and by numbers of peculiar small "thumb-nail" scrapers, etc.

In some areas, as in South Africa, they seem to have been introduced by an advancing race, while elsewhere, as in parts of North Africa, they seem to be merely a local development of the Aurignacian, which seems probably to be the case in Kenya. In Europe it seems to be the general view that such microlithic industries as the Azilian and Tardenoisian represent a northerly migration from North Africa. It has been claimed by M. Vignard[4] that these microlithic cultures all have their origin in his upper Sebilien, and he regards Sebil as the cradle where such industries developed and whence they spread. I have already indicated my own view, that they represent rather the natural and independent evolution of the Aurignacian culture which took place at about the same time in several areas, but M. Vignard's line of argument may be indicated.*

He finds in the final phase of his Sebilien, which seems to be a derivative of a very late Mousterian culture, a large number of so-called "Tardenoisian burins" which he designates "mêches à percer". He regards these as such a highly specialised tool that their occurrence in the microlithic industries in widely separated areas can only be due to the directly common origin of these industries from a single cradle. He says, referring to the Tardenoisian burins, "Elles sont pour nous la preuve la plus convainçante de la parenté étroite de ces industries", and he goes on to quote l'Abbé Breuil as saying— "Cette forme est beaucoup trop spéciale, et, en apparence trop insignifiante pour que sa répartition puisse être due à un phénomène de convergence, il faut donc admettre que l'une au moins des industries tardenoisiennes qui s'étend de Sahara central à l'Ecosse, indique pour sa répartition un mouvement migrateur". To me the frequent occurrence of this tool in industries which always also include small pointed notched blades or flakes is best explained on the ground that it is a broken tool and not the complete tool, and that the so-called "Tardenoisian burin facet" is no more than a special kind of fracture due to usage in a particular way. At any rate the "Tardenoisian burins", though not common, certainly occur in the upper Kenya Aurignacian, and it would be absurd to regard that as derived from the upper Sébilien, and I believe that they are also not unknown in upper Aurignacian sites in Europe.

The relation of the culture which I have named Gumban to the Wilton of Kenya is not clear. I have for the present divided the Gumban into two divisions A and B. This division is based upon the differences in the method of burial between the two divisions and upon the fact that a peculiar type of pottery, which is associated with Gumban A, does not seem to occur with Gumban B. Unfortunately the number of tools which can with certainty be

* Since writing this discussion of M. Vignard's views on Tardenoisian burins I have had a long discussion with him and find that he has considerably modified his views. I understand that he is now preparing a new paper on the so-called "Tardenoisian burins" of the Sebilien which will in great part bear out my contention that these things are not in themselves tools but merely the result of certain techniques of usage.

associated with Gumban A is so small that any comparison on that basis is impossible at present. In attempting to discuss the relation of the Gumban to cultures in other parts of the world, I propose to deal only with Gumban B. It should be noted here that the name of this culture has been derived from a Kikuyu term which is applied to-day primarily to a semi-mythical race of small people who are said to have been in occupation of much of the Kikuyu country before the Kikuyu first arrived. In using the word for this culture, I am not referring to this, its primary meaning, but to its present more usual meaning, that is in reference to any people who preceded the Kikuyu. From the moment that I first started excavations, old Kikuyus who visited the camp used to talk of my "search for the Gumba", and when thinking of a name for this comparatively recent culture the word Gumban seemed to be not inappropriate.

The obsidian industry of the Gumban B phase is mainly a microlithic industry which if taken alone is not very unlike such other microlithic industries as the Azilian, Tardenoisian, Kenya Wilton, or the Magosian of Uganda. But the associated finds mark it as distinct from these other cultures. Pestles and mortars, and saddle querns seem to indicate some sort of agriculture, while the well-made stone bowls are a decidedly interesting feature. Even more interesting, perhaps, is the occurrence at the Nakuru burial site of two beads which are certainly indicative of outside influence. It is not unreasonable to believe that the idea of stone bowls and the agriculture are due to the same source as the beads, and that we have in this Gumban culture evidence of the contact of a late stone age people with one of the early civilisations of the world.

We know that the Gumban B culture is associated with the Nakuran wet phase, when Lake Nakuru stood some 145 feet above its present level and contained fish. We know from the beads that the date cannot be much earlier than 3000 B.C., while from the other evidence a date of *circa* 1000 to 850 B.C. seems most probable. Unfortunately the evidence of the beads themselves is insufficient to give an exact date, or even a definite indication of origin (there are only two of them from this site). They were submitted to Mr Horace Beck, and his note on them appears in Appendix F. The bead which is of agate recalls some early Mesopotamian beads, while the other which is of faïence most nearly resembles some beads from a late Neolithic site in Algeria. Nor, unfortunately, do the stone bowls tell us very much, for even though they may be due to an outside influence, the ones which we have found were locally made by men still in a Neolithic stage of development.

It is very tempting to indulge in speculation, and to suggest that the traders were from Mesopotamia or from Egypt. Stone bowls are characteristic of some early Mesopotamian periods, and were introduced from there into Egypt apparently about the time of the First Dynasty. But such speculations are not yet justifiable and we must await further evidence. All that can be said at present is that if the dating of the Nakuran wet phase as about 1000 to 850 B.C. is correct, then it is not unreasonable to look to Egypt as the probable place whence these early trade beads arrived, as also agriculture and the use of saddle querns, mortars and stone bowls. Sooner or later further evidence is certain to clear up this particular problem, since I know of many sites of Gumban B type, and it is hoped that investigation of some of these will be possible next season.

The Njoroan culture with its polished axe and its full-length burials in cemeteries also needs much more investigation before it can be definitely correlated with finds from other areas. Polished axes have not been found at all frequently in Kenya or in South Africa, although they are not uncommon in the Congo and in West Africa. I only know of one place in Africa south of the Sahara in which they have been found in definite association with burials and other cultural objects, and that is at Gebel-Moya in the Sudan. Full details of the Gebel-Moya site have not yet been published, but the available information5 indicates that the polished axes are there associated with full-length burials in cemeteries. It is probable that a direct connection between the Njoroan and the Gebel-Moya cultures will be shown when further work has been done on this period in Kenya and when the Gebel-Moya material has been published in full. Certainly the possibility of such a connection must be borne in mind and it is interesting to note that Gebel-Moya is dated as about 800 B.C.

REFERENCES

1. "The Stone Age Cultures of South Africa", by A. J. Goodwin and C. van Reit Lowe, in *Annals of South African Museum*, 1929, vol. XXVII; and *South Africa's Past in Stone and Paint*, by M. C. Burkitt.
2. *Annual Reports of Geological Survey Department, Uganda*, 1927, p. 34, and 1929, p. 36; also note in *Man*, July, 1929, by E. J. Wayland.
3. *Une Nouvelle Industrie Lithique le "Sebilien"*, by E. Vignard, 1923 (Cairo).
4. *L'Anthropologie*, vol. XXXI, p. 35, a paper by H. Breuil.
5. *Transactions of 17th International Medical Congress*, 1913. *Historical Section.* Paper on Gebel-Moya, by M. B. Ray and L. H. Dudley Buxton.

THE GEOLOGY OF THE IMPLEMENTIFEROUS DEPOSITS IN THE NAKURU AND NAIVASHA BASINS AND THE SURROUNDING AREA IN KENYA COLONY

By J. D. SOLOMON, B.A., F.R.A.I., F.G.S.

THE Nakuru and Naivasha basins furnish an extremely suitable field for investigating the relations of man's cultural stages with the pluvial periods which have plainly occurred in the area, which latter have resulted in an enormous extension of the lakes, and in the deposition of a considerable thickness of strata. The Nakuru basin in particular, having had no outlet, provides a complete record of the fluctuations of the lake, and hence also of the climatic changes which have occurred.

We have thus been able to adopt the following classification for these strata, drawn up by the method of checking the sequence of human cultures against the stratigraphy in the two basins, and based on the major pluviations. The boundary between each division is drawn at a maximum of inter-pluvial aridity, and each division is named after an area where its corresponding deposits are typically developed.

Climatic conditions	Division
Second post-pluvial wet phase	Nakuran
Dry period	
First post-pluvial wet phase	Makalian
Dry period	
Second major pluvial	Upper Gamblian
	Pause
	Lower Gamblian
Dry period, marked by volcanic activity, rift faulting, etc.	
First major pluvial	Kamasian

The Kamasian is an extension of the term used by Gregory to describe a thick series of flood gravels, clays, etc., which occur at such a height above Lake Baringo that it is plain that they were deposited in lake basins much greater than those which now exist within the Rift Valley. They have also been considerably affected by faulting. With these he correlated the series of tuffs and gravels exposed in the Njorowa Gorge near Naivasha and (although somewhat tentatively) the older series of lake deposits exposed by the Kariandusi River near Gilgil. In this correlation we follow him, but as we have obtained a series of Acheulean implements from the last-named site, we do not feel inclined to follow him in putting the whole series into the Miocene. It is true that the base of the series may be of any age, and we do not make any assertions on that point, as no fauna has as yet been discovered in the beds.

APPENDIX A

The Kamasian beds were not laid down in lake basins with a similar configuration to those of to-day, but rather in one enormous lake which stretched in any case from Baringo to the Kedong Valley, and probably still farther. They are affected by a considerable amount of faulting, and always contain a significant proportion of coarse tuffaceous material, the fragments of which are often unrounded, showing that they have not been re-deposited.

The term "Gamblian" is derived from Gamble's Cave and Gamble's Drift, Elmenteita, the most important exposures of deposits of this period. It includes the earliest and most important series of post-Kamasian lake deposits. Nowhere has faulting been detected in these beds, and what tuffaceous material they contain is generally re-deposited.

In the middle of the series is an unconformity, found both in the Nakuru and Naivasha basins: in places a land surface deposit occurs at this horizon in the former district. This must mark a retreat of the lake in both cases, and is useful as providing a sub-division for the period.

The Makalian refers to the Makalia river, which flows into the south end of Lake Nakuru. The Makalian deposits are notably diatomaceous, and rest, sometimes unconformably, upon a red, weathered surface of Gamblian beds. They contain an ashy band which is traceable over a distance of some miles.

There is also some evidence for a subsequent epi-pluvial of minor importance. It will be referred to as the Nakuran, and probably fell almost within historic times.

NAKURU BASIN

This basin includes the Lakes Nakuru and Elmenteita; it is bounded to the north by the crater of Menengai, to the south by Eburru, also of volcanic origin; while to the east and west are important fault scarps.

In the south-east corner of the basin, near Lake Elmenteita, the watershed between the Nakuru and Naivasha basins is low, being formed by the Gilgil Escarpment, a fault belonging to the latest series traceable in this part of the valley, with a strike some 10° east of north. This watershed stands at a height of some 6600 feet above sea level, the height of Lake Nakuru being 5776 and of Lake Elmenteita 5825 feet.

Both lakes are shallow, the maximum depth of Nakuru in May 1929 was 9 ft. 2 in. and that of Elmenteita 6 ft. 4 in. The waters of both lakes contain a large percentage of soda, and possess nothing but a microscopic fauna, composed of diatoms and rotifers, etc.

Lake Nakuru is fed by three rivers; the Njoro, which enters at its north-west corner, and the Enderit and Makalia, which both enter from the south. The latter two rivers pursue a roughly parallel course; they rise in the Mau Hills, and flow roughly from west to east until clear of the lowest of the Mau fault steps; they then turn abruptly northwards and pursue their meandering course to the lake. These meanders are incised in the soft lake deposits which they here traverse, and it is in the gorges thus produced that the best exposures are seen.

APPENDIX A

The topography of this basin suggests the presence of three principal rest levels of the lake; but no widespread beach has as yet been found to correspond to the highest of these, although various high-level terraces and beaches have been found, notably on Lion Hill in the centre of the basin, where the highest terrace stands 750 feet above lake level. Another is known at about 600 feet, while the beach found in Lion Hill cave stands at 620 feet.

The most widespread rest level is that represented by the beach in Gamble's Cave (see below) and dated as Upper Gamblian in age. It has been discovered and levelled by Mr D. G. B. Leakey at the following points:

Locality	Height above present lake level
Gamble's Cave	500 ft.
Above the precipice west of Lake Nakuru	490 ft.
Terrace at foot of Lion Hill	510 ft.
Beach and terrace on Gilgil Escarpment	530 ft. (?)

These results suggest a slight tilt subsequent to the formation of the beach; the distance between the precipice west of Lake Nakuru and the Gilgil Escarpment beach is about 17 miles.

The lower terrace occurs at approximately 375 feet above the present level of Lake Nakuru, and is known near Elmenteita Camp, at Nakuru on the slopes of Menengai, and at the Kariandusi River. Its Makalian date is established by the absence of Makalian deposits above this level; in any event, it clearly represents the most important post-Gamblian wet period.

A terrace and beach at a height of 145 feet above present lake level is known near Major Macdonald's farm, Nakuru. This is associated with an industry which is dated as not more than 3000 years old; it corresponds to a post-Makalian wet phase, which is known as the Nakuran.

The sections at Gamble's Cave have already been dealt with by Leakey. They establish clearly the correlation between the advanced Aurignacian of the fourth occupation level of Gamble's Cave II and the second maximum of the Gamblian lake; they also show evidence of the presence of men with Mousterian affinities towards the close of that pluvial (second occupation level). Gamble's Cave provides clear evidence of the subsequent aridity, and supports the correlation of the Elmenteitan industry with the Makalian wet phase.

The deposits in Lion Hill Cave also provide interesting evidence. The lowest deposit in the cave is a beach gravel which is some 620 feet above present lake level and probably represents a rest level during the decline of the Lower Gamblian, above this is an occupation level with upper Kenya Aurignacian tools, but with a curious fauna consisting almost entirely of Hyrax (of which many hundreds of jaws were found) and small mammals and fish with a very few ungulates at the base. The beach of the second Gamblian maximum lies immediately below the cave, but 100 feet lower.

During both the Gamblian maxima Lion Hill must have been an island, and we know from other evidence that during the pause between the two Gamblian maxima the lake dropped sufficiently low for the hill to be connected up with the mainland. It would seem that during the pause a family of upper Kenya Aurignacians established themselves in Lion Hill Cave and were subsequently cut off by the Upper Gamblian rise of the lake. Hence the very limited fauna.

Overlying this upper Kenya Aurignacian level is a bed of reddened soil, and that is followed by deposits containing Elmenteitan and later tools, thus confirming the sequence in Gamble's Cave II.

DETAILS OF SOME IMPORTANT SECTIONS
IN THE PLUVIAL DEPOSITS

Enderit Drift

This is the point at which the road from Mau Narok to Elmenteita Station crosses the Enderit River. The river is flowing nearly due north at this point, and floods have cut a transverse valley on either side of the main stream and approximately at right angles to it. The section given here is necessarily composite, being built up out of the various small exposures produced by the rapid erosion.

The sequence is as follows:

Makalian (?)

(6) Sand, not always present; occurs in irregular hollows overlying the Makalian silts. It is not well stratified, but is probably water deposited, up to 14 feet.

Makalian

(5) Evenly bedded diatomaceous silts, white in colour. Variable in thickness; they seem to thicken as the present river is approached. Up to 6 feet. The base is often very unconformable to the underlying beds.

(4) Grey unstratified ash, occurring in irregular patches and often absent. This is well exposed in the cutting for the fuel railway which crosses the river at this point, and has here yielded a number of implements. Up to 3 feet.

Upper Gamblian

(3) Series of sands, silts and gravels, the latter particularly well developed towards the top of the series. Towards the base diatomic material predominates. The upper part of the series is intensely reddened and contains great quantities of kunkar. Implements of Aurignacian and late Mousterian type have been obtained, in somewhat rolled condition, from the gravels in the upper part of the series.

This series, in contrast with the Lower Gamblian, does not appear to contain much obviously pumiceous material, and the gravel pebbles are all of lava. Thickness up to 30 feet.

Mid-Gamblian Pause

(2) Loamy sand, with unrounded stones, passing laterally in places into a coarse rubble gravel, with large pebbles of lava and rounded tuff; this latter is almost un-

APPENDIX A

stratified, and seems to be in the nature of a flood gravel filling in a river valley of mid-Gamblian date which did not coincide with that of the present river.

The loamy sand contains rootlets, which do not penetrate the overlying beds, thus showing that it represents a mid-Gamblian land surface, and that the Gamblian lake must at one time have retreated at least as far as this point. The gravel has yielded a few implements of Aurignacian type.

The maximum thickness of these beds is approximately 7 feet.

Lower Gamblian

(1) Series of well-stratified diatomaceous silts, ashes and gravels; the latter chiefly near the top of the series, where false bedding is very marked. The base of the series is not exposed. No implements or fauna are known from this horizon.

This section, of which a diagrammatic representation is given in Fig. 46, illustrates the separation of Gamblian and Makalian, and also the mid-Gamblian unconformity.

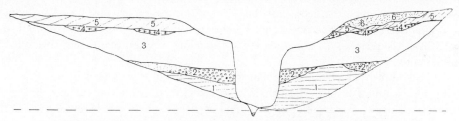

Fig. 46. Diagrammatic representation of Section S. of the roadway of Enderit Drift.
Approximate scale: Horizontal 1 inch = 100 yds.
Vertical 1 inch = 60 ft.

The mid-Gamblian river seems to have flowed WSW.–ENE. judging by the distribution of the flood gravel.

The deposits exposed at the Enderit Drift have no consistent dip, and show no signs of any disturbance due to earth movements.

SECTIONS NORTH OF ENDERIT DRIFT

Proceeding northwards down the Enderit we find a series of flood cuttings similar to that at the Enderit Drift itself. But the exposures are by no means so satisfactory as at that place.

The mid-Gamblian unconformity is not well marked, although discernible at the site known as "Juma's Drift". The Upper Gamblian deposits thin out somewhat, but can still be readily distinguished by the reddening which affects their upper portions.

The Makalian, however, thickens and becomes gravelly towards the top; an ashy bed also appears near the base.

At "Long's Drift" the section is as follows:

Makalian

(6) Wash, deposited on an uneven (land) surface. Up to 9 in.

(5) Stratified silts. A stage in the retreat of Makalian lake, due to temporary rise. Up to about 3 ft.

(4) Wash, deposited on uneven (land) surface. Up to 1 ft. 6 in.

(3) Diatomaceous silts. Up to 20 ft.

(2) Fine, water-stratified ash. Up to 4 ft.

(1) Diatomaceous silts (base not exposed).

Bed (4) has yielded numerous implements of Tardenoisian appearance, described as Kenya Wilton.

The gravels and silts of the Gamblian and Makalian north of Enderit Drift have yielded fossil remnants of hippopotamus.

SECTIONS SOUTH OF THE ENDERIT DRIFT

South of the Enderit Drift are a number of further "drifts", few of which show a complete section of the beds. All the deposits thicken except the Makalian, which consists entirely of diatomaceous silt and disappears a little to the north of the spot known as "Cut-off boulder"—*i.e.* a large block left standing between the present river and its former course.

The land deposit of mid-Gamblian times is still quite well seen in the first two drifts; on account of its unstratified character it gives rise to weathering rather reminiscent of that of the loess. Beyond Cut-off boulder, however, the sequence becomes, for a time, rather obscure, owing to the scrappy nature of the exposures.

The Lower Gamblian becomes much more gravelly; a few flakes have been obtained from the gravels, but no determinate implements and no fauna. It includes a poorly stratified ash, which is exposed at the bottom of the first drift south of the Enderit Drift.

The next section of importance is that at Gamble's Drift; the highest beds exposed are here nearly 500 feet above present lake level. About 200 feet of deposits are here shown.

The sequence is as follows:

Upper Gamblian (reddening at top due to post-Gamblian aridity)

Brilliant red soil on the highest points both east and west of the drift, with which is associated a very evolved industry of Mousterian type, characteristic everywhere of the latest Gamblian deposits. Up to 1 foot in thickness.

Diatomaceous silts, with bands of sand, composed of tuffaceous material, near the base. Thickness, up to 15 feet.

Mid-Gamblian pause

Ashy, unstratified loam with many obsidian flakes in places. These are, however, very brittle, and the only important finds are a few flakes with prepared striking platforms, indicating the presence of a Mousterian facies.

The base of this bed rests on a very uneven surface, and the underlying deposits are sometimes somewhat weathered. Thickness, up to 3 feet.

APPENDIX A

Lower Gamblian

Thick series of diatomaceous silts, volcanic sands and pumiceous gravels; the coarser deposits predominate in the lower part of the series. A few flakes have been obtained from the gravels, but are not determinate in character.

Thickness, about 70 feet.

Thin red bed, apparently due to sub-aerial weathering of the underlying tuffs. It contains rootlets. It appears to be conformable to the beds above and below, and would not seem to represent any lengthy retreat of the Gamblian lake. 1–2 feet in thickness.

Lower Gamblian (?), *Kamasian* (?)

Thick series of stratified tuffs and diatomite, with inter-stratified gravels in places. This series is banked up against a lava cliff which may be seen 50 yards east of the river crossing, and contains pebbles derived from that cliff, but apparently no implements.

Fossil bone has been found in one of the gravels of this period, but is unfortunately too fragmentary for identification.

Thickness, upwards of 100 feet.

A short distance above Gamble's Drift the river makes a right-angled bend, where it flows out from the west through a gap in one of the fault scarps. The lower deposits are, unfortunately, no longer well exposed; and the relations of the Lower Gamblian and the Kamasian, which here begins to appear, are undecipherable, particularly as implements are wanting and the former deposit does not differ markedly from the latter, consisting, as it does, largely of the same material re-deposited.

The Upper Gamblian and mid-Gamblian deposits persist, and can be detected at several points both north and south of the river; they have yielded a few implements to the south in the fairly near neighbourhood of Gamble's Cave, described above.

The Kamasian deposits here consist of a great thickness of stratified tuffs with some inter-stratified boulder beds. In the neighbourhood of Gamble's Cave they are affected by numerous small faults, and they contain no diatomitic horizons. In these two latter characteristics they differ from the Gamblian deposits already described.

They rise to a height of more than 750 feet above the level of the present lake; this is higher than any beach as yet identified with certainty in the Nakuru basin.

FORMATION OF THE VALLEY OF THE ENDERIT

The Enderit at present flows in a deep gorge which is in places cut into an older valley at a level about 70 feet above that of the present river; the course of the older valley does not coincide altogether with that of the newer one, and the older course is not traceable above the point where the river makes its right-angled bend.

That much of the lower part of the valley is recent is shown from the following considerations:

(i) The evidence from Enderit Drift shows that in mid-Gamblian times the direction of drainage was not similar to that of to-day.

(ii) The Makalian deposits above Enderit Drift do not thicken towards the river, or dip towards it; and the development of a gravelly facies within this series has no relation to the course of the present river.

It is thus seen that the lower part of the river system is post-Makalian in date. The younger valley may belong to a later phase in the Makalian retreat, or else to the Nakuran period. It may be noted that erosion is still proceeding, although not with much speed in the lower portions of the valley.

The river would seem to owe its peculiar course to having cut its valley during a period when the lake was retreating from south to north; the consequent stream ran out on to the lake flats and meandered about the plain in a direction which was on the whole naturally from south to north; after a dryish interval, during which erosion was slow, the meanders were incised during another period of somewhat increased rainfall.

The upper section of the Enderit is in part pre-Gamblian; as the terrace and beach of the Upper Gamblian period may be followed for a short distance (but not far) up its course. But such Gamblian deposits as occur are very thin and sparse, from which it may be deduced that before the Gamblian period the river had not cut its bed down much below the level of the Gamblian beach, *i.e.* 510 feet above present lake level.

EXPOSURES IN THE MAKALIA VALLEY

These exposures comprise chiefly Upper Gamblian and Makalian deposits, although mid-Gamblian and Lower Gamblian beds probably occur at least at one point, and Kamasian beds are known to be exposed at one point and have been proved in pit sections in this area.

As mentioned above, the Makalia bends abruptly northwards shortly after traversing the lowest of the Mau fault steps: but between the bend and the scarp it has evidently meandered, and the resulting erosion of the soft lake deposits has given rise to a "Bad Land" topography. At the time of the meandering the river was evidently adjusted to a higher base level than at present, and this correlates well with the river terrace of the Enderit, which is either late Makalian or Nakuran in age.

The most easterly exposure is that known as "Terraced Cliff", which occurs exactly at the chief bend of the river.

The sequence here is as follows:

Makalian

Well-bedded diatomaceous silts.
Fine, poorly stratified ash, probably laid down in still water. Up to 10 feet.
Diatomaceous silts, with gravel at the base.

Upper Gamblian

Silts, and some gravel, reddened and with some development of kunkar in the upper part. Upwards of 50 feet.
The gravelly beds in the Gamblian and at the base of the Makalian have yielded

tools both of upper Aurignacian and upper Mousterian type. (The reddening and kunkar at the top of the Gamblian beds indicates the post-Gamblian arid period.)

When traced southwards the Makalian beds show very little variation; at a site known as "MacInnes Site", some 400 yards from Terraced Cliff, the ash has yielded an interesting assemblage of human and animal remains; the human type is very similar to that found elsewhere associated with the "Elmenteitan" culture (see Bromhead's Site, described below).

A few hundred yards west of the above-mentioned sites further exposures occur. The lower series of Makalian silts is here absent and the ash shows no signs of stratification; in the more northerly sites, such as "Red Cliff", which are nearer to the present course of the river, it is absent, the total thickness of the Makalian being reduced to some 3 feet. It invariably rests on a strongly reddened surface of earlier deposits.

The Gamblian is similar to that of Terraced Cliff; but the exposure at Red Cliff shows some extraordinary pockets of gravel, which would seem to have been deposited in small ravines contemporaneously cut through the lake deposits, or else to be due to removal of sand by percolating underground water, thus causing a concentration of coarse material.

The gravels have yielded a few rather indeterminate implements.

The lower part of the deposits consists chiefly of silts with very well-marked planes of stratification, which at one site have yielded numerous leaf impressions. At one site (known as "Pepperbox") these silts are seen to rest on an unstratified sandy loam with unrounded stones, similar to the mid-Gamblian deposit at the Enderit Drift; and it may represent this horizon. This loam rests on another series of well-bedded silts, which are poorly exposed.

This stony loam has yielded a few implements, but they are not sufficiently typical to establish its horizon.

The Gamblian deposits, when traced westwards, develop a marked easterly dip; it is possible that this is due to a slight subsequent movement along the fault line which here brings an ancient lava flow to the surface; but the dip does not exceed the probable angle of rest for these generally fine sediments, and banking up against the lava cliff is probably sufficient to account for it. There is in any case no faulting observable in the beds and the development of a gravelly facies in the immediate neighbourhood of the scarp sugggests that the latter was already in existence in Gamblian times.

A small pit, sunk near the foot of the lava cliff in order to determine the section there, went through two feet of white silts, presumably of Makalian date, and then struck a gravel, followed by yellowish stratified silts. The gravel yielded some very fine implements of Kenya Stillbay type, thus confirming the association of this culture with the latest Gamblian times.

In the immediate neighbourhood of the waterfall by which the Makalia descends the lava scarp, the Makalian contains some thickness of re-deposited tuffaceous material.

The succession of beds above the scarp differs from that below in that the Makalian lake rose above the scarp for a short time only; and the ash, which is subaqueous at

Terraced Cliff, was here deposited on a land surface. A generalised succession is as follows:

Makalian silts.
Ash and tuffs.
Red Bed.
Silts, gravelly towards the top, diatomaceous in the lower levels.

The Makalian silts occur in very few places, and are there seen to be banked up against the ash. This latter forms in places a little cliff, which often has a small gravel deposit at its foot, and was probably formed during the maximum of the Makalian lake, as no Makalian deposits are known above its level.

The most important Makalian site is that known as "Bromhead's Site". This occurs a short distance down stream from a small waterfall, caused by the cutting of the river through the relatively hard ash. Here, banked against the ash, were a thin series of fine, well-bedded silts, almost certainly of lacustrine origin. These covered a human burial site, from which Leakey obtained several human skeletons, implements and pottery of the "Elmenteitan" culture. The skeletons undoubtedly belong to the species *Homo sapiens*, but have markedly primitive characters and are non-negroid.

The Makalian ash is very variable in thickness; it varies from some 20 feet near the river to nothing on the higher ground. It shows no sign of stratification; but the upper layers are usually finer textured than those below. It rests on an extremely uneven surface, plainly one with a topography generally similar to that of to-day; it would seem that it must have been concentrated in the valleys chiefly as the result of wind action, perhaps aided by occasional storms; this hypothesis alone serves to account for its peculiar distribution.

It possesses the peculiar quality of hardening when exposed to normal weathering, particularly under moist conditions; and as it is easily dressed when fresh, it is much used locally for building purposes.

The "Red Bed" is a soil of brilliant red colour, generally about 6 inches in thickness. It occurs only on the high ground, and is everywhere overlain by ash. It has yielded a peculiar series of implements, comprising Kenya Stillbay types together with rather crudely made Aurignacian ones; Leakey inclines to regard it as a variation of the Kenya Stillbay. This red bed represents the arid period at the close of the Gamblian.

The Upper Gamblian deposits are entirely similar to those below the lava scarp. Unfortunately, where super-position by the "Red Bed" can definitely be proved, they have yielded no good implements; but gravels in this neighbourhood, which correspond to them both in lithology and position, have yielded some late Mousterian forms.

The presence of Lower Gamblian beds is somewhat problematical, and Kamasian deposits are doubtfully represented in Pit No. 1. If this latter identification is correct, we have distinct evidence of desiccation between the Kamasian and Gamblian periods.

APPENDIX A

HISTORY OF THE MAKALIA VALLEY

There is nothing to suggest that the history of that part of the Makalia Valley below the waterfall differs from that of the Enderit, except that rough mapping shows that the base of the Makalian deposits dips slightly towards the present river.

The upper part of the valley is, however, probably somewhat older; the reasons for this statement may be given as follows:

(i) About $1\frac{1}{2}$ miles to the west of the waterfall referred to above, which has not cut back to any marked extent, the river flows over a higher scarp, into which it has cut a considerable gorge.

(ii) The distribution of the Makalian ash demonstrates that the valley was in existence in pre-Makalian times.

The sequence of events would seem to have been as follows:

(1) Deposition of Kamasian beds and formation of faults.

(2) Rise of Gamblian lake as far as the foot of the higher (western) scarp; during this period the upper gorge was being cut, while the lower scarp was well beneath lake level.

(3) Fall of Gamblian lake, resulting in gravelly facies of latest Gamblian deposits, formed near the Gamblian shore line.

(4) Period of desiccation, during which the Gamblian beds were reddened and the 'Red Bed' formed.

(5) Period of valley cutting, during which the Red Bed and underlying deposits were cut through and the present valley formed between the two fault scarps.

(6) Eruption of the ash, and its concentration in the valleys on the higher levels. At lower levels it was deposited in the rising waters of the Makalian lake.

(7) Maximum of Makalian lake, some erosion of the ash, deposition of upper Makalian silts and formation of Makalian cliff and beach.

(8) Fall of Makalian lake, with a pause, during which the meander belt below the eastern scarp was formed.

SECTIONS EAST OF LAKE ELMENTEITA

The lake beds in this locality are twice mentioned by Gregory. He says of them (p. 116): "At the Kariandusi they include diatomites or diatom clays...as the diatoms belong to living species, these clays are apparently of recent age; and that they are a younger series than those of Lake Kamasia is further indicated by their position, since they are faulted against the Elmenteita quartz-trachyte".

The force of this latter argument is hard to see; for even if the quartz-trachyte is subsequent to the Kamasia series, which is by no means proven, the fact that the lake beds are faulted against it merely proves that the faulting, and not the deposits, is post-Kamasian in date.

Elsewhere (p. 200) he says: "In the basin of Lake Elmenteita is a thick series of

255

lake deposits which appear to be of two ages; some are quite modern, but some of the older, as around Soit Sambu and east of Lake Elmenteita, may belong to the Nyasan (Kamasian) series". The present writer's observations agree entirely with the latter statement of Professor Gregory.

The sequence at the Kariandusi River is as follows:

Gamblian

(6) Grey silts, with intercalated ferruginous gravels, particularly near the base; these chiefly occur in valleys cut in the older deposits, and contain unrolled implements of Aurignacian types; a few rolled and rather crude Mousterian flakes have been recovered from the basal gravel.

Kamasian

(5) Fine stratified tuffs, with a little intercalated sandy material.

(4) Tuffaceous gravel, with abundant lower Palaeolithic implements in obsidian and other lava, both rolled and unrolled. Thickness variable, but of the order of 10 feet near the river.

(3) Diatomite, 6 feet.

(2) Stratified tuffs, total thickness not exposed, but probably more than 100 feet.

(1) Lava.

The Kamasian deposits are here affected by a fault with a throw of more than 100 feet; the fault which affects them belongs to the series which forms the Gilgil Escarpment, which has separated the lake basins of Naivasha and Nakuru. The relations of the beds are best shown diagrammatically. (See Fig. 47.)

The implements from the Kamasian deposits have been described by Leakey in Chapter v.

When traced southwards the diatomite and gravel disappear after a mile and a half; but the lower series of tuffs (in which ripple-marks may be seen a mile to the south of Cole's farm) occurs at the top of the Gilgil Escarpment, where it is faulted against the lavas; the fault is well seen in the shallow railway-cutting between the level-crossing near mile 408 on the Uganda Railway and Gilgil Station.

At the Kariandusi itself, however, the diatomite and gravel are perfectly conformable with the underlying tuffs, and there is no doubt that there has been no break in the deposition of the beds. It would seem that they were laid down in that remnant of the Kamasian lake which was left subsequent to the second great epoch of faulting.

The sudden incoming of detrital material of other than pyroclastic origin is probably due to the initiation of the Kariandusi River by faulting; for the gravel only occurs in the neighbourhood of the river, the source of which is probably plutonic, as it consists of warm springs which are not noticeably affected by changes of rainfall. These rise at a point on the line of the principal fault of the Gilgil Escarpment; and this also points to the latter feature having been formed at about this time.

Patches of Gamblian deposits occur to the south of the Kariandusi River, and their

APPENDIX A

final disappearance, at the Gilgil Scarp, coincides with a lake-beach and terrace the level of which corresponds well with that of Gamble's Cave and elsewhere.

To the south-west of Lake Elmenteita the older tuffs are overlain by the basalt flows mentioned by Gregory, while these in turn are overlain by later sediments which have, however, yielded no implements.

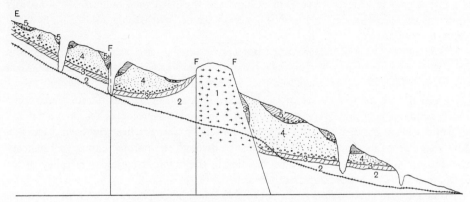

Fig. 47. Diagrammatic section from the road bridge over the Kariandusi River to the Eastern shore of Lake Elmenteita.

Approximate scale: Horizontally 3 in. = 1 mile.
Vertically 1 in. = 200 ft.

5 = Gamblian gravels and silts.	F = Fault.
4 = Upper Kamasian gravels, volcanic sands and tuffs.	E = Level of river bed.
3 = Diatomite.	
2 = Lower Kamasian volcanic sands and tuffs.	
1 = Lava.	

SECTION AT THE MERORONI RIVER

An exposure of lacustrine beds occurs at the spot where the Gilgil-Nakuru road crosses the Meroroni River, a few miles to the north-east of Lake Elmenteita. The sequence is:

Makalian

(3) Makalian ash, up to 6 feet in thickness.

Gamblian

(2) Ferruginous gravels, some 10 feet thick.

(1) Diatomaceous silts, base not exposed.

The gravels yielded implements of types characteristic of the fourth occupation level in Gamble's Cave, and are therefore referred to the Upper Gamblian.

NAKURU NEIGHBOURHOOD

There are no river-sections here, and the lacustrine deposits are all covered by a thick layer of tuff and agglomerate; a "Red Bed" beneath this deposit has, however, yielded a few implements of similar type to those of the "Red Bed" at Elmenteita.

257

APPENDIX A

NAIVASHA BASIN

This basin includes the lake of the same name; it is bounded to the north by Eburru and the Gilgil Escarpment mentioned above, to the east by the Kinangop faults, to the south by the extinct volcano of Longonot and the ridge of high ground on which it stands, and on the west by the Mau range.

The lake is fed by two rivers, the Gilgil and the Malewa (sometimes erroneously known as the Morendat). It is practically fresh water, is drinkable, and contains a fish and molluscan fauna.

The rivers enter the lake near the northern end; they are permanent streams, and draw their supplies from the Laikipia ridge and the Kinangop plateau and Aberdare mountain, which lie to the north and east of the basin.

From the freshwater character of the lake, it would seem that it must have some outlet, but none is visible. Its depth does not in most places exceed 34 feet, but a "hole" 60 feet deep is known. The 500 feet crater quoted by Gregory has now been disproved. The water probably finds its outlet by seepage through the porous Kamasian beds; this may account for the presence of a water-table in the lower lying and arid valley of the Kedong, which lies immediately to the south.

The Naivasha basin differs from that of Nakuru in having had an outlet, the Njorowa Gorge, which has been amply described by Gregory[1]. The top of the gorge stands at a slightly lower level than the watershed at the northern end of the basin; and as the evidence of the lake-beaches in the basin seems to preclude the possibility of much tilting, it would seem that no overflow can have taken place at the latter spot, and that Nilsson's conclusions on the subject are ill-founded.

TERRACES IN THE NAIVASHA BASIN

No caves have yet been excavated in this area, and the most important sections are those shown in the gorge of the Malewa, which has cut through a thickness of some 150 feet of lake deposits in its lower course.

Three terraces can be clearly distinguished; the two higher ones are lake terraces with river terraces grading into them when traced upstream, while the third is a river terrace some 40 feet above present river level and grades into a corresponding flat plain. The age of the two higher terraces is clearly shown by the fact that each terrace possesses a corresponding series of implementiferous deposits which occur up the level of the terrace but not above it; and as the basin possessed an outflow, there can be no question that the higher terrace is not in every case the earlier.

The highest terrace has been levelled at three widely separated points within the basin, with the following results:

Top of cliff in Njorowa Gorge	6560 ft.
Beach on flat-topped hill by Beale's Farm	6575 ft.
Beach behind Gilgil Hotel	6600 ft. approx.

These figures show a reasonably close approximation, and appear to show a slight southerly tilt, of about 40 feet over a distance of 25 miles.

APPENDIX A

The figures for the lower lake terraces are:

Present entrance to Njorowa Gorge	6375 ft. mean*.
Terrace and beach at foot of cliff, east of Nairobi Road	6380 ft. approx.
Terrace inside Njorowa Gorge	6380 ft.
Beach on Sikukuu Road near Naivasha	6386 ft.
Terrace at foot of hill on Beale's Farm	6400 ft. approx.

These figures again show evidence of a slight southerly tilting, of similar magnitude to that shown by the upper terrace.

The presence of a terrace inside the Njorowa Gorge indicates that the watershed at that time must have been somewhat south of the present entrance to the gorge. It is clear that the gorge was cut at the time of formation of the highest terrace; and this latter, as demonstrated below, belongs to the Lower Gamblian period.

Now the gorge itself cuts through Kamasian deposits; it follows therefore that there was no pluvial period of major magnitude between Kamasian and Gamblian times; a result which will be subsequently referred to.

The height of the lake at present is 6203 feet above sea level; it has been subject to fluctuations of level of some 10 to 20 feet within the last twenty years. The two main terraces are thus at heights of approximately 380 and 180 feet above present lake level.

SECTION OF THE MALEWA GORGE

It is impossible to describe this section in great detail owing to its length and the rapid lateral variation of many of the beds. Kamasian and Gamblian beds are exposed, and a generalised sequence is as follows:

Upper Gamblian

(3) Gravels and silts, with much re-deposited tuffaceous material and, in places, a thin band of almost pure diatomite near the base. Up to 15 feet.

Lower Gamblian

(2) Large thickness of silts with impersistent gravels, especially near the top of the series; the gravels are often cemented together with ferruginous material, and have yielded a large fauna and many implements; but no sub-division of the series is possible by means of the gravel bands, as no single band can be traced for more than about half a mile. Thickness probably up to some 200 feet, but the whole series is nowhere exposed.

Kamasian

(1) Series of well-stratified tuffs, best exposed in the gorge to the north-east of Beale's farm; these have plainly been affected by the faulting which has produced the Kinangop escarpment, and have a westerly dip of some 30°.

The Upper Gamblian deposits, when traced upstream, consist chiefly of ashy muds; these nowhere rise above the level of the lower lake terrace, which is here cut through Lower Gamblian beds.

* The gorge has two entrances, which differ slightly in level.

APPENDIX A

From the Upper Gamblian deposits a large series of upper Mousterian and Aurignacian implements has been recovered, which serve to determine its horizon with respect to the sequence in the Nakuru basin. A fairly considerable fauna has also been recovered, and it may be mentioned that the fossil buffalo obtained by Nilsson[2] in this area came out of late Gamblian river muds.

The obviously ashy character of the Upper Gamblian beds is in marked contrast to that of the lower series.

The unconformity between the Upper and Lower Gamblian deposits is in places very marked indeed, at one site a half mile north-east of the Government Farm a channel 50 feet deep has been cut through the Lower Gamblian and filled up with the ashy deposits of the later series. This would seem necessarily to imply a retreat and re-advance of the lake. In places, however, the unconformity is difficult to detect; it would appear that conditions of erosion must somewhat have resembled those of to-day, namely, the local cutting of steep-sided channels through the soft lake deposits, without much general erosion on the plains.

The Lower Gamblian deposits have yielded implements of early Mousterian and early Aurignacian type; this association occurs down to the lowest levels examined, although the Mousterian industry predominates. The specimens of both types are often much rolled, and it seems impossible to doubt that the men who made them were living side by side in the district. No lower Palaeolithic implements have been found in the Gamblian deposits.

None of the Gamblian deposits have been faulted, and all are horizontal except for slight local variations due to false bedding, etc. The Lower Gamblian beds become increasingly gravelly when traced upstream.

The Kamasian beds are yellow in colour and mostly rather fine textured. They harden on exposure to moist weathering. Their relations here are somewhat obscure, but there is little doubt that they belong to the series which underlies most of the Kinangop plateau to the east, and which is so well exposed in the higher portions of the Malewa gorge.

HISTORY OF THE MALEWA RIVER

The Malewa rises in the Aberdare range; the tributaries flow westwards from the fault-scarp, and then turn northward, and pursue their course in shallow valleys cut into the Kinangop plateau. At a point close to the swampy lake of Ol Bolossat the river turns abruptly eastward for a short distance, and then falls into a gorge and takes a southerly course, which it preserves until it emerges from the high ground on to the lake-flats of Naivasha. Its tributaries behave in a very similar manner, and it would seem that the northerly flowing streams, which originally must have reached the Uaso Nyiro, have been captured by the Malewa, which has been more active owing to its lower base-level.

The rejuvenation which has produced the gorges is plainly of comparatively recent date; for it has not had time to affect the whole of the ancient drainage system, in spite of the soft strata (Kamasian ashes, tuffs and gravels) through which the streams are cutting. Further, the Lower Gamblian terrace is not traceable for more than about five miles north of Beale's farm, Naivasha, although to-day a rise of the lake to the height of the terrace would result in a much greater drowning of the valley. It follows, then, that much of the post-rejuvenation erosion is of Gamblian and post-Gamblian date. Now it is clear that the steeper gradient of the Malewa is due entirely to the formation of the Kinangop faults; these are therefore not much earlier than the Gamblian pluvial.

LITTLE GILGIL RIVER SITE

This site is mentioned by Gregory as yielding obsidian implements, which were thought to be Neolithic. A thickness of some 30 feet of deposits is exposed a little to the west of the spot where the Naivasha-Gilgil road crosses the Little Gilgil river.

The deposits consist of diatomaceous silts inter-bedded with several impersistent bands of unstratified stony sand with rootlets. These latter have yielded implements of late Mousterian and Aurignacian type, and are therefore referable to an Upper Gamblian horizon. They probably represent old soils formed near to the shore of the lake during its temporary oscillations.

KAMASIAN DEPOSITS OF OLEONDO, ETC.

Near Oleondo station on the Thomson's Falls branch line, some 10 miles north of Gilgil, there occur some good exposures of the Kamasian deposits. These here consist chiefly of water-stratified ashes and tuffs, considerably disturbed by minor faults, and with intercalations of sandy and gravelly beds. Near the base they are markedly cherty, and contain silicified wood, thin bands of white lateritic deposit and some Manganese ore which is probably also of lateritic origin.

The topmost part of the series consists of thick-bedded tuffs which are apparently not of sub-aqueous origin.

Unfortunately, when these beds were examined, the writer had not seen any reason to doubt their Miocene date; and therefore he did not search the gravels for implements; some chert flakes recovered from the immediate neighbourhood may, however, be derived from these beds.

MISCELLANEOUS AREAS

MOUNT KENYA

Investigation of the ancient moraines of the mountain was unfortunately impracticable owing to the rains, and only a few scattered observations have been collected in this area.

The area is essentially one of young rivers, which are actively cutting down vertically, not only through lava beds, but also, as near Fort Hall and Tumu-Tumu, where they are flowing over crystalline schists. As the present is by no means a period of large rainfall for this climatic zone, it follows that this rejuvenation is due to an uplift with respect to the base level of the river systems, *i.e.* to sea level.

A certain amount of aggradation has taken place round the foot of the mountain in the Nanyuki region. Since the rivers here are far from being graded, it follows that this aggradation is the result of overload. This in turn seems to be due to one of two causes.

(i) An excess of hardly transportable coarse gravel in the immediate vicinity of the mountain, which is brought down the valleys in time of flood.

(ii) Diminution in the volume of the streams due to decrease of rainfall and probably accompanied by an increase in wind-borne material.

In the valleys of the Liki and Nanyuki rivers there is exposed the following section:

(7) Unstratified red sand and loam with few stones.
(6) Yellow sand with some stones.
(5) Unstratified thin red sand and loam.
(4) Thin gravel and false-bedded sand (up to 3 feet).
(3) Unstratified red sands and loam.
(2) False-bedded sands.
(1) Coarse, very rolled gravel, more than 20 feet thick.

The unconformities shown are not large; the upper one, indeed, is more in the nature of a surface of weathering; but both can be followed for considerable distances.

It would appear that there is evidence here for three periods during which floods occurred, following each of which was a period of comparative aridity. This sequence only represents the immediate neighbourhood of Nanyuki; higher up the course of the rivers it is to be expected that the gravels would thicken and the sands thin out; it might, indeed, be possible to trace the gravels into the corresponding moraines which are known to occur on the mountain.

Only one Palaeolithic culture has been discovered here as yet; examples of it occur in the sands, and none have yet been discovered in the gravel. The industry has been provisionally named Nanyukian. It consists of well-made coups-de-poing associated with flakes and side scrapers. On grounds of typology it would be referred to the period between the Kamasian and the Lower Gamblian. This industry is not known to exist anywhere within the Rift Valley; and it seems likely that during the period following the Kamasian (which, since the Rift Valley lakes were low, was presumably one of aridity) man left the dry and inhospitable valley in search of better hunting grounds, such as would be found near Mount Kenya. This latter district, on the other hand, would be cold and ill-stocked with game during a pluvial period, and this would explain why none of the exact equivalents of the industries known in the Rift Valley have been discovered in the highlands on either side.

CORRELATION

Mr Hopwood* has made a preliminary investigation of the mammalian fauna obtained from the Gamblian deposits at Naivasha and Elmenteita, and says that few, if any, of the species represented are extinct, and that the fauna is definitely later in date than that of Kaiso, Oldoway, which are considered as early to middle Pleistocene.[3]†

* See also Appendix C.
† Most of the fossils come from the Upper Gamblian. (L.S.B.L.)

APPENDIX A

The Gamblian pluvial therefore falls within late Pleistocene times; and it would seem that the Kamasian must be equated with the Sangoan terrace of Lake Victoria, the Kaiso bone beds at Lake Albert,[4] the Chiwondo bed[5] in Nyasaland and the lake beds of Oldoway.[6]

It would seem fairly certain that a period of aridity occurred between the Kamasian and the Gamblian; for the bone beds of Kaiso contain in themselves evidence of contemporary desiccation, if Wayland's interpretation is correct. The Gypsum bed of Homa[7] and the aggradation of the valleys near Mount Kenya point to a similar conclusion.

We thus seem to have the following succession of events in East Africa during the Pleistocene:

(i) Wet period, during which the peneplaination of Uganda was completed, and which coincided with the epoch of the man who made pebble-tools (Kafuan).

(ii) (?) Dry period. (There are no data covering this inter-pluvial gap.)

(iii) Wet period (Kamasian). This was a period of great sedimentation within the Rift Valley, and we have the Kaiso, Kamasian, Oldoway, Omo and Chiwondo beds which probably all belong to this horizon. These are contemporaneous with lower Palaeolithic man as represented by Wayland's Sangoan and our Kenya Chellean and Acheulean tools, but *Homo sapiens* (as represented by Reck's specimen from Oldoway) was already in existence, if Reck's interpretation and not Leakey's (see Chapter II) is correct.

(iv) Dry period, during which we have a culture of transitional type. Partly contemporaneous with this was a period of considerable earth movement, resulting in the faulting of the Kamasia, Oldoway and Chiwondo deposits, and in the cutting of the outlets of the lakes Victoria and Albert, etc.

(v) Wet period (Gamblian), unrepresented in the Victoria and Albert basins owing to the presence of an outlet; also apparently absent from Oldoway, probably for the same reason. This period may be represented in Nyasaland by the Chitimwe beds, but as no implements have been obtained from the latter, this must remain uncertain. The cultures include Kenya Aurignacian and Kenya Mousterian, contemporaneous in this area.*

(vi) Dry period, lasting to the present day, but broken by two minor wet phases (Makalian and Nakuran). There are indications that the climate is not now at a maximum of aridity, but it is impossible to say whether it is proceeding towards or away from that maximum. The cultures are mostly degenerate upper Palaeolithic, sometimes with Mousteroid influences.

* An explanation is here necessary if the correlations are to be understood. Wayland regards his Sangoan apparently as "Essentially le Moustier in facies and locally characterised by large coups-de-poing (*sic*) and picks" (*Report of Geological Survey of Uganda* 1927, p. 34). We regard his Sangoan rather as partly local Chellean and partly local Acheulean with possibly a hint of Levalloisean. Mr Wayland's Sangoan compares culturally rather with our Kenya Chellean and Kenya Acheulean, and is quite distinct from our Kenya Mousterian, and therefore deposits which contain Sangoan tools (unless the latter are derived fossils) must be equated with our Kamasian pluvial.

APPENDIX A

Little is known about the Pleistocene history of South Africa; but the work recently done by Mr C. van Riet Lowe[8] is of the utmost importance. He has studied the terraces of the Vaal River, and finds the following state of affairs.

(i) High terrace, with coarse gravel containing what may be a pebble-culture.

(ii) Middle terrace, also with coarse gravel, and an early Chellean culture (Stellenbosch A).

(iii) Low terrace, approximately at present river level, with coarse basal gravel containing advanced Acheulean types (Stellenbosch B and C); this is overlain by a firm gravel, with Fauresmith (Micoque) implements, and this in turn by sands. On the surface, overlying the sands, occur factory sites of the Smithfield culture.

The lowest terrace gravel has yielded a fauna which includes several primitive forms of elephant, and is plainly of Pleistocene date.

These terraces, with the exception of the highest, do not extend laterally to any great distance from the river; they are not, in fact, well marked as topographical features and therefore do not appear to correspond to a marked pause in valley cutting. But the coarseness of the gravels bespeaks a very strongly flowing river, in view of the flatness of the country. The deposition of the gravels must therefore have coincided with very wet conditions. There is no evidence to show whether, between these pluvial periods, there were conditions of aridity. On the other hand, after the formation of the lowest terrace gravel the river seems to have silted up; this implies conditions more arid than at present, for it is now degrading its bed.

It is tempting to correlate the two upper terraces with the Kafuan and Kamasian wet periods of East Africa, and the lowest with the Gamblian period. This would imply that each successive culture either arrived or persisted later in South Africa than in East Africa. This is by no means unreasonable, considering that the former area is essentially a cul-de-sac.

In Rhodesia the writer has observed distinct evidence of climatic change in Palaeolithic times. In the neighbourhood of Bulawayo there have been three distinct periods of valley aggradation by fine-grained material; that is to say, under arid conditions, since the rivers are now degrading their bed, and aggradation can only be ascribed to overload.

These dry periods were separated by periods of valley cutting, *i.e.* of relative wetness. This process is now proceeding, but somewhat slowly.

The second arid period is associated with a Mousterian type of industry; at the Chelmer Spruit near Bulawayo were found implements and a fauna which included some extinct forms (*e.g. Equus Capensis*) at the base of a red alluvium which must be attributed to this period.

This has also been confirmed by Mr L. Armstrong in the neighbourhood of Bambata cave in the Matopos. He has, in addition, found implements of Wilton (Tardenoisian) type in the most recent of the alluvia there. The sequence here would seem to fit those to the north and south if the first arid period be considered pre-Gamblian and the second post-Gamblian in date; the third is in any case subordinate in magnitude, but may correspond to the post-Makalian dry period of Kenya.

COMPARISON WITH EGYPT

It is generally agreed that the present aridity of the Sahara did not set in until post-Mousterian times; and the terraces of the Nile point to a similar conclusion. But there is considerable difference of opinion as to whether the climate was uniformly moist throughout early Pleistocene times; Miss Gardner[9] considers that it was not, while Sandford and Arkell[10] think that it was.

It is not the writer's intention to enter into this dispute; but he would point out that the statement by Sandford and Arkell, that the degradation of the Nile Valley and the formation of terraces therein seem to be "equally Pluvial in character" needs amplification, unless explained simply by changes of sea level. Miss Gardner has already pointed out that the climatic changes postulated by her fit very well with those found in East Africa. It is, however, impossible to postulate anything but moist conditions during the late Chellean and early Acheulean period in this area, in view of the large numbers of implements of these types which have been obtained from the Sahara and the arid regions of Somaliland, and in consideration also of the coarse gravel terraces of the Nile, some of which are referable to this age.

The period of desiccation would therefore seem to fall in late Acheulean and early Mousterian times, a result which agrees well with those obtained from farther south.

If the "Sangoan" industry of Wayland is considered as a local variant of the lower Palaeolithic similar to the Victoria West industry of South Africa, a reasonable working hypothesis can be drawn up to explain the relation of human migrations to the pluvial and inter-pluvial periods.

In the first place, we have the pebble-culture, probably of long duration and widespread, coinciding with a pluvial period during which migration could take place freely.

It is possible that the supervening of a dry period isolated the moist temperate belts from the zone of tropical rainfall, thus giving rise to differentiation in the evolution of the next (pre-Chellean) stage.

A further pluvial occurred in Chellean times, lasting on into the Acheulean, and resulting in the wide distribution of a very uniform industry. But desiccation again took place, with the probable result that very advanced Acheulean types occur only in the northern and southern temperate belts, and probably also in the tropical rainfall zone; the very diverse modifications of the Acheulio-Mousterian cultures may also be due to isolation.

During this dry period it is probable that the Mousterian and Aurignacian cultures were evolving in those regions which were still habitable; on the advent of another pluvial period they spread widely, the Mousterian in most cases preceding the Aurignacian, although the opposite seems to have been the case in Spain[11] and they seem to have arrived almost simultaneously in Kenya.

Subsequent further desiccation resulted in further differentiation of these cultures,

APPENDIX A

until a minor increase in rainfall allowed the spread of the Tardenoisian, which persisted in South Africa until comparatively recent times.

The question of correlation between Africa and Europe is one for the meteorologist, and is being dealt with by Dr C. E. P. Brooks. With his conclusions the present writer is in general agreement; but he would point out that it is possible that the Kamasian has a major sub-division as suggested by Wayland's Kafuan and Sangoan divisions.

REFERENCES

1. *The Rift Valleys and Geology of East Africa*, by Prof. J. W. Gregory, 1923.
2. "Preliminary Report on the Quaternary Geology of Mt Elgon and some parts of the Rift Valley", by E. Nilsson in *Geologiska Föreningens Stockholm Förhandlingar*, March–April, 1929.
3. "Review of the Fossil Mammals of Central Africa", by A. T. Hopwood, in *American Journal of Science*, vol. XVII, February, 1929.
4. E. J. Wayland in *Man*, July, 1929. See also annual reports of the Geological Survey of Uganda, 1924–29, and also *Petroleum in Uganda* and *The Geology and Palaeontology of the Kaiso Bone Beds*, both published by the Uganda Government. An earlier article occurs in the Prehistoric Society of East Anglia's *Proceedings*, 1923.
5. "The Tertiary and Post-Tertiary lacustrine sediments of the Nyasan rift valley", by F. A. Dixey, in *Q.J.G.S.* 1927.
6. "Erste und zweite vorläufige Mitteilungen über den Fund eines fossilen Menschenskelets aus Zentralafrika", by H. Reck, in *Sitzungsberichte der Gesellschaft naturforschender Freunde*, Berlin, 1914, No. 3.
7. "The Miocene beds of Karungu, etc.", by F. Oswald, in *Q.J.G.S.* 1914.
8. "The Archaeology of Sheppard Island", by C. van Riet Lowe, in *British Association Report*, Section H, 1929 (Johannesburg).
9. "The Origin of the Faiyum Depression", by Miss E. W. Gardner, in *Geographical Journal*, vol. LXXIV, No. 4, October 1929.
10. K. S. Sandford and W. J. Arkell in *Nature*, April, 1928, p. 670; *Man*, April, 1929; *Q.J.G.S.* January, 1930, and discussion.
11. *Études sur le Terrain Quaternaire de la Vallée du Manzanares*, by J. P. de Barradas, Madrid, 1926.
    Reallexikon der Vorgeschichte, by H. Obermaier. Section dealing with the Iberian Peninsula (Pyrenäenhalbinsel).

THE CORRELATION OF PLUVIAL PERIODS IN AFRICA WITH CLIMATIC CHANGES IN EUROPE

By C. E. P. BROOKS, D.Sc., F.R.Met.Soc.

IT is now generally agreed that the "Pluvial Age" which occurred at the end of the geological record in low and middle latitudes in all continents was of Pleistocene date, and to that extent roughly synchronous with the "Ice Age" of higher latitudes. One can go further; pluvial and glacial phenomena are typically developed in different regions, but in the few cases in which a direct connection can be traced the heaviest rainfall is found to coincide with the greatest development of ice. Thus in western U.S.A. the greatest extension of the Sierra Nevada glacier ended in old Lake Mono when the latter also attained its maximum area. In Egypt a succession of dry and pluvial periods has been demonstrated, the later members of which can be correlated on archaeological grounds with the closing stages, from Würm II onwards, of the glaciation of Europe, and here again glaciation coincides with pluviation.

Theoretical considerations also lead us to expect a parallelism between glacial and pluvial periods. Both the North American and the European sides of the Atlantic Ocean were heavily glaciated by ice which underwent four main cycles of advance and retreat. In the Alps Penck and Brückner have named these cycles the Günz, Mindel, Riss and Würm periods. The inter-glacial periods between the Günz and Mindel, and between the Riss and Würm, were relatively short; that between the Mindel and Riss was much longer. The Antarctic and the southern part of South America were also far more heavily glaciated than at present, and traces of ice-sheets or glaciers have been found in Africa, New Zealand and many parts of Asia. Although the glacial deposits in the two hemispheres cannot be directly correlated, it is highly probable that the major advances and retreats of the ice were synchronous all over the world.

In addition to the extensive sheets of land ice there were great icefields in higher latitudes in both the North and South Atlantic, and probably to a less extent in the other oceans. On the other hand the marine fauna of the equatorial shores shows very little trace of a cold period, and the increased glaciation on high equatorial mountains was probably due mainly to increased precipitation above the snow-line. There can be no doubt that the gradient of temperature between low latitudes on the one hand, and middle to high latitudes on the other hand, was greater than at present, and this must inevitably have caused an increased flow of air into the equatorial belt of low pressure and hence an increased rainfall over the equatorial parts of the continents. This line of argument leads directly to a correlation between glacial and pluvial periods.

The most recent theory of the cause of Ice Ages is that developed by Dr C. G.

APPENDIX B

Simpson,* which finds the initial cause in cycles of solar radiation. High radiation is associated with high temperature and heavy precipitation; the latter in turn causes increased snowfall on the mountains and hence glaciation, but at the crest of the radiation and precipitation cycle the temperature becomes so high that snow is replaced by rain and an inter-glacial results. In the lower part of the radiation cycle the precipitation is too scanty for glaciation. Thus we have the following scheme:

> Würm glaciation.
> Warm rainy inter-glacial.
> Riss glaciation.
>
> Cold dry inter-glacial.
>
> Mindel glaciation.
> Warm rainy inter-glacial.
> Günz glaciation.

Dr Simpson's theory gives two pluvial periods centred on the first and third inter-glacials. On the other hand the secondary effect on the circulation of the globe which I have outlined above would give a pluvial period to each glaciation. From the combined action of these two factors we should expect a pluvial period to begin in the Günz glacial and to continue through the Günz-Mindel inter-glacial to the Mindel glacial. Then would follow a long dry period during the Mindel-Riss inter-glacial, followed by a second pluvial covering the Riss glacial, Riss-Würm inter-glacial and Würm glacial. If, as I think probable, the secondary effect on equatorial rainfall due to the presence of the ice-sheets was rather stronger than the primary effect due to the radiation cycle, each pluvial period would be interrupted by one period of slightly decreased rainfall in East Africa, either synchronous with the warm rainy inter-glacial or lagging somewhat behind it. On these grounds we may correlate the pluvial periods in East Africa as follows:

Nakuran pluvial	
Dry period	
Makalian pluvial	Post-glacial
Dry period	
Upper Gamblian pluvial	Würm glacial
Moderately dry period	Riss-Würm inter-glacial
Lower Gamblian pluvial	Riss glacial
Dry period with earth movements	Mindel-Riss inter-glacial (with earth movements)
	Mindel glacial
Kamasian pluvial †	Günz-Mindel inter-glacial
	Günz glacial

The Mindel-Riss inter-glacial was a time of earth movements in many parts of the world, giving increased support to the correlation.

The events of the post-glacial period have to be treated rather differently. The succession in central and north-western Europe shows first a series of moraines marking halts in the recession of the ice-sheets and glaciers, followed by a series of alternating

---

* *Past Climates*, The Alexander Pedler Lecture, London, British Science Guild, 1929.

† The Kamasian pluvial probably has sub-divisions, but these have not yet been worked out in detail. Possibly Wayland's Kafuan pluvial equals the first part of the Kamasian and so equals Günz.

dry and wet periods. Ignoring minor details, we may make out the following general scheme:

Date, B.C.	Climatic period
850– 0	Sub-Atlantic, wet
2,500– 850	Sub-boreal, dry, "Climatic Optimum"
5,500– 2,500	Atlantic, wet
6,500– 5,500	Boreal, dry
8,000– 6,500	Finiglacial retreat of ice and Ragunda pause
10,000– 8,000	Fennoscandian moraines; probably Bühl ice advance
13,000–10,000	Gothiglacial retreat; Achen oscillation

It will be convenient to begin with the latest changes and work backwards. The change from the sub-boreal to the sub-Atlantic period appears to have been in the direction of rainier and stormier conditions in all parts of the world for which information is available, including the north of Africa. It seems reasonable to infer, therefore, that the Nakuran pluvial period was part of the same series of events, and began about 850 B.C.

The sub-boreal dry period is also widely distributed; in Egypt Lake Moeris was completely dry, and the very dry period between the Makalian and Nakuran evidently represents this period, from about 2500 to 850 B.C.

The change from Boreal to Atlantic periods, *i.e.* from dry to wet, in north-west Europe appears to have been more of the nature of a local oscillation of climate due to geographical changes in the Baltic, and to have little relation to changes in other parts of the world. There is, for example, little evidence of a dry boreal period in the west of Ireland, where I think the early post-glacial was mainly wet. On the other hand, there is evidence of a generally cold and stormy period between about 9000 and 6500 B.C. In north-west Europe this is represented by the great Fennoscandian moraines, the Finiglacial ice retreat and the Ragunda moraines. E. Antevs* considers that the Finiglacial retreat was caused by the breaking in of the Atlantic into the Baltic rather than by a general amelioration of climate, and in North America the whole period was probably occupied by a prolonged halt of the ice. In the Alps this period may be represented by the various re-advances of the ice known collectively as the Bühl Stadium. In Egypt Miss G. Caton-Thompson and Miss E. W. Gardner have proved the existence of a high level stage in Lake Moeris and the Nile from about 9000 to 6000 B.C., which reached a maximum about 7500 B.C. Conditions round Lake Moeris did not become really dry until about 3000 B.C. Hence it seems that the Makalian pluvial must have coincided with this generally wet period, commencing about 9000 B.C., reaching a maximum about 7500 B.C., and continuing with decreasing intensity until about 3000 B.C.

The dry period between the Upper Gamblian and Makalian must then represent the drying up of Lake Moeris from 13,000 to 9000 B.C., the Achen oscillation between the Würm glacial and the Bühl re-advance in the Alps, the Gothiglacial retreat in Scandinavia, the corresponding retreat in North America, and especially the period of tundra and steppe climate in central Europe. In fact this period was generally dry everywhere in the Northern Hemisphere for which we have data.

* *The Last Glaciation*, American Geogr. Soc. Research Series, No. 17, New York, 1928.

APPENDIX B

The correlation of the whole East African series may therefore be set out with a high degree of probability as follows:

East Africa	Europe	Date, B.C.
Nakuran pluvial	Sub-Atlantic	850– 0
Dry period	Sub-boreal	2500–850
Makalian pluvial	Atlantic Boreal Ragunda pause } Bühl Finiglacial retreat Fennoscandian halt	10,000–2500
Dry period	Gothiglacial retreat Achen oscillation	
Upper Gamblian	Würm glacial	
Lower Gamblian	Riss glacial	
Dry period	Mindel-Riss inter-glacial	
Kamasian pluvial	Mindel glacial Günz glacial	

PRELIMINARY REPORT ON THE FOSSIL MAMMALIA

BY A. TINDELL HOPWOOD, M.Sc., F.L.S.

(Published by permission of the Trustees of the British Museum)

IN the following report I have dealt mainly with the larger mammals, the rodents and insectivores are reserved for future consideration. There are two reasons for this: first, the obvious one of greater rapidity of working with material which does not need microscopic examination, and secondly, that, despite the volume of literature published on the microfauna of Central Africa, there is so much yet to be done that it is undesirable to publish results derived from fossils contained in beds as recent as those examined by Mr Leakey.

All the mammals identified up to the present, with possibly two exceptions, are referable to recent species, and it does not seem likely that any of those yet to be studied will prove to be extinct.

The arrangement of the report needs explanation. I have endeavoured to make it useful to archaeologists and geologists, as well as to zoologists. To this end the localities are arranged according to the age of the deposits, the youngest first, and under each locality is given a list of the animals found there. This should enable the fauna associated with any culture to be ascertained with a minimum of trouble.

(i) LOCALITIES IN MAKALIAN DEPOSITS

BROMHEAD'S SITE, MUNROE'S FARM, ELMENTEITA

Specimens from this site have a fresher appearance than those from other localities. In part, at least, this is due to the absence of charring and other signs of heat.

Phacochoerus africanus Linné. Skull, lacking the left half of the brain-case, and mandible of a very young animal. In the upper jaw the deciduous canine and the first three deciduous cheek-teeth are just entering into wear; in the mandible the first two cheek-teeth of the deciduous series are in wear, and the third is still in the crypt.

Antilope sens. lat. At least four species of antelopes are present.

Bos sp. Part of a left maxilla with M^{2-3} appears to be referable to this genus.

Procavia sp. Remains of hyraces are very frequent; there are over fifty pieces of lower jaws, pieces of more than a dozen skulls, and numerous parts of the skeleton of the trunk and limbs. Four of the skulls and one palate enable the essential characters to be distinguished. Adopting the terminology proposed by Oldfield Thomas (1892, *P.Z.S.* p. 53) one skull is at stage IV, two are at stage VII, and one perfect skull is at stage VIII: the palate is at stage VIII.

271

APPENDIX C

The species is megadont and hypsodont. All the skull sutures are persistent so that none of them is closed, even when the third molar is half worn. In the dentition and structure of the skull there are points of resemblance to *P. mackinderi*, *P. erlangeri* and *P. abyssinica*. For example, the form of the occipital is that of *P. erlangeri*, the paroccipital processes are nearer those of *P. mackinderi*, and the teeth most nearly resemble those of *P. abyssinica*. It is probable that the specimens constitute a new species, but, for the moment, it is preferable to wait for additional material, both fossil and recent, from the same locality.

Papio neumanni Matschie. A badly broken skull of an old male, together with the almost complete lower jaw, raised hopes of learning something about the past history of the baboons in Kenya, but the characters agree so closely with those of specimens obtained by Mr Leakey in the Mau forest that they clearly prove the fossils to belong to *P. neumanni*.

DECKERVILLE SITE, ENDERIT DRIFT

The bones from this locality were obtained in a cutting through the silts at the Enderit River Drift. They are extremely fragmentary, and mostly unidentifiable.

Hippopotamus amphibius Linné. Represented by an astragalus, and the anterior portion of a left mandibular ramus from which all the teeth have been broken off.

Antilope sens. lat. The occipital region and the bones of the right half of the brain-case of a hornless female antelope of medium size.

Elephas (?). Part of a large rib.

MacINNES SITE

In many ways this material is the most satisfactory of all. It was washed into position by flood waters, and any breakages are due to that cause. Hence the specimens are not so fragmentary as those which have been found in the caves, and which have been broken for the sake of the marrow they contained.

Crocuta crocuta (Erxleben). The brain-case wanting most of the roof, together with the associated atlas and axis. This represents a young individual in which the basilar suture is still open.

A canine and third upper incisor probably belong to this species.

Equus quagga sub-sp. Five teeth from either side of the upper jaw agree very well with those in skulls from Ankole, Uganda, which have not been determined. The skulls were obtained by Capt. C. R. S. Pitman and are registered 27.7.3.57 & 58 in the Zoological Department of the British Museum.

? *Bos* sp. There is a moderately hypsodont animal which appears to be some kind of ox. It is a small beast, rather less than the Celtic Short-horn, with the truncated occipital contour which helps to distinguish the oxen from the antelopes. Apparently the females had no horns, and in the males the horns were very small. One maxilla shows a heavy coating (of cement?) on the cheek-teeth, and all the other specimens indicate the former presence of this.

APPENDIX C

At present there is no small race of wild cattle in Africa with hornless cows, and the four species of large antelopes in which the female is hornless differ from this form in almost every respect. It is most important to make an effort to obtain further material, especially the skull of an adult male.

Antilope sens. lat. The palate and part of the face of a small antelope.

Papio neumanni Matschie. The palate and muzzle of a young adult female baboon is probably referable to this species. The differences from the male found on Bromhead's Site are not more than can be accounted for by differences in age and sex.

EUPHORBIA FLATS

Hippopotamus amphibius Linné. The greater part of the skeleton of a large hippopotamus was obtained from this locality.

HIPPOPOTAMUS SITE

As its name implies, this site is noteworthy for the remains of *Hippopotamus amphibius* which were found here. These consisted of the skull of a large adult male, and, some distance away, a lower jaw. The skull was complete when found, but became broken during transportation to the camp. Mr MacInnes has reconstituted it with considerable patience and skill.

The main dimensions are:

Condylo-basal length	650 mm.
Zygomatic breadth	390 ,,
Greatest width across the glenoid fossae	483 ,,
Greatest width across muzzle	400 ,,
Rostral constriction	140 ,,
Length of premolar-molar series ...	270 ,,
Width of palate at rear of M^3 ...	92 ,,
Least width of palate	80 ,,

These measurements are well within the limits of variation of the recent hippopotamus.

(ii) LOCALITIES IN UPPER GAMBLIAN DEPOSITS

Most of the material was obtained from the fourth occupation level in Gamble's Cave, but a certain amount was found in Lion Hill Cave. Apparently the latter was in the possession of an impoverished tribe whose sole means of subsistence was to feed on snails, hyraces, and occasional fish, for the poverty of the fauna is in striking contrast to the richness of that found in Gamble's Cave.

GAMBLE'S CAVE II, FOURTH OCCUPATIONAL LEVEL

From the point of view of the archaeologist this level may be divided into upper and lower parts, but from the geological viewpoint it is all one, and so I have gathered the fauna together as a whole.

Thos adustus (Sundevall). The side-striped jackal is represented by fragments of the upper and lower jaws. It is readily separated from *T. mesomelas* by its upper molars, which are more square and compact than they are in the latter. From the East African forms of *T. aureus* it differs in the shape of M², which is larger relative to M¹ and not so definitely kidney-shaped.

Lycaon pictus (Temminck). An isolated left first upper molar agrees with the same tooth in a skull from Soy, Kenya Colony, which is preserved in the Zoological Department of the British Museum (regd. no. 28.11.6.1).

Lutra maculicollis Lichtenstein. There are several specimens of this animal, and the variation among the different individuals is exactly comparable with that found among the living animals.

Aonyx capensis hindei Thomas. A fragment of a right maxilla with P⁴–M¹ undoubtedly belongs to *A. capensis*. Apart from the fact that the teeth are slightly larger, it agrees with a skull of *A. capensis hindei* from Lake Naivasha (B.M. Zool. Dept. 4.9.29.1).

The fossil differs from the recent specimen in the development of the cusps, which are stouter in the fossil. This is of no significance, for comparison shows that there is considerable individual variation within any sub-species of the Cape otter.

Atilax paludinosus Geoffroy & Cuvier. The water mongoose is represented by a left mandibular ramus lacking the incisors and the last molar.

Felis sp. There are two species of medium-sized cats in the collection, but the fragments are not sufficient to allow of specific identification.

Tachyoryctes sp. The mole rats are represented by numerous specimens of both the upper and lower dentitions.

Pedetes sp. The jumping hare does not appear to be common in the collection.

Hystrix galeatus? A right lower mandibular ramus appears to be referable to this species. The specimen is somewhat smaller than the average of those in the Zoological Department of the British Museum.

Thryonomys swinderianus (Temminck). Common. Both upper and lower dentitions are well represented.

Choeromys sp. The small cane rat is also fairly common.

Lepus sp. There are several species of hares found living in East Africa, and until they have been carefully revised and monographed it is almost impossible to identify the fossils. The commonest fossil form appears to be close to *L. crawshayi*, but there are several points of difference.

Orycteropus aethiopicus Sundevall. The ant bear is represented by a single molar.

Primates. There are two or three species of monkeys as yet unidentified. Apparently the large baboon found in the Makalian deposits has not been seen in the Gamblian up to the present.

Choiropotamus choiropotamus (Desmoulins). Several isolated upper and lower teeth.

Hylochoerus meinerzhageni Thomas. Several isolated teeth and tusks.

Phacochoerus africanus Linné. Part of a third lower molar.

Hippopotamus amphibius Linné. A single unworn lower premolar.

APPENDIX C

Bovidae. There are several species of antelopes represented by teeth and bones. The most useful portions for identification, namely the horn cores, are missing, except for two specimens of *Redunca* sp.

Procavia sp. Hyrax remains are not rare in the deposits, but are not definitely identifiable.

Lion Hill Cave

The remains found in this cave were mainly hyraces. The number of individuals represented was enormous. It is not possible to identify the species as yet, but perhaps another season may produce some skulls so as to allow of comparisons with those found in the Makalian.

The other remains are of small rodents, insectivores, and a monkey.

(iii) Localities with Exposures of Upper and Lower Gamblian Deposits

Most of the bones were unaccompanied by any teeth. They were mainly found in a quartzose ferruginous sand.

Malewa River, Naivasha (= Morendat River)

Hippopotamus amphibius Linné. Numerous limb bones and vertebrae, and some teeth.

Diceros bicornis (Linné). Numerous limb bones and teeth from the upper and lower jaws.

Bovidae. There are two bovines, one of large size.

Conclusions

From the lists given above it will be seen that none of the animals, except perhaps the hyrax and a bovine, is extinct. This indicates that these deposits are far younger than those at Kaiso and Oldoway, and that they are upper Pleistocene, or possibly later. Until fossils are found in the Kamasian, I do not propose to make any wider correlation.

NOTE: Other tentative correlation based upon climatic considerations as well as on the Archaeology is that the Upper Gamblian is the equivalent of the Würm glaciation, and that the Makalian phase is the equivalent of the Bühl stadium. This would seem to fit in with Mr Hopwood's conclusions based upon the fauna. It is very regrettable that the Lower Gamblian fauna found last season was very sparse, and that none was found in the Kamasian deposits. I am not at all certain that Oldoway will not turn out to be the equivalent of Lower Gamblian. (L.S.B.L., Jan. 1931.)

THE MOLLUSCA FROM DEPOSITS OF GAMBLIAN PLUVIAL DATE, KENYA COLONY

By M. CONNOLLY

I APPEND nominal lists, in so far as approximate identification has been possible, of the mollusca collected by Leakey in the above-mentioned deposits; a query denotes that the specimens are too weathered or fragmentary to admit of exact determination.

A. From the beach gravel at 510 feet above present lake level in Gamble's Cave II = maximum of the Upper Gamblian pluvial.

    (i) *Lymnaea elmeteitensis* ? Smith, rare.

    (ii) *Bulinus* sp., fragments.

    (iii) *Melanoides tuberculata* (Müll.), very abundant.

    (iv) *Corbicula africana* (Krs.) (= *radiata* Phil., pre-oc.).

B. From "fourth occupation level" immediately over the beach gravel in Gamble's Cave II = Elmenteita.

    (v) *Planorbis nairobiensis* Dautz.

    (vi) *Segmentina planodiscus* ? (M. & P.).

The single example collected agrees in form with that of this Natal species, which has recently been found in Albert Nyanza, but the shell is too calcined to show presence of septa; it has not been recorded hitherto from Kenya Colony.

    (vii) *Bulinus* sp.

    (viii) *Melanoides tuberculata* (Müll.).

    (ix) *Mutela bourguignati* Ancey, fragmentary.

    (x) *Aspatharia* sp., fragmentary.

    (xi) *Halolimnohelix bukobae* (Mts.), juv.

    (xii) *Cerastus lagariensis* (Smith).

    (xiii) *Homorus* sp., indet.

    (xiv) *Homorus* sp., fragmentary.

    (xv) *Subuliniscus adjacens* ? Conn.

    (xvi) *Opeas aphantum* Conn.

    (xvii) *O. psephenum* Conn.

    (xviii) *O. tangaense* d'Ailly.

A race apparently inseparable from this little-known species has lately been collected in recent condition at Naivasha, so its occurrence at Elmenteita is not remarkable; Leakey's singleton agrees exactly with the Nairobi form, which, until better examples come to hand, I would not venture to identify as other than d'Ailly's species.

APPENDIX D

C. From upper levels of the "fourth occupation level" in Gamble's Cave II = Elmenteita.

(xix) *Bulinus syngenes* ? (Preston).

(xx) *Halolimnohelix bukobae* (Mts.), juv.

(xxi) *Cerastus lagariensis* (Smith).

(xxii) *Subuliniscus adjacens* ? Conn.

(xxiii) *Subulina* sp.　　　(xxiv) = (xiv).　　　(xxv) *Opeas aphantum* Conn.

D. From Lion Hill Cave in deposits above a beach gravel 620 feet above present lake level, which equals a rest level of the first maximum of the Gamblian pluvial; the deposits are probably of Upper Gamblian maximum date.

(xxvi) *Melanoides tuberculata* (Müll.).

(xxvii) *Gulella ugandensis* (Smith) (= *optata* Preston).

(xxviii) *Marconia elgonensis* (Preston).

(xxix) *Limicolaria flammea* ? (Müll.).

This race occurred in large quantity, but all are now in such faded condition as only to show the well-known terra-cotta flames on a white ground, which are characteristic of bleached Limicolariidae, and it is safest to assign to them the oldest applicable name, which is that given by Müller; the shells accord well with others of this widely distributed species. It might have been considered probable that the aborigines used to collect these large snails for eating purposes, as they do even now, but some of those from the above locality were full of eggs, which militates against this theory, and it is equally probable, as in the case of the other terrestrial molluscs collected, that they merely crawled into it by force of circumstance or for purpose of aestivation.

E. From lake silts and muds at Enderit Drift, Elmenteita, period of the Makalian wet phase.

(xxx) *Helicarion ugandensis*? Thiele.

A single shell with smooth, rather prominent apex, probably belongs to this species, which belies its name by having been described from the Mau Escarpment and not Uganda, but it is too badly broken to admit of exact identification.

(xxxi) *Cerastus lagariensis* (Smith).

(xxxii) *Limicolaria martensiana* (Smith).

(xxxiii) *Homorus margaretae*? Conn.

Here again, the examples are too weathered and damaged for exact identification, but I would not venture to separate them from *margaretae*, while the presence of two eggs, less than 4 mm. in length, supports this view, as the small eggs are a feature of this species.

All the species named above are still found living in East Africa, and the distribution of some is more or less widespread. They serve no useful purpose for determining the approximate date of the deposits, since some are of extreme antiquity, *M. tuberculata* and *C. africana*, for instance, dating back to the Pliocene;* the presence or absence of the *aquatic* mollusca, however, may be instructive as a rough guide to the point at which Lake Nakuru attained its highest level, and provide some evidence relative to its periods of desiccation.

* *Journal of Conchology*, vol. XVIII, 1928, p. 207.

PREHISTORIC MAN IN BRITISH EAST AFRICA*

By J. W. GREGORY, F.R.S.

(By permission of the Publishers and Author.)

EVIDENCE of recent geographical changes along the Rift Valley is abundant and conspicuous. Volcanic eruptions and earth-movements have taken place at a date which, geologically speaking, is quite modern; and that some of the changes have happened during the human occupation of the area is shown by the stone implements, which are widely scattered through the district and are buried in the beaches of the ancient lakes. The first prehistoric stone implement found in B.E.A. was apparently a chipped flake of obsidian which I picked up in the Ulu Mountains in 1893. The adjacent rock was gneiss, so that the piece of obsidian had been clearly carried there artificially; but it seemed possible that this might have been made for use as a gun-flint, as the main Suahili caravan route to Uganda passed a few miles away. Subsequently, however, I found obsidian flakes of a Neolithic type on the Athi Plains, on the summit of the Kikuyu Uplands; on the beaches of the extinct Lake Suess; on the plateau S. of Lake Hannington, on the lake terraces round Lake Baringo; on the Lobat Pass leading from Baringo northward to the Sugota; on the summit of the pass from Baringo on to Laikipia; and at numerous places on that plateau. The best collection was obtained on the floor of the Rift Valley beside the Gilgil River from an ancient camp where the implements were made; for I obtained there numerous flakes and scrapers as well as the cores and lumps of obsidian from which the implements had been struck. Many of the flakes were of the shape useful as skin-scrapers, and for scraping wood to be used as spcar- and arrow-shafts; others were of forms suitable for knives, arrow- and spear-heads. A series of these implements is figured in *Great Rift Valley* (Fig. 19, p. 234).

These obsidian implements were clearly of considerable antiquity, for they were found buried in the soil on the platform above the Kedong Basin, and in the high level beaches of Lake Baringo, where they were associated with broken pottery at a camp site inhabited when the lake was much larger than at present. None of the Masai, or the people of Njemps, or the Kikuyu, whom I asked about them, had any traditions of these implements having been used or made by man. They were of the Neolithic type— that of the Newer Stone Age. During recent years they have been found abundantly and widely distributed through the interior of B.E.A. Some of the most perfect were collected by Mr Tunstall at an old obsidian implement factory at Njoro, W. of Lake Nakuru.

Hobley (1912, p. 21) has figured an obsidian implement from Kisumu, and (*ibid*

* Reprinted from *The Rift Valleys and Geology of East Africa*, pp. 219–222.

APPENDIX E

Figs. 1 and 2) a series of those from Njoro that were found by Mr Tunstall; also beautiful pointed arrow-heads from Kinobop, and from Kyambu, and more roughly chipped flakes from near Kikuyu Station (*ibid*. Fig. 3). Obsidian flakes of a crude type made of chert, sandstone, quartzite, and quartz-porphyry were found by Dr Oswald near Karungu (Appendix, Hobley, 1912, pp. 27–28).

To the Neolithic age probably also belong some stone bowls and rings which have been found in Western B.E.A. Mr Hobley in his book on the Akamba (1910–1911, Plate XXVI) has figured a stone hollowed into a bowl, found 4 ft. deep at Naivasha. A similar stone ring and a bowl were found in Sotik and described by Mr C. M. Dobbs (1914, pp. 145–146) covered over with a few inches of loose soil; they are regarded by Mr Hobley as Neolithic. A similar bowl found at the depth of 10–12 ft. in a salt cave near the Government Bungalow at Sotik has been described by Mr Dobbs (1918, pp. 265–266).

Conclusive evidence of the Neolithic character of the obsidian implements is given by the discovery of two ground stone axes. The first, which has a weather-roughened surface, was found by Major C. Ross in 1913 at a depth of 3 ft. at the Eldoma Ravine. It has been described by Mr Hobley (1913, pp. 60–61), who regards it as the same age as the obsidian implements found at Njoro, only 25 miles distant.

In 1919 I found an obsidian axe with a ground front edge on a raised beach near the south-western end of Lake Naivasha, where it was associated with chipped flakes of the type common in the district. Its ground edge is clear evidence of Neolithic workmanship.

This Neolithic axe helps to fix the date when Lake Naivasha was at its greatest extension; it was found at a camp 50 ft. above the present level of the lake, so that Neolithic man was living beside Lake Naivasha after its waters had fallen about 100 ft. below their highest level, and long after the end of the overflow down the Njorowa Gorge. This axe shows that the maximum extension of Lake Naivasha was pre-Neolithic.

Though implements of the Paleolithic or Older Stone Age are widely distributed in Africa, none appears to have been found in B.E.A. until 1913, when a settler named Harrison took a series of roughly flaked axes to the Nairobi Museum. He was told that they were worth a good price, so he refused to say where he had obtained them, as he thought the discovery would be as valuable as a gold mine. He left the collection on loan at the Museum, went to the war where he was killed, and the secret of the locality was lost. The circumstances of their deposit at the Nairobi Museum and a plate illustrating five of them have been published by Mr Hobley (1917, p. 189), who suggests that the stone is like the phonolite of the Yatta Plateau.

During our journey from Naivasha to Magadi Mr Hobley and I found independently near our camp at the Ol Kejo Nyiro, at the northern foot of Mount Ol Gasalik, some roughly chipped axes similar in size and character to those found by Harrison. The specimens collected (Plate IV, Fig. C, reduced ⅓ dia.) were lying on a bank of white diatomaceous earth which seemed to have been dug by such implements. The earth was probably used as a paint, and these thin stone axes would make effective hand hoes in digging it. One specimen was in two pieces lying 4 ft. apart, showing that it had been broken at the place. These flakes are certainly suggestive of Paleolithic workmanship. They are not to be explained as unfinished implements which were to be ground and used elsewhere, since no ground stones of this type have been found in the country. They indicate the occupation of the Rift Valley N. of Magadi by Paleolithic man.

Further evidence of the presence of men of the Older Stone Age in the Rift Valley is given by the implement from the Murendat River near the Government Farm N. of Naivasha. Mr Dowson there found a series of rough flakes of amber-coloured chert in gravels beside the Murendat River, in the same bed as a fossil bone, identified by Dr Smith Woodward as that of some species of rhinoceros. They came from the same gravels as part of the lower jaw of a fossil zebra, which Prof. Ridgeway (1909, pp. 586–588) has described as an extinct species, *Equus hollisi*, and as more nearly related to Grevy's zebra than to the species now living in B.E.A. At the same locality Mr H. J. H. Stedman found an implement, also of amber-coloured chert, similar to that of the flakes collected by Mr Dowson. Mr Stedman's specimen may have been made for use as a spear-head; it is three-ridged and triangular, 3 ins. long, $1\frac{3}{4}$ ins. wide at the lower end, and $\frac{3}{4}$ in. thick. The chert may have come from the beds beside Lake Magadi. The implement strikingly resembles those of the Magdalenian, the uppermost division of the Paleolithic (exclusive of the Azilian). This specimen indicates the existence in East Africa of late Paleolithic man, for in addition to the difference in workmanship, it, and Mr Dowson's flakes, came from a lower horizon than that of the Neolithic implements which are numerous on the surface.

NOTES ON BEADS FROM THE UPPER KENYA AURIGNACIAN AND THE GUMBAN B CULTURES

By H. C. BECK, F.S.A.

BEADS FROM GAMBLE'S CAVE II, ELMENTEITA (WITH THE UPPER KENYA AURIGNACIAN CULTURE)

THESE are small disc beads which vary in size from 0·2 inch to 0·3 inch in diameter and from 0·04 inch to 0·065 inch in length. They vary greatly in colour, some are white, some grey and some black.

A microscopic examination shows that they are all made from ostrich shell. The thin ones seem to have split and a portion to have flaked off or corroded away.

The black ones are coloured by iron*, the metal is in the form of small opaque granules. It is difficult to see how the colouring matter has been introduced. The particles are very numerous and close together, so that a piece 0·003 inch thick is quite opaque.

A sufficiently thin section however shows under polarised light the characteristic marking of ostrich shell.

The white and black beads are exactly similar to the beads found by Prof. Seligman in the Faragab Mound in Northern Kordofan.

One similar black bead has been found by Prof. Sir William Flinders Petrie in Palestine. (1929 Expedition.)

Blackened sea shells are found in Egypt and Mesopotamia at an early date, but the black is not nearly as dense.

BEADS FROM NAKURU BURIAL SITE WITH THE GUMBAN B CULTURE

Only two beads were discovered here.

(1) Agate bead. A very well-made circular barrel bead. (I.C.1.b.) Length 0·311 inch. Diameter 0·289 ± 0·006 inch.

Perforation about 0·07 inch diameter, drilled from both ends, very good workmanship; the two holes are practically parallel except at the extreme ends and meet with only a slight displacement.

The ends of the perforation are slightly rounded or chamfered, probably partly done intentionally, and possibly partly due to wear, as it seems unequal in different parts.

The outside of the bead has been ground mainly by a motion at a considerable angle with the axis of the bead. The grinding was rather rough, leaving many small holes,

---

* I am indebted to Mr F. A. Bannister of the Natural History Museum, South Kensington, for finding that the colouring matter in these beads is iron.

but the polish is very good, having been continued for a long time with a soft material. This has had the effect of polishing away more of the soft parts of the agate, than of the hard parts, and the latter stand above the former on the surface. There is no trace of patination.

It is difficult to suggest where this bead comes from. I do not think it is Egyptian, and although many beads of similar material come from Mesopotamia, I have not seen one from there which is quite similar to this.

(2) Short cylinder faïence bead. (I.B.2.b.) Length 0·148 ± 0·002 inch. Diameter 0·254 ± 0·001 inch.

This is a well-made bead and in extremely good preservation. I do not think it is Egyptian. It resembles to a certain extent faïence beads from Mycenean tombs of about 1500 B.C. Some beads from a late Neolithic site in Algeria have a considerable resemblance to this bead, but the Algerian beads are in a very bad state of preservation. This may be due to a different technique, but it is not certain, as a difference in the soil that beads have been kept in greatly affects their state of preservation.

EXTRACT FROM THE *EAST AFRICAN STANDARD* ANNOUNCING THE DISCOVERY OF THE NAKURU BURIAL SITE

To the Editor,   AN INTERESTING FIND

SIR,

I wonder whether any of your readers could give me any idea of the likely explanation of the following finds I have recently made. I can discover little information from any of the books on this country to which I have access, nor can I elicit anything save murmurs of "long ago very", from any of the natives in my employ.

Some little time ago, the grass having been burnt off a little hill, I happened to notice against the face of an upheaved strata of rock an area of at least 25 by 15 feet which had obviously at some time been filled in with loose stones, although several large boulders from the face of the cliff had since fallen on top.

To cut a long story short, for interest sake, I had a bit of excavation made which has now reached some 9 feet below the original surface, although not over the whole area of the filling. Up to to-day there have appeared six stone cooking pots or vessels, a portion of a staff, the balance of which was dust, and a flat pestle and mortar, besides a quantity of bones, some in process of petrification, so far as I can see.

It would almost appear from the face of the rock as if the mouth of a cave was nearly bared. The artificial filling continues below for several feet at least yet, judged by probing. But the feature which seems strangest is that so far the interstitial dust or earth is of fine division as Fullers earth and has obviously been fired. How this has been accomplished under the mass of debris defeats me.

It may be to the expert or the older settler that there is little of interest in this matter, for there may be some practice of the native tribes which simply explains what is to myself hardly clear. Another detail which may have some bearing is that near by are remains, which to myself look like samples of the stone erections of those earlier inhabitants referred to in Sir Charles Eliot's book, although so far as one may judge from the illustration in the book mentioned, these latter are in a far better state of preservation. Their dimensions are far from inconsiderable, and they bear the same features of "bastions at the corners". (*Vide* p. 87 of the *East African Protectorate*, by Sir Charles Eliot, 1905.)

I should be more than grateful if any of your readers could throw some light on the whole question, for it is not unnaturally of some interest to myself, however simple the explanation may be.

Yours, etc.

Box 22, Nakuru.   JAS. ALEX MACDONALD.

(This may prove to be a most interesting discovery, and we would suggest that the spot should be left *in statu quo* as much as possible, till some expert can take the matter in hand—EDITOR.)

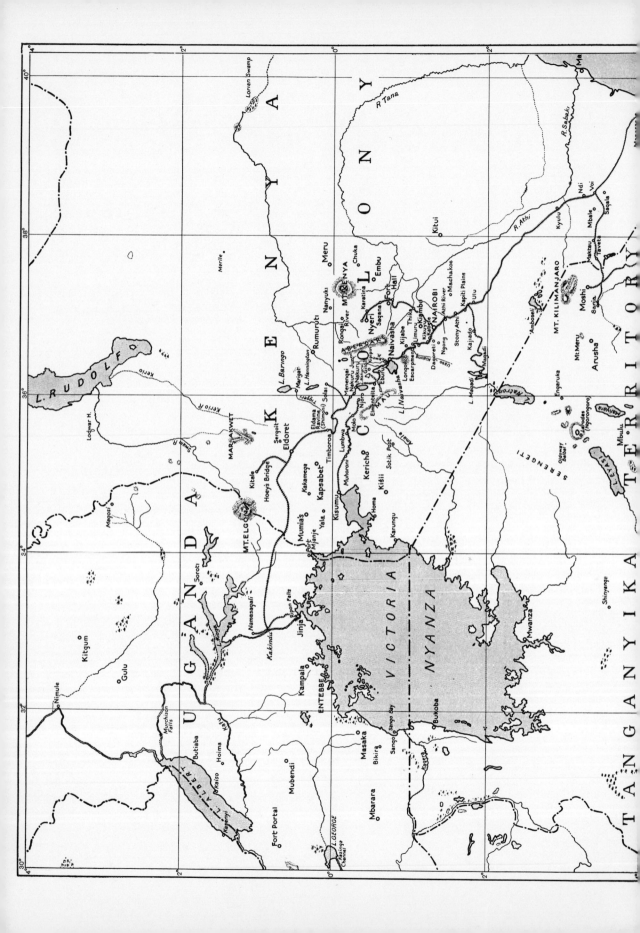

*Lists of principal places which are referred to in the book,
and which are shown on this map*

Aberdare (VII. *e*)

Albert, Lake (I. *c*)

Balbal (VI. *g–h*)

Baringo, Lake (VII. *d*)

Eburru (VII. *e*)

Eldama Ravine (VI. *d*)

Elgon, Mt (V. *c*)

Elmenteita (VII. *e*)

Gilgil, River (VII. *e*)

Homa (V. *e*)

Kaiso (I. *c*)

Kenya, Mt (VIII. *e*)

Kedong (VII. *b*)

Kiambu (VII. *f*)

Kilimanjaro (VIII. *h*)

Kipipiri (VII. *e*)

Magadi (VII. *b*)

Malewa or Morendat (River) (VII. *e*)

Manyara, Lake (VI. *h*)

Menengai (VI. *e*)

Nairobi (VII. *f*)

Naivasha (VII. *e*)

Nakuru (VII. *e*)

Nanyuki (VIII. *d*)

Ngorongoro (VI. *h*)

Njoro (VI. *e*)

Oldoway (VI. *g–h*)

Ulu, Mts (VIII. *f*)

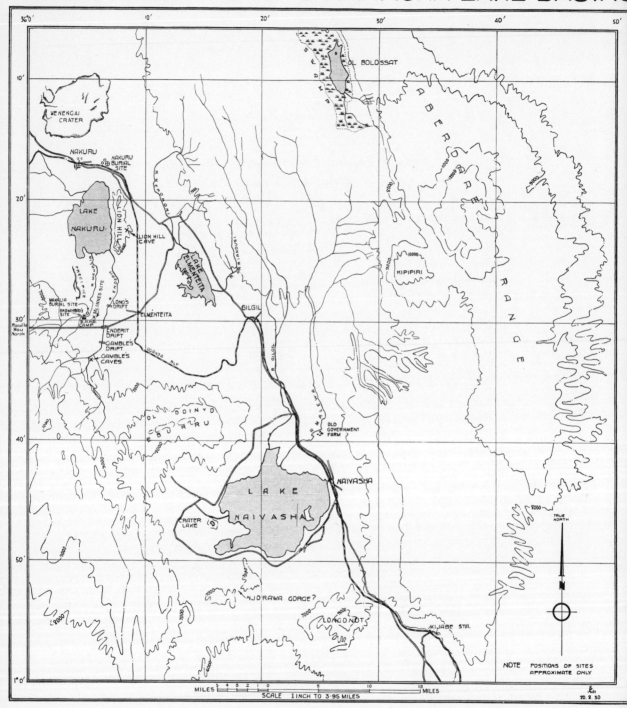

INDEX

INDEX

Elmenteitan, 31, **172–175**
Endariki Valley, 8
Enderit Drift, 176, 248
Enderit River, 90, 91, 176, 198, 246, 248
Enderit Valley, formation of, 251
Equus capensis, 264
Equus hollisi, 3, 24
Equus stenonis, 23
Euphorbia Flats, fauna from, 273
Evans, Sir J., 1
Eyzies, Les, 95

Fabricators, 96–97; making and use of, 97–99.
　See also Lames écaillées
Fauna, 7, Chapter III; use of, for dating, 19–20;
　list of, 25–26; Appendix C, p. 271
Fauresmith, 234, 264
Fishhoek, 234, 235, 241
Fleure, Dr, 20, 103
Fort Hall, 261
France, 238

Gamble, A., 91
Gamble's Cave, 17, 31, 78, 80, 90, **91–94**; views
　and sections, 113–119; fauna from, 273–275
Gamble's Drift, 246
Gamblian, 12, 14, 16, 17, 22, 29, 30, 38, 78, 90,
　92, 246
Gamblian fauna, **24–26**
Gardner, E. W., 265, 271
Gebel-Moya, 244
Geology, Appendix A, p. 245
Getulian, 236
Gibraltar, 20
Gilgil, 245, 246, 256
Goodwin, J. H., 233
Gravette points, 95; use of, 104–105. See also
　Backed blades
Gregory, Prof. J. W., 1, 2, 3, 8, 9, 10, 11, 12, 245,
　253, 261, Appendix E
Grimaldi, 237
Gumban A and B, 31, 32, **198–203**
Günz, 7, 17, 232, Appendix B

Hammer stones, 39, 101
Hannington, Lake, 278
Harrison, 2, 279
Hipparion, 15, 16, 23
Hippopotamus hipponensis, 23
Hippopotamus site, 273
Hobley, C. W., 1, 2, 3, 278, 279
Homa, 24, 263
Homo Rhodesiensis, 30, 80. See also Broken Hill
　skull
Hopwood, A. T., 24, 262, Appendix C, p. 271
Howieson's Poort, 236, 241
Human remains: Aurignacian, 108–109, 127, 129;
　Elmenteitan, 175, 191, 193; Gumban A, 199–
　201, 213; Gumban B, 204, 229

Illustrated London News, 4
India, 239
Ireland, 269
Italy, 238

Johannesburg, 100
Jordan Valley, 17
*Journal of East Africa and Uganda Natural
　History Society*, 2, 8
Juma's Drift, 249

Kafuan, 4, 263, 264, 266
Kaiso, 13, 14, 16, 23, 263
Kalahari, 22
Kamasian, 10, 11, 12, 17, 24, 29, 30, 33, 34, 38, 91,
　232, 263, 264, 266
Kariandusi River site, 34, 35, 36, 37, 245, 247, 255;
　sections of, 256–257
Karungu bone beds, 10, 14, 279
Kedong, 244
Kenya, Mt, 8, 12, 13, 22, 38, 240; geology of, 261
Kerr, Seton, 3
Kikuyu, 243, 278
Kilimanjaro, Mt, 12, 13, 22
Kinangop, 260, 279
Kipipiri, 3
Kisegi, 13
Kisumu, 24, 278
Koru, 34
Kyambu, 2, 279

Laikipia, 278
Lames écaillées, 174
Land bridges, 20–22
Leakey, D. G. B., 10, 247
Le Moustier, 80, 233
Levalloisian, 233, 234
Levels of Lake Nakuru, 247
Lindi, 4
Lion Hill, 247
Lion Hill Cave, 24, 247; fauna from, 275
Little Gilgil River, 261, 278
Long's Drift, 177; section, 249
Longonot, 258
Lonnberg, 12
Lowe, C. van Reit, 118, 233, 264
Lunates. See Crescents

Macdonald, Major J., 3, 200, 247; reprint of
　letter, Appendix G, p. 283
MacInnes site, 253; fauna from, 272
Magadi, 2, 279, 280
Magdalenian, 240, 280
Magosian, 4, 241, 243
Makalia Burial site, 177, 198, 199
Makalia Valley, 246; exposures of, 252; history
　of, 255
Makalian, 12, 14, 16, 33, **91–94**, 232, Appendix B

286

INDEX

Malewa River, 3, 24, 78, 90; section of, 259–260; history of, 260, 261; fauna from, 275, 279
Mammalia, Appendix C
Man, 2, 3, 9, 13
Manyara, Lake, 14
Masai, 278
Matopos, 234
Mau, 246
Menengai, 246, 247
Meroroni River, 257, 259
Mesolithic, Chapter VIII, p. 172
Mesopotamia, 239, 243, 244
Micoque Is., 264
Microliths, 95
Mindel, 6, 7, 17, 22, 232, Appendix B
Miocene, 10, 245
Moeris, Lake, 269
Mollusca, 25, 93, Appendix D, p. 276
Mono, Lake, 267
Montague, Capt., 2
Morendat River. See Malewa
Morocco, 236
Mousterian, 29, **30–31**, 38, **78–82**, 233 *et seq.*

Nairobi, 3
Nairobi Museum, 2, 279
Naivasha, 3, 10, 24, 78, 90, 279
Naivasha Lake, 9, 11; geology of the basin, 258; terraces of the basin, 258–259
Nakuran wet phase, 12, 14, 16, 33, 94, 177, 232, 243, Appendix B
Nakuru, 3, 200
Nakuru burial site, **200–204**. See Gumban B; Appendix G
Nakuru culture. See Gumban B
Nakuru Lake, 9, 32, 92, 243; geology of basin, 246; terraces of the basin, 247
Nanyuki, 38, 262
Nanyukian, 29, **37–39**, 78
Nature, 11
Neanderthal, 20, 79, 80, 236
Neolithic, 1, 3, 32, Chapter IX, pp. 198–205, 243, 278
New Zealand, 267
Ngorongoro crater, 4, 201
Nile, 265, 269
Nilsson, Dr Erik, 10, 12, 24, 260
Njemps, 278
Njoro, 1, 2, 204, 278, 279
Njoroan, 32, 198, **204–205**, 244
Njorowa Gorge, 10, 11, 245
North Africa, 23, 24, 37, 233, 234, 236, 237, 238, 241
North America, 267
Nyasaland, 17, 263
Nyasan, 10

Oakes, C. J., 204
Ochre, 101, 109, 201

Ol Bolossat, 260
Oldaway, 4, 19, 23, 109, 263, 275; sections, 14–16
Oldaway skeleton, 15–16
Old Government Farm, 3, 81, 90
Older Diluvium, 17
Oleondo, 261
Olgasalic, 2, 279
Ol Kejo Nyiro, 2, 279
Omo, 263
Oswald, 279
Ovate, 38

Palestine, 234, 237, 238
Passemard, Dr, 233
Peake, Dr, 20
Peers, 80, 235
Penck, 6, 267
Pendants, 103, Plate, p. 125
Pestles, 203, 243
Péyrony, 80, 233
Pitman, Capt., 272
Pluvials. See Climatic changes
Polished axes. See Axes
Pottery: Aurignacian, 103–104, Plate, p. 121; Elmenteitan, 175, Fig. and Plate, pp. 187, 189; Wilton, 176, 206; Gumban A, 199, 208, 210; Gumban B, 204
Prehistoric Society of East Anglia, 9

Querns, 202, 203, 221, 243, 244

Raised beaches of Mediterranean, 238
Ramsden, Sir J., 2
Reck, Dr Hans, 4, 14, 15, 16, 23, 109, 201, 263
Rhinoceros merkii, 21, 23
Rhodesia, 17, 79, 176, 234, 236, 241; correlation with, 264
Ridgeway, Prof., 24, 280
Riss, 6, 7, 17, 22, 232, Appendix B
Romer, Dr A. S., 20
Ross, Major, 1, 3, 279
Ruenzori, 22

Sahara, 9, 22, 238, 239, 242, 244, 265
Sandford, K. S., 265
Sangoan, 4, 263, 265, 266
Sawmills, 236
Scandinavia, 269
Scrapers, 96; use of, 107–108; Elmenteitan, 173
Sébilien, 102, 242
Sewall, 204
Shells from Gamble's Cave II, 93, Plate, p. 125, Appendix D
Sierra Nevada, 267
Simpson, Dr, 22, 24, 268
Sinew frayer, 99–100
Smith Woodward, Sir A., 280
Smithfield, 236, 241, 264
Solomon, J. D., 10, 12, 14, 38, Appendix A

INDEX